LATINO COMMUNITIES

EMERGING VOICES
POLITICAL, SOCIAL, CULTURAL, AND LEGAL ISSUES

edited by

ANTOINETTE SEDILLO LOPEZ
UNIVERSITY OF NEW MEXICO

A GARLAND SERIES

CHICANO PROFESSIONALS

CULTURE, CONFLICT, AND IDENTITY

TAMIS HOOVER RENTERÍA

GARLAND PUBLISHING, INC.
A MEMBER OF THE TAYLOR & FRANCIS GROUP
NEW YORK & LONDON / 1998

Library of Congress Cataloging-in-Publication Data

Rentería, Tamis Hoover.
    Chicano professionals : culture, conflict, and identity / Tamis
Hoover Rentería.
        p.   cm. — (Latino communities)
    Includes bibliographical references and index.
    ISBN 0-8153-3093-6 (alk. paper)
    1. Mexican Americans in the professions. I. Title. II. Series.
HD8038.U5R46 1997
331.7'12'0896872073—dc21

                                                    97-35336

Printed on acid-free, 250-year-life paper
Manufactured in the United States of America

Contents

Preface

I began to wrestle with the issues in this book on my first day as an undergraduate at Stanford in September 1972. Eighteen, dressed in a mini-skirt, blonde hair swinging and my arms loaded with suitcases, I walked into the lobby of Casa Zapata, the Chicano Theme House and dormitory, full of naive excitement about my anticipated encounter with the Mexican cultural Other.

The Chicanos at Stanford quickly set me—and my WASP assumptions—straight. An encounter with the Other, if it is genuine, may begin with giddy attraction, but will inevitably evolve into something more difficult and profound if pursued.

I owe thanks and continued dialogue to all the Chicanos, and the handful of Anglos, with whom I argued and discussed into the wee small hours, in dormitory halls and rooms, those ideas which challenged my perspectives and opened me up to a whole new world view. I feel particularly grateful to Ramon Flores, Jose Padilla, Mickey Baeza, Sylvia (Martina) Puente, Arturo Pacheco, Gayle Turner, Nancy Mayans, and Elena Robles. I don't hold any of these ex-Zapatistas responsible for the analysis developed here; in fact, I feel sure that every one of them would find things with which to argue. I would feel disappointed if they didn't.

A few of the people I knew at Casa Zapata became subjects for this dissertation study. To them, and to all my other friends and the generous strangers who opened up their lives and ideas to me during the course of my fieldwork, I offer heartfelt thanks.

I am grateful to Jane Collier, George Collier, Renato Rosaldo, and Donald Donham, my teachers, for helping me take the raw clay of my fieldwork experience and shape it into the dissertation which formed the basis of this book.

I owe thanks to Susan Bibler Coutin, my fellow graduate student, who painstakingly helped me clarify my thinking in the early stages of writing and empathized with me over the trials of fieldwork and writing. Thanks are due also to Martha Luemers who helped me trim the jargon for non specialists (although I'm sure there is still plenty of it), and to Blair Pleasant for her editing suggestions. Kristi Long and Antoinette Sedillo Lopez, editors for this series, asked questions and made suggestions that helped me to clarify many issues.

I owe hours and hours of lost time to Lucas Emiliano and Elijah Martin, my sassy, sweet sons who will undoubtedly someday ask their parents what this "Chicano" stuff is all about.

And of course, I owe my sanity, my love, and the very substance of this book to my husband, Beto. He has suffered without complaint in the three demanding roles of "native" subject, fellow ethnographer, and everloving husband over the last several years. I asked him at the outset of this project how he would feel about being a primary subject and participant, and whether or not he might feel threatened by my scrutiny, analysis, and exposure of the Chicano professional community of which we were both a part. He answered that he looked forward to getting some of these issues we were constantly talking about "out in the air," into public discourse. He has since that time never indicated any regrets, whether or not he felt them. I am deeply grateful for his gentle, supportive presence in my life.

Tamis Hoover Rentería
August 1997

Introduction

Writing about Chicano[1] professionals in Los Angeles proves timely for many reasons. Anthropologists now venture into the ethnic borderlands of their own western countries rather than encroach on the flexing ethnicities of the third world as they have traditionally done. The Mexican American community in the United States is particularly important as an arena of study because its numbers are increasing rapidly, and its culture is densely entangled in the history as well as the contemporary reality of the American Southwest. While various subgroups of this community have received a fair amount of scholarly attention, the focus has been primarily on working-class Mexican Americans. White-collar professionals, who for the most part are the product of affirmative action in the last twenty years, have been neglected. This generation of Chicano professionals deserves study because 1) it is a historical product of the creative, political ferment of the sixties, 2) it defies assumptions about assimilation and class mobility, and 3) its members claim to represent and provide leadership to the working-class Mexican American masses. Their leadership claims are shaped by a unique cultural imperative, born and nurtured within the Chicano Student Movement of the 1960's and 70's, when the core of these professionals attended universities and negotiated a shift in class identity from blue-collar to white.

Chicano doctors and lawyers make particularly interesting groups on which to focus, since they are two of the most politically active and prestigious groups of Mexican American professionals in Los Angeles. Their lives and work are already making an impact on the politics and culture of the Southwest and will continue to do so in the upcoming decades.[2] The story of this ethnic elite begins in the 1960's and 1970's when Mexican American students from blue-collar backgrounds first entered California colleges and universities in significant numbers due to affirmative action [Muñoz 1989:1-12].[3] This generation of Mexican American students is important, however, not merely for its increased numbers, but rather for the *culture* it created, the culture of "*Chicanismo.*"

Chicanismo, the culture of the nationalist Chicano Movement, was shaped by a constellation of forces. First were the challenges experienced by the members of the Movement cohort as the first in their blue-collar families to attend colleges and universities. In this new academic, pre-professional environment they felt their identities being hammered into the shape that professional status required, and they responded in a way that earlier generations of Mexican American students had never done—they rebelled. They were children of the sixties, sparked by the overall spirit of challenge which typified an entire generation of young people. Their rejection of university and establishment values shared certain elements with other youth movements like those of the white middle-class "hippie" counter-culture and drug culture, or the Vietnam protest, or Black Power. However, while usually overlooked by chroniclers and historians of the sixties, the Chicano Movement was a powerful youth movement shaped to address issues of racism, assimilation, class, and cultural identity through the unique cultural language of the blue-collar Mexican American/Chicano university student. The fact that this movement has been largely ignored by the media is perhaps partially to explain why this generation, now that it has grown up and become professional, is largely misunderstood, ignored, and underestimated in terms of its actual and potential power to influence the culture and politics of the Southwest today.

What needs to be understood is that the culture of *Chicanismo,* shaped by the Chicano Movement student generation roughly between the years of 1966 and 1975, constitutes the formative experience of an entire generation of Mexican Americans who are now professionals. Furthermore, this youth culture, shaped by Chicano students as an alternative to what they perceived as White Anglo Saxon Protestant middle-class/professional values, continues to shape and constrain Chicano behavior even now when Chicanos have successfully negotiated their way into middle- class, professional lives.[4]

What makes this retention of "Chicano" values different from similar retentions of ethnicity by other upwardly- mobile groups, is that Chicano professionals are not simply clinging for comfort to some blue-collar ethnic practices learned from parents and family back in the "barrio." The culture which continues to influence their everyday lives is one that they created themselves as students within the Chicano Movement, a culture that addresses the issues of American identity in a profound way and which commands an ethic which, in many ways, challenges their successful negotiation into the professional class.

Thus even the most basic retention of blue-collar Mexican cultural practices, like serving tortillas and beans at every social function, has a significance beyond ethnic/class nostalgia. It is rooted in a Movement culture which challenges the dominant American myth of assimilation at several levels, including the "simplest" level of food habits. This culture suggests that social mobility in America need not mean replacing tortillas with white bread, or Spanish with English. Even more significantly, it suggests that achieving "success" in American society and shifting class affiliation need not mean that one forgets the interests and needs of the blue-collar, ethnic community from which one comes.

What sustains this ethic of concern for the blue-collar Mexican is the belief that racism continues to limit the opportunities of Mexican people in every class. Thus the Chicano professionals from the Movement generation are that rare beast—a bourgeoisie which does not fully believe in its own legitimations, which does not act simply out of its own class interests.

Of course, cynics and social scientists will immediately pounce here, gleefully eager to watch me hang myself for appearing to suggest that Chicano elites are constrained by an ethic of unselfish concern for a class which is not theirs. But allow me to explain. On the one hand, I *am* suggesting that Chicano doctors and lawyers of the Movement generation are constrained and motivated in much of their lives by an ethic of concern for the Mexican American masses. However, the Movement culture affects people in different ways. Some appear to make choices in their careers and lives out of a genuine, deeply-felt commitment to this value. Others appear to simply manipulate the value for their own class and career ends. The vast majority, however, appear to make choices out of mixed motives and values, all of which at some level are affected by the Chicano Movement ethic of concern for blue-collar Chicanos.

The tensions that result from this continued influence of *Chicanismo* are due to competing ideas about what "success" means.

On the one hand, Chicanos, like any other blue-collar American who "makes it" into the professional class through the educational system, view themselves within the pattern of the classic American success story; they are intelligent, hard-working individuals who have raised themselves up "by their own bootstraps," beyond the level of the lazy, unfortunate masses, and therefore deserve increased prestige and monetary remuneration as professionals. Concomitant with this attitude in the extreme is the notion that those Mexican Americans who have not "made it" have simply not tried hard enough to obtain an education and take advantage of opportunities provided them.

On the other hand, when Chicano professionals view themselves through the culture of *Chicanismo*, their hard-won success looks more contradictory. In this story, they view themselves as the "lucky" ones who have either escaped the barriers of racism and discrimination that have traditionally kept Mexicans and other minorities out of the professional class, or overcome them through great hardship. This view characterizes the blue-collar Mexican American as the unlucky brother, the fellow sufferer of discrimination due to physiognomy, skin color, religion, or culture, the one who must be helped by those who have already "made it" to overcome the barriers to social mobility.

While the contradictory tensions of these two stories are felt and expressed most uniformly by members of the Chicano Movement generation who were educated in the sixties and seventies, they also have a widespread influence over all professional Chicanos who network with other professional Chicanos in Los Angeles. These include 1) the pre-Movement generation—those small numbers of Mexican Americans that became professionals before the sixties, affirmative action and minority political activism and 2) the post-Movement generation—those Mexican Americans who were educated in the late seventies and eighties after the peak of the Chicano Movement.

This strong influence of Chicano Movement culture on the wider Mexican American professional community is due to several factors. Perhaps the most important is that the Movement generation shares a powerful generation *culture*—set of shared memories, expectations, perspectives, and practices—which bonds its members more strongly than the members of either of the other generations. Furthermore, unlike the generations before and after it, the Movement generation carries a sharply articulated vision and language of political responsibility and community identity which serves as a powerful rallying cry for the political claims of all Mexican American elites to represent and lead their people. No other generation has yet shaped such a compelling discourse of solidarity and political destiny for the Mexican American. The influence of this generation's culture is compounded by the fact that the Chicano Movement cohort currently dominates Chicano elite politics in Los Angeles. The cohort holds this position for three reasons: 1) its numbers, which are greater than the generation before it due to affirmative action and Chicano political activism; 2) the fact that its members are in their thirties and forties[5] and reaching influential positions in their professions and political careers and are thus more powerful than the generation after them, which also has large numbers, and 3) its closely-knit networks which were generated in colleges and professional schools, and bonded tightly through the shared culture of the Movement. The latter is something that neither other generation shares, although individual members of both cohorts may identify strongly with the Movement generation and its culture, and may network with members of that cohort.

Thus, carried by the intricate networks of the Chicano Movement generation, the transformed culture of *Chicanismo* continues to wield a force in Mexican American life in Los Angeles, shaping a powerful and controversial discourse about ethnic identity and class politics with potentially tremendous implications for the Southwest. It is a force felt both in the most personal spaces where people weave stories about the intimate meaning of their own lives, and in the most public places where Chicanos use it as a powerful ideology of political unity and a basis on which to make claims on the wider society as representatives of blue-collar Mexican Americans.

METHODOLOGY: A "CULTURE AND POWER" APPROACH

Social analysis, particularly as practiced within the anthropological tradition, has been undergoing a tremendous shift in the last ten to fifteen years. Where once structural and synchronic analysis dominated, a new interest in process and diachronic analysis— history—has emerged. Where strictly interpretive and symbolic analysis prevailed, a new concern for how meaning is shaped by relationships of power has surfaced. Where the claims of objectivity once held authority, the frank recognition of observer subjectivity has pulled back the curtain on omniscience.

The theoretical approach of this book is the fruit of several years immersed in the intellectual waters of Stanford University's anthropology department during the 1980's, where all these new trends were blending a distinct kind of social analysis.[6] Some of the students casually referred to these intermingling tributaries of thought as the "Culture and Power School." My own work is heavily indebted to professors Renato Rosaldo and Sylvia Yanigasako who were merging their interpretive, symbolic approaches with an interest in structure and power, and Jane Collier and Donald Donham who were beginning to cross their structural, political approaches with more interpretive work. No less influential, although never encountered in the flesh, were mentors Raymond Williams the literary critic, and E.P. Thompson the historian.

Those readers looking for a statistical, structural, objective study will be disappointed with this book. This is an interpretive cultural analysis. I *begin* with *structure* in that I identify these Chicanos as members of a particular class—the professional class—living within a particular geographical location called the city of Los Angeles, in a region called the Southwest, in a country called the United States of America. However, "class", "city", "region," and "country" are all actually conceptual models, reifications of relationships which are in reality much more fluid and amorphous than any models could accurately represent.[7] The group I study in Los Angeles is not a concretely, statistically cohesive group, but rather a network of people who identify as Mexican American, who are doctors and/or lawyers, and whom I have divided, for my own analytical convenience, into generations. The key generation, or cohort around which Chicano professional life centered at the time of this study, includes those Chicanos who were the first affirmative action generation, who experienced university life in the sixties and seventies, and who created the Chicano Movement. Their language, ideas, feelings, perceptions and practices, including the claims they put on each other—i.e. their *culture*—reflect that mutual experience.

The study is also structural to the extent that it relies on analysis of two particular professional organizations, the Mexican American Bar Association and the Chicano/Latino Medical Association of California. However, I did not originally intend to make these associations central to my study. I actually stumbled on them through networks. They were important to me mainly because they were important to so many Chicano doctors and lawyers whom I encountered. Happily, these organizations were the generators of many of the most interesting *rituals*—that staple of the anthropological diet—where meanings and practices intersected revealingly.[8]

Also true to recent anthropological trends, this is a historical analysis. I did formal fieldwork between January 1988 and May 1990, and I do not pretend to explain what the culture of Chicano doctors and lawyers in Los Angeles will be like for all time. It is also an interpretive, subjective study, in which I place myself as the ethnographer squarely and transparently within the analysis. I am frank about my own experiences with the Chicano Movement and the Chicano professional community, and about my biases. Like many contemporary anthropologists, I believe that done with discretion, such openness—while it may not be helpful for political purposes which require statistics and claims to scientific objectivity—produces richer, thicker, and more subtle analysis and understanding.

COHORT ANALYSIS

The Chicano Movement culture, which shaped the consciousness of a generation, continues to influence not only the practices and beliefs of the doctors and lawyers who are the subject of this book, but also the analysts and academics who study Chicano professionals in their work. In broad terms, approaches tend to line up on two opposing sides. On the one hand, some analyses not only question the long-term political impact of the Chicano Movement, characterizing it as a "romantic" phase [Gann and Duignam: 1986: 183-194], but also seek to discredit the claims of Movement generation professionals to represent blue-collar Mexican Americans [Gann and Duignam 1986; Chavez 1991]. I suggest that these studies are defensive, politically motivated works whose popularity reflects a growing unease among many politically-aware Americans with the very real threat of ethnic claims to power—in this case, that of Mexican Americans/Chicanos—to politics as usual in the United States.[9]

On the other hand, there are the equally politically-motivated explanations of those social analysts who were themselves shaped by the Chicano Movement, who are concerned that its values not be lost by their fellow Chicano professionals. The dominant model underlying their analyses, with slight variations, depicts working-class Chicanos entering white-collar universities, experiencing an identity crisis, and shaping a working-class youth Movement and culture in response to that crisis [Muñoz: 61; Limón 1982]. The subsequent movement of these youths into the professional class is viewed in terms of whether or not, or to what extent, they "assimilate" and take on the values of the White Anglo Saxon Protestant (WASP) professional class [Barrera 1982: 52-53].

While these assimilation models rely primarily, and I believe, appropriately, on class analyses, they do not delve deeply into the subject of the relationship of the Movement to current Chicano professional dynamics. Barrera [1979] suggests that Chicano identity is maintained by Chicano professionals in two ways: 1) in the recognition that despite their class identity, they share with Chicanos of all classes the experience of racism, or class segmentation and 2) in the maintenance of a common culture [1979: 216]. While Barrera adequately demonstrates how racial segmentation is imposed on all classes of Chicanos through the systemic, historical processes of capitalism, he does not demonstrate the mechanisms of how Chicanos themselves create solidarity across class lines, or even within classes, in terms of either the shared experience of racism or the sustaining of a common culture.

Limón [1982] explores some of the dynamics of shared culture as it was practiced within the Chicano Movement at the University of Texas in Austin. For Limón, this culture is largely a revitalized and partially transformed blue-collar culture. He suggests that Chicano Movement students have continued as professionals to be influenced by this ideology created in their university years, thus sustaining their alliance with the Mexican working-class [161].

While both Barrera and Limón suggest that maintenance of at least certain aspects of Chicano ideology is possible for Chicano professionals, what is lacking is an analysis of what actually has happened to the Chicano Movement generation and the unique culture they created since its members have become professionals. In approaching this question, I found that after a certain point, class analysis obscures rather than illuminates the dynamics of Chicano social mobility since the sixties. What "class" Chicanos belong to in a socioeconomic sense does not predict either their cultural practices or their sense of to which collective they belong. Chicano professionals in the eighties and nineties are creating their own kind of cultural identity and are not becoming carbon copies of the image of American success. Furthermore, they are in many cases acting out of a loyalty to a community which is defined across class lines. What is needed is historical analysis which takes culture as well as human agency—both individual and collective—seriously.

Cohort, or generational analysis offers a structural way to introduce history into the analysis of class and cultural dynamics, and makes possible a compelling explanation for the current dynamics of Chicano professional culture in Los Angeles and possibly throughout the Southwest. While it has been used in the fields of demography, sociology, and social history, anthropologists are only recently beginning to use cohort approaches to the benefit of cultural analysis [Rosaldo 1980: 110-218; Yanagisako 1978; 1985].

In one pertinent recent case, an analysis of Japanese American kinship, the anthropologist Sylvia Yanagisako [1978] suggests that social structurally defined units—in her particular case, that of the United States as a "nation"—are perhaps not appropriate units for cultural analysis, since the diversity of particular historical experiences are obscured by such structuralist definitions. She critiques the notion that there is some "American" system of kinship by describing how Japanese Americans shape their kinship practices as individuals in terms of context, and as members of particular immigrant generations according to their historical experiences. In terms of Chicano professionals, I similarly question the utility of using a unit of analysis which is structurally defined—in this case, "class"—for my cultural analysis. Like Yanagisako, I look at both individual cultural practices and collective practices within a set of unique, historical circumstances, questioning the assumption that there is one "American" way to be a member of the professional class. Also like Yanagisako, the social unit I employ for this analysis is that of cohort, or generation.

Cohort analysis works on two levels.[10] On one level, it concerns the generational dynamics of history, as one cohort succeeds the next and wrestles out its place in relation to other generations. The focus is on how a particular generation both creates and conceives of itself in unique cultural terms, particularly in relation to the generations which come before and after it. These generational cohorts are defined not so much as people who are born at the same time, but rather as individuals who come of age from youth to adulthood at the same time, experiencing similar historical forces and shaping a common culture and group identity in response to those forces.

Cohort analysis is also concerned, at another level, with the biological movement from youth to age; that is, what happens to the culture shaped by a generation of youth when it becomes the culture of a generation of middle-aged elders. The time of youth is generally considered the moment where the new generation confronts the culture of the generation before it, experiencing that culture and perceiving it differently from the way it is perceived by the generation (now older) which shaped it. In this confrontation of generations, the youthful cohort shapes a new culture out of both the material inherited from its elders, and the unique social forces of its own time. Eventually, when this particular cohort passes from youth to middle age, it must confront the challenges of the new upcoming generation as they too begin to shape their collective identity in relation to the cultural and historical status-quo.

This analysis focuses primarily on those members of the Chicano Movement generation who are now professionals in their middle years, at the peak of their political and cultural power. This group is an example of the kind of unique generation which may emerge during times of social upheaval and rapid change, often producing a cohort culture with long-lasting and wide-reaching influence on the members of other generations. I argue that the culture of the Movement generation, forged in the fire of historical forces which characterized the sixties and early seventies, linked its members in a more cohesive, compelling, and widespread collective identity than had been created by any other Mexican American generation. Furthermore, because of its unusual cultural force, its influence has subsequently spread to such a degree that members of both the generations before it—the pre-Movement generation, and after it—the post-Movement generation, are deeply compelled by its dynamics.

THE MOVEMENT

While this is not a work about the Chicano Movement itself, but rather about the continued influence of the Movement on Chicano professional culture,[11] it may be helpful to sketch out some basic details about Movement culture and its historical setting. While I discuss trends that happened across the southwest, I take my specific examples from Stanford University where I was a student living in the Chicano Theme House dormitory, Casa Zapata, for three years between September 1972 and June 1975.[12]

In the mid 1960's, when Chicanos first began matriculating to California campuses in post-affirmative action numbers, there were no

Chicano research centers, dormitories, theme houses, Chicano Studies departments or classes, and no Chicano student organizations. Chicanos of that immediate pre-Movement era describe an intense feeling of alienation from campus life. They were surrounded by Anglos[13] who knew nothing about them, and they had no places to go which were their own. The sense of not belonging was not only cultural, but also for the majority of them, class-based.

It was bolstered by the fact that until the early seventies, the numbers of Chicano students were minimal. At Stanford, for example, in 1968 there were fifty-seven Chicano students, graduates and undergraduates. The following year there were approximately 160. It was not until 1974 that there were about 600 Chicano students on campus out of approximately 10,000 total students, with nine faculty members, and twenty-one staff members. The feeling of being a minority was not merely a feeling—it was an overwhelming fact for many years.

By 1966 the students of several California schools began coordinating Chicano student political organizations and in 1969 at the C.C.H.E. (Chicano Council on Higher Education) Santa Barbara Conference, they placed all campus organizations under one name, *Movimiento Estudiantíl Chicano de Aztlán*, or MEChA [Muñoz 1989: 75-79]. At Stanford, the Mexican American Student Confederation (MASC), founded in 1967, was replaced by MEChA in 1969. Chicano nationalism became the dominant theme of the Movement culture, the celebration and glorification of being a Mexican in the United States, defiantly bilingual, bicultural, and proud to be Brown/Bronze/Mestizo/Indian.

Belonging to this culture involved people in a flourishing range of activities. These included political protest over campus policies toward Chicanos and other minorities, tutoring students in barrio communities, painting murals, dancing *folklórico*, celebrating *Cinco de Mayo*, creating Chicano literature and history classes, inviting barrio artists to teach sculpture and silk-screen, coordinating Chicano pre-med, pre-law, and pre-engineering societies, publishing Chicano campus newspapers and literature magazines, supporting worker strikes on campus, teaching each other the latest "*corrido*," "*cumbia*," and "*salsa*" steps for the upcoming dances, programming Chicano radio shows, and just as importantly, hanging around Chicano centers catching up on gossip, cracking jokes in Spanish and code-switching slang, and otherwise creating Chicano community life.

Of course, on most college campuses today you can find many of these same activities, including political activism. However, the years between 1966 and 1975 had a unique quality to them for Chicano college students. A cauldron of energy boiled up out of Chicano campus life, a biting, hot anger at "The System," "The *Gavacho*",[14] and a burning sense of being caught up in something important, historic. The Movement was sparked in part by the sixties ferment and in Vietnam War protest. People in my dormitory at Stanford before 1974 bandied the word "revolution" around freely, feeling with all the self-assurance, vision, and rebellion of youth that they were somehow on the verge of turning the world upside down. Students sported Che Guevara beards and berets and decked their halls and walls with murals and posters of Emiliano Zapata and Pancho Villa, the Mexican revolutionaries.

It was not simply an "arm-chair" kind of radicalism. Inspired by their heroes, Chicanos walked picket lines, organized protest marches, made alliances with Chicano prisoners at Soledad, performed street theater, and wrote articles in their student newspapers about strikes, farm worker exploitation, and medical research on Chicano communities.

Chicanos were not only concerned with forging links with the political struggles of the larger community, but were actively committed to transforming the university and college environments around them. At Stanford, by 1974 Chicanos had pushed for a Chicano Theme House, founded a Chicano Library, and organized the Chicano Fellows Program which was designed to intimately involve Chicano Graduate students in organizing Chicano activities and classes for undergraduates on campus. There was a Pre-Med Society, a Pre-Law Society, a Farm Workers Committee, a Barrio Assistance Program which did tutoring in nearby East Palo Alto, a *Chicana Colectiva* women's group, and numerous graduate student organizations. A maxim of Movement culture was that truly committed Chicanos would sacrifice their schoolwork for political activism.

Protest was not limited to political activities, however. Another hero of the movement was the Chicano street gang member, the "*vato*" and the "*vato loco*" the crazy guy who would rip Anglos off, smoke marijuana, and do other off-the-wall, dangerous acts that contributed to the revolution.[15] As part of the sense of solidarity with that attitude of rebellion, the everyday exchanges and greetings at Casa Zapata, the

Stanford Chicano Theme House dormitory, leaned heavily on East Los Angeles street slang: "*!Orale, ese! ¿Qúe pasa, carnál?*[16] As late as 1972, an air of danger and rebellion lingered around the Stanford Chicano student community, stories told about students getting kicked out of the Residency program, rumors about the fire at the MEChA house, whispers and allusions to the heroic craziness of the really "heavy" Chicanos who had first broken the trail into Anglo Stanford by "kicking ass" and doing "*chingazos.*"[17]

I didn't know too many of these "heavies" personally, since most of this was before my time at Stanford, but I did know a lot of the stories and the names. Once several years later during fieldwork I struck up a conversation with a couple of Stanford graduates who were a few years older than me, now successful lawyers, at a Stanford Chicano Alumni Association meeting. I asked what had happened to "so and so" and "so and so." They started to laugh and warm up to me as I reeled off several names. One of them, shaking his head with a smile, said something about how he couldn't really get into "all that" because the "statute of limitations" hadn't run out on some of the stuff they were all involved in.

The sense of rebellion, of being *in* the university but not *of* the university, permeated Chicano student life. Said one student in an essay she wrote in a Chicano student-designed class in 1974:

> In trying to define my role and reality at Stanford, I come a little closer to defining my role in society. Because of the fact that in four years I will be a product of the university, I must struggle to preserve my "natural resources" (which I consider to be those things in me which stem from my culture, i.e. attitudes, beliefs, ideals, values) so that they will not be altered or assimilated to manufacture the Stanford "middle-class American" student. Part of my role, as I see it, is to prevent this from happening to me.[18]

Students felt that Chicanos in the university were part of a wider community of blue-collar Mexican Americans. Every Chicano touched by the Movement was forced to deal with the idea that their education was not simply theirs as an individual, but that they owed something to the communities from which they had come.

Another important aspect of the Movement was how widely the networks between members of this generation were spread across the Southwest, and how the ideas of Chicanos from different regions cross-fertilized each other to create a cultural richness and excitement. Conferences in Denver and Santa Barbara, where manifestos about Chicano identity and political action were drawn up, drew students from across the country. Chicano graduate students and academics formed alliances and created their own organization in the early seventies called The National Association for Chicano Studies (N.A.C.S.). Students were inspired by political leaders like Corky Gonzalez in Denver, Reies Tijerina in New Mexico, and Cesar Chavez in California. At Stanford, I remember tremendous excitement over the visit of Texas poet Ricardo Sanchez, and the ideas of Tomás Atencio and *La Academia de la Nueva Raza* in New Mexico.

Of course, like any political Movement, a hegemony was created which some Chicanos embraced, some partially accepted, and others outright rejected. In fact, many people were just as alienated from "Chicano" life on campuses as they were from "Anglo" life, because there was pressure to conform to certain dominant modes of behavior, speech, and thought. The street-fighting *cholo* was the most-imitated cultural hero, and the blue-collar Mexican lifestyle the only one any Chicano would admit to having enjoyed back home. Those Chicanos who did not conform sometimes felt snubbed or ostracized by others. There were also sub-groups of Chicanos—Texans vs. Californians; Mexican-born vs. American-born; women vs. men; middle-class vs. working-class—who often wrestled out their differences and didn't always agree.

However, the culture was coherent and compelling enough to be deeply imprinted on the collective consciousness of an entire generation. Its influence would follow them not only from youth into middle age as a cohort, but would cast its pattern on other generations who had played no part in its creation.

THE CHICANO PROFESSIONAL CULTURE OF LOS ANGELES

Around the time when I first chose Chicano professionals as a research topic, I ran into a fellow student in my department, and in the course of our conversation, told him about my choice. He looked at me with a blank expression, and said, "What's so interesting about that?" In response, I sputtered something which was probably unintelligible and scurried off to hide my crushed feelings. The fellow student was a Chicano. If *he* didn't understand what was "interesting" about Chicano professionals, who would?

I hope to pique the interest of the perhaps still skeptical reader with the first section of the book which outlines the "cultural territory" in terms of Generations, Networks, and Identity. In the first chapter, *"Ritual Politics: Of Grapes and Glitter,"* I describe the elegant exuberance of two typical Chicano professional "rituals," trying to capture the excitement and expectation which this emerging elite feels about standing at the edge of a political future full of possibilities. I also begin to lay out the internal political territory by analyzing these rituals in terms of the intricate warp and woof of generational politics, with the Movement generation culture as the dominant pattern.

The following two chapters similarly set out some of the more important cultural motifs which make up Chicano professional culture. In Chapter 2, *"The Familia: Cohesion and Conflict,"* I describe how the densely intricate networks of Movement Chicanos, reaching back into their undergraduate years, sustain and shape the culture and politics of that generation. Movement Chicanos define this sense of network community in terms of the metaphor of family, or *"familia ."* The problem of who belongs to this "family" and who doesn't is taken up in Chapter 3, *"What's in a Name? Chicanos, Latinos, Mexican Americans and Hispanics,"* where I discuss the intricate linguistic politics of ethnic labeling and identification.

Section Two, *Race and the Roots of Resistance*, cuts to the heart of Chicano Movement culture by addressing the question of how Chicanos use racial metaphors and stories about the shared experience of racism in constructing their Chicano professional ethnicity. In Chapter 4, *"Race and Gender: The Body Language of Ethnic Unity,"* I show how Chicanos within the Movement used body metaphors, shaped in terms of race and gender, to fashion a sense of ethnic "racial" pride as a countering response to centuries of Anglo American racism directed against Mexican Americans. The legacy of this "racial" sense of unity in the professional culture is a contradictory one, lending a close feeling of ethnic identification at the same time masking internal conflict under the blanket of "racial" unity.

In Chapter 5, *"Race, Racism and the Power of Stories,"* I describe how Chicanos from diverse backgrounds, across campuses, during the Movement years created the discourse of "Experienced Racism" through telling each other stories about their own experiences of racism. I show how Movement generation Chicanos continue to use such storytelling forms to both tell their own individual "success" stories (against the odds of racism), and to collectively reinforce and pass on to the next generation the Movement ethics of responsibility for blue-collar Chicanos who continue to suffer disproportionately from racism.

The succeeding Section III, *Negotiating a New Class Identity*, describes how Chicano professionals feel about and deal with conflicts surrounding the issue of their social mobility, particularly the clash of values between their youth Movement ideas and their middle-aged professional perspectives. While those that identified with the Movement generation culture most strongly in their youth are usually the most troubled by these tensions, all Chicano professionals who network within Chicano professional circles are affected by them.

In chapter 6, "*Status and the Trappings of Class,*" I describe how Movement generation professionals wrestle with the contradictions between the blue-collar, barrio ideal of Movement culture and the reality of their own white-collar professional lives. In the following chapter 7, "*Serving the Gente: An Alternative Professionalism,*" I demonstrate how professional Chicanos balance their Movement sense of suspicion and critique of professional work values with the demands and pressures of professional life. In the process, some Chicanos actually create distinctly Movement-oriented ways of practicing their professions.

In the last Section, *The Assimilation Myth*, I collect and sharpen my arguments about assimilation. First, in "*Tortillas, Beans, and Bilingualism: Transformed Meanings,*" I continue the earlier argument that Movement Chicanos are creating a unique professional culture. This culture is not merely a matter of practicing remnants of a blue-collar ethnicity and gradually culturally assimilating into the middle-class melting pot, according to the typical model shared by sociologists and popular American culture. What is different is that this culture is rooted in a Movement world-view through which Chicanos self-consciously think of themselves as different from, or actually in opposition to, the dominant Anglo American model. In this vein, eating blue-collar Mexican foods is more than nostalgia; it is a practice of opposition and a reminder that Chicano professionals are culturally different and proud of it, and that they feel a responsibility to, and affinity for, their fellow Mexican Americans who are predominantly blue-collar in a way that is unusual for successful ethnics.

In Chapter 9, *Assimilation Reevaluated*, I talk more specifically about the problems of the classic assimilation myth and continue to argue that the behavior and beliefs of Chicanos professionals, at least in Los Angeles, cannot be predicted by typical sociological and political models. By drawing from the rich, cultural explosion of their Movement years, and blending these elements with the new realities of life as bicultural professionals, Chicanos are not simply "assimilating" as they work their way up the class ladder. They are creating a new culture, a culture with a distinctly "Chicano" flavor and a strong ethic shaped by their involvement in an unprecedented social movement which has changed the shape of Mexican American politics forever. No wonder so many Chicano professionals are enthusiastic about their lives and their futures. Most feel a heady excitement about being bicultural professionals with a strong sense of alternative ethnic identity in the current climate of world politics and, more particularly, in the ethnic fomentation of Los Angeles today.

NOTES

1. Throughout this work I use "Chicano" and "Mexican American" relatively interchangeably as terms. However, as I explain in chapter 3, ethnic labeling in the Chicano community is complex and tricky and my own nuanced usage in this dissertation sometimes reflects those subtleties. The use of terms is not referential, but contextual. For example, there are instances in which I would never use the term "Mexican American;" like where I describe the members of the Movement generation who coined the term "Chicano" to describe themselves.

2. This book does not explain exactly how Mexican American professionals will impact the politics and culture of Los Angeles and the southwest. The point is that as Latinos, primarily Mexicans, increase in population proportionate to Anglos and other minority groups in the southwest [see Hayes-Bautista 1992] I am assuming that their cultural practices will continue to impact the groups around them increasingly. Also, those Mexican Americans in leadership positions, as representatives of those masses, will be able to have increasing influence on wider political arenas, particularly if they can harness the voting power of the voting-eligible population.

3. To be accurate, the movement also began, at least in Los Angeles, on high school campuses, as witnessed by the example of the high school walk-outs of 1968. It can also be argued that the Movement had its roots in Mexican American activism going back to the nineteenth century. However, I agree with Muñoz [1989: 5-8] that there was a qualitative shift which occurred with the Student Movement's call for Chicano nationalism.

4. This idea, that Chicano Movement students have retained values and culture from their university experiences and transformed them in the professional context as a continuing "counter-hegemonic" is the underlying theme of this book. In this argument I differ from the assessment of Jose Limón, who has also examined this question. In his 1981 essay, "The Folk Performance of 'Chicano' and the Cultural Limits of Political Ideology," he contends that little of the Chicano nationalism of Texas university students from the sixties and seventies was retained in professional life. Maybe Texas is different from Los Angeles, or maybe we differ in what we mean by "counter-hegemonic." I do think that Los Angeles is unique. Chicano professionals in San Francisco do not have anywhere near the cultural cohesion as those in L.A. As to the nature of a cultural counter-hegemony, I do not believe that resistance to the dominant culture can only be manifest by members of the working-class. Professionals experience, suffer, and culturally respond to the oppressive, limiting aspects of their own class lives, and may, as I argue in several places in this book, identify across class lines.

5. By the time of publication, some will be in their fifties, and few in their thirties.

6. Renato Rosaldo's 1989 book, *Culture and Truth* (Boston: Beacon Press) discusses these theoretical shifts in depth.

7. For those concerned with my methodology as an anthropologist studying urban groups, the recent trends I describe erase the classic dichotomy between the study of urban plural societies and the allegedly whole, rural, primitive societies which were the meat and potatoes of early anthropology. Contemporary anthropologists are increasingly skeptical about their forebear's claims to being able to identify and isolate discrete, concrete human communities. These "wholes" were actually complex networks of people who shared experiences and meanings.

8. Rosaldo (1989) talks about ritual as intersection p. 17.

9. The fear concerns the possibility of a separatist cultural and/or political movement along the lines of Quebec in Canada. This possibility has been discussed by Chicano nationalists.

10. For this discussion of cohort analysis, I have relied mainly on Rosaldo 1980, Mannheim 1952, and Ryder 1965.

11. A historical ethnography of the Movement across the Southwest, or individual ethnographies of particular campuses in which people's memories of the Movement are recorded and placed within an appropriate cultural analysis, are sorely needed. Alice Reich's book, *The Cultural Construction of Ethnicity: Chicanos in the University*, 1989, an ethnography of the Movement culture on one campus, is a good beginning. José Limón's two essays, "El

Meeting: History, Folk Spanish, and Ethnic Nationalism in a Chicano Student Community," [1982a] an analysis of the use of Spanish within the Movement at the University of Texas at Austin, and "History, Chicano Joking, and the Varieties of Higher Education [1982b] are two exciting examples of this kind of work. Carlos Muñoz's book, *Youth, Identity, Power: The Chicano Movement* details many of the important historical events, but does not describe the taste and texture of the Movement culture.

12. My sophomore year I did not actually have a room in the dormitory. However, I ate most of my meals in the Zapata dining room, and spent almost all my free time hanging around and participating in house activities.

13. "By "Anglo" I mean anyone not "Chicano" or "Mexican." I borrow here from Chicano classifications.

14. "Gavacho" is a derogatory term for Anglo.

15. Arturo Islas explains the role of the "vato loco" in an introduction to a story by Jose Razo, called "Curadas" in *Miquitzli: Un Cuaderno de Arte, Poesia, Cuento, y Canto*. Vol. 2, Issue 1, Winter Quarter, 1974. Stanford: Chicano Press, Stanford, p. 5.

16. A loose translation would be: "Alright, guy! What's happening, brother?"

17. I find this difficult to translate. It means roughly, "blows" but is related to the verb "chingar" which is slang for "fuck," and as Octavio Paz explains in great detail in *The Labyrinth of Solitude*, 1961, pp.73-88, this verb for Mexicans is loaded with cultural baggage having to do with masculine roles.

18. Angelina Briones, "A Token Education," in *Chicanismo*, Vol. 6., Issue 2, Spring Quarter. 1974. Stanford: Chicano Press Stanford.

Chicano Professionals

CHAPTER 1

Ritual Politics:
Of Grapes and Glitter

Banquets and barbecues, receptions and meetings. As with any cultural group, the thick tapestry of Chicano professional life is most visible in its community rituals.[1] What stands out in these rituals is the political tug and pull between generations, particularly between the Movement generation culture now in power and its rivals. Some rituals demonstrate the Movement culture in its full strength, presenting Chicano culture as a virtually seamless texture of shared meanings and invoking in their participants a feeling of belonging to a community with a heroic past and a grand destiny. Other rituals manifest the Movement culture at its weaker points, revealing the more raveled edges of the culture where power struggles fray the fabric and new threads challenge the well worn pattern.

Both types of ritual are crucial to understanding contemporary Chicano professional culture and its generational struggles. It is currently the Chicano Movement generation which holds power, but, as its rituals reveal, this cohort must strive to maintain hegemony. Its leaders must jockey not only among themselves to determine who and what ideological emphasis will dominate within particular organizations, but must also vigilantly defend the hegemony of their generation's culture from that of the upcoming generation.

Those rituals that successfully manage to present the professional culture as a "whole" demonstrate the enduring power of the Movement myth and its values, particularly among those of the generation who participated in and created the Movement culture during their college years. Through careful management of Movement symbols, the leaders who create these professional rituals invoke not only deep nostalgia and bonhomie among participants, but may also motivate participation in Chicano organizations by those Chicanos who may have been distracted from their youthful ideals by the pressures and "temptations" of professional life.

These rituals may even reach out to educate and inculcate Movement values in members of the post-Movement generation who participate in them. The rituals can be powerfully persuasive when carefully designed, presenting the Movement in all its glory as a brilliantly colored tapestry which gathers up all loose threads and mends all tears in a mythic story of grand proportions transcending generations.

No less important to understanding Chicano professional culture however, are those rituals whose purpose is not to glorify Movement culture and celebrate the unity of generations, but rather to challenge the dominance of the Movement generation. The Movement generation was shaped by the particular circumstances and combined forces which its members confronted in their youth and through which they forged a unique culture. Like many of the youth cultures which were created during the sixties and early seventies—the counterculture, drug culture, Anti-War Movement—this Chicano culture has had a lasting impact not only on its own generation's members as they shift class position and surrender their youth to middle age, but also on the members of the Mexican American generations which came before and after them. Yet, while Movement culture still wields its power across generational lines within Chicano professional circles, as these more conflictive rituals reveal, the Movement culture does not necessarily have the last word on how Mexican American politics will be shaped in the future.

The following two stories describe two different rituals whose purposes and results contrast sharply. The first, a reunion of C.M.A.C. and C.M.S.A. (Chicano/Latino Medical Association of California and the Chicano /Latino Medical Students Association) was held during the second annual C.M.A.C. conference at the Los Angeles Airport Marriot hotel on November 3 and 4, 1989. This ritual effectively invoked certain key tropes of Chicano Movement culture and subsequently managed to evoke in most of its participants (including me) an intense feeling of euphoria and unity by making us feel as though our individual stories were woven into the texture of a much larger collective story.

The second event was the Latino Lawyer's Association Second Annual Latino Summer Associates Reception, held in the Los Angeles City Hall Tower room on Friday evening, August 5, 1988. This ritual subtly challenged those same tropes on several different levels and left both its organizers and many of its participants (including me) with ambivalent feelings as we felt tugged and pulled by the warp and woof of a new pattern emerging within Mexican American professional culture.[2]

THE SECOND ANNUAL C.M.A.C./C.M.S.A. CONFERENCE

All day I had been trailing various C.M.A.C. members with my notebook in hand and a baby on my shoulder, in and out of the conference room, the lunch room, the bathroom, the halls. This was the nuts and bolts of fieldwork, not to mention motherhood. But tonight I was putting on my new dress, tucking my notebook discreetly into a small black purse, and leaving the baby home with a sitter. Tonight was the C.M.A.C./C.M.S.A. reunion, "Circles from the Past," an event that had everyone excited because of rumors that Chicano doctors from all over California and several eras of Chicano medical student activism would be there in force.

As I first walked into the hotel that evening around 7:30, I ran into my friend, (Dr.) Miranda Hinojosa,[3]dressed to kill in a tight fitting black cocktail dress and high heels. "Isn't this a great conference?!" she exclaimed, "This is so amazing! I've been to medical conferences before and this one really is professional!" Her obvious pleasure in the fact that Chicanos had finally "arrived" and could produce a proper professional conference (in contrast to the ad-hoc student meetings she was accustomed to) was contagious. In high spirits, we sailed arm in arm into the reception room seeking out my husband and the rest of our friends.

The room that had earlier served as lunchroom was transformed. The lights on the crystal chandeliers were lowered and the large banquet tables had been replaced by small, nightclub style tables with white tablecloths and vases of flowers. A trio playing soft Mexican music stood in one corner and about fifty people milled nearby around a large buffet table set with wine, sodas, and hotel style munchies like lunch meats, cheeses, and tiny *empanadas*.

At the door we discovered a table set with baskets full of brightly colored buttons, each with a logo and the name of one of the

California pre-medical school and medical school organizations which had preceded C.M.A.C. and C.M.S.A.[4] A smartly dressed medical student behind the table directed new arrivals to choose the buttons representing all the organizations to which they had belonged and to wear them.

It was amazing. All these dignified doctors in their suits and dresses, strolling around like college kids, proudly decked out in two inch orange, pink, chartreuse, blue, and yellow buttons and joshing with each other over the memories they evoked. These buttons were a stroke of genius, for they set the tone of the evening. It was to be a genuine celebration of unity; all the quarrels, misunderstandings, and political fights which those buttons represented (for the organizations had formed, melted, splintered, and transformed over the past twenty years in various rows over political turf) were to be forgotten in the larger call of a united history as Chicanos in medicine. The theme was to be repeated throughout the evening.

Miranda dressed herself in the appropriate buttons and we drifted apart as we ran into old friends, met new people, or huddled in corners to catch up with the gossip. Eventually we met up again with my husband, Beto, and another handful of doctors and friends at a table near the podium. I noted that Beto was festooned with at least four different buttons with a pocket full of several others. "Just for the sake of history," he confided. "These are gonna be collector's items."

The room had filled by the time the speakers began. There were around a hundred people before the evening was over. I periodically pestered Beto with whispered questions about who was who as I spotted various interesting looking people at the tables around us. From what he told me it was apparent that the event had successfully lured doctors and students from all over California, even some who had been unable to attend the conference that day.

The conference had been planned by a C.M.A.C. committee of nine people plus a hired conference coordinator. Eight of the committee members were doctors (and one director of a medical school health resources program) who knew each other through University of California at Davis networks going back to the mid seventies. It had been sponsored with donations of either staff or money by various pharmaceutical companies, hospitals, and medical groups.

Historical circumstances and extensive advanced planning by the president of C.M.A.C. in particular had paved the way for this to be a successful conference, both in attendance and in the enthusiasm it could generate for the organization.

I was particularly aware of the significance of this event since I was a friend of the current C.M.A.C. president, Ignacio Garcia. In fact, over coffee several years before, we had talked about the problems that Chicano doctors had encountered in sustaining a powerful professional organization. At least one other attempt had been made earlier with the Pacific Medical Association. Why had it been so difficult, I asked him, to keep a *professional* organization going, in contrast to the Chicano undergraduate and medical student organizations which were thriving?

He suggested that while Chicanos were students their activism on behalf of other Chicanos in medicine corresponded with their own ambitions, i.e. it looked good on resumes, and it created networks where they could get help in school as well as recommendations and advice about residencies and jobs. Once these same active students finally became physicians, they were too busy working, having fun, getting married, buying first houses, and so on to be interested in an organization that did not appear to directly benefit them. What was different now, in the late 1980's, Ignacio claimed, was that a substantial amount of Chicano physicians had been in practice long enough to have indulged in satisfying much of that "delayed gratification," and might now be ready to "help the community" again.

Ignacio Garcia was also central to another recent development which enhanced the possibility for the conference's success. He and seven other Chicano and Latino physicians had in the last year created the first Chicano residency training program and large medical practice group in Los Angeles. They had organized a medical group among friends and acquaintances and contracted with White Memorial Hospital, a hospital with a primarily Latino clientele, to bring their patients exclusively there and to run a residency training program for doctors who wanted to train in the barrio.

This program had been going well for about a year, generating much excitement in the Chicano physician community since it was the first such attempt to create a (predominantly) Chicano residency program.

These recent developments in the Chicano professional community in Los Angeles helped to conjure up a feeling among many people present that day that the fruits of all their labor as medical school activists were beginning to ripen. Perhaps this conference was the beginning of a vital physicians organization which could have a major political impact on a statewide and perhaps even national level.

However, Ignacio and his committee were not leaving the success of the conference as a vehicle for the boosting of C.M.A.C. to chance. Great care was taken to orchestrate the evening to enhance the standing of C.M.A.C. as the appropriate organization to strengthen and unite the political power of the Chicano medical community.

The mood was set by focusing on a narrative theme of which everyone felt a part, a myth formed in the heart of the Chicano Movement culture. This was the story of *"The Struggle to Make It."* It was a story told on two intertwining levels. At one level the story concerned the endeavor of every individual there to "make it" through the medical education system. At the other level, it concerned the wider undertaking of their collective organizations, which in the last twenty years, had formed and fizzled and formed again in the intense efforts of getting more Chicanos successfully through medical training.

The speakers and their subjects had been carefully chosen to enhance this theme. The first was a veteran member of several of the student health organizations, a doctor with a Masters degree in public health who was widely known as a firmly entrenched Chicano nationalist with an activist student past in the Movement. It was his task to gather up the various threads of Chicano medical history since the Sixties and to present it as a unified story.

His speech emphasized two themes. One was how the earliest Chicano pre medical school and medical school organizations of the late sixties and early seventies had evolved from back-pack conferences of militant students (he had dredged up old health organization literature on how to make mace and how to behave when you're arrested) to the current hotel hosted assembly of full-fledged doctors. He emphasized that although appearances had changed, this was still the same group of people, the same ongoing organization in a new form: "You're not attending a new meeting here. We go back a long way."

His other theme was that the struggle for equal representation in health care professions continued even after two decades of progress: "It's the same issues at these meetings twenty years later: retention, recruitment, financial aid, people not applying still. In 1989 that's still happening." In other words, people should not feel that just because

there were larger numbers of Chicano physicians in California, that
the struggle for affirmative action was won.

The choice of the speaker, and the speech itself, were key to
successfully projecting a unified history in the spirit of the Movement.
First, the speaker represented the first generation of affirmative action
medical students. Second, he had been active in the leadership of
many of the organizations named that night. Third, he had always
projected his image as the "Movement Activist Chicano", the rebel,
the die-hard Nationalist, the Movement in its hot, potent youth. And
last, he was a controversial figure and the fact that he could make a
speech which effectively projected unity somehow made the history
that much more credible.

The speech itself nostalgically evoked the good old days of student
organizing, "when we didn't know anything," and "we slept in gyms"
when attending conferences on other campuses. He mentioned a litany
of names, the founders of various organizations, a patriarchal lineage
of heroes in the struggle. One name he mentioned in particular was
that of Saul Nevarez, an M.D. with a Masters degree in public health,
who had been seminal during the Brown governorship in getting more
Chicanos into medical schools.

I was impressed by the speech, but still a bit skeptical about the
entire project, especially since he had neglected to mention some of the
women that I knew were important in the history, one of whom was
Miranda sitting next to me, who had been a founder of C.M.S.A. I
leaned over and whispered in her ear, and she nodded. (Later we found
her name on the display which had been set up to illustrate the history
of the organizations, but we were only partially mollified).

The next speaker was the director of the Office of Minority Health
in the Office of the Assistant Secretary for Health, Public Health
Services, from Washington D.C. The doctor shaped his speech in tune
with the theme of the evening by talking about his own experiences as
an African-American pre-professional and medical student during the
Sixties in the days of the "Great Society." He emphasized how the
early organizing of Blacks in the health field was a similar story to
that of the earlier speaker, one of struggle, internal disagreement, and
ultimate working together to increase access to medical education. He
too mentioned some of the earlier Chicano health organizers, praising
Saul Nevarez in particular, as had the earlier speaker. He topped his
speech off by urging the audience to participate in their organization,

C.M.A.C., and assuring them that the government would try to be responsive to the organization.

The last speaker was introduced by the C.M.A.C. president as a "full blooded Pueblo Indian dentist" who was a former Assistant Surgeon General during the sixties. The man had convened the first Special Career Grants Committee which was to disperse five million dollars granted by a health allocations bill to increase minorities in health care. This was a program, all the doctors in the room were aware, that had made it possible for the first of them to go to medical school, and the audience recognized him as one of the "old timers" of the health careers struggle.

He was a soft-spoken man, probably in his mid sixties if not older, wearing a rumpled suit of no particular color and a large circular turquoise and coral pendant hanging around his neck. The fact that he was recognized as a "revered elder," along with his quiet manner and gentle humor (and I suspect the fact that he was a Native American, a group which is strongly attractive to Chicanos in their idealization of their Indian heritage) immediately caught the crowd's attention. The room became silent to hear him speak.

He wove a story going back to the "exciting times" of the sixties when the committee was first convened in Washington, citing names which for me, via my husband, were like a chronicle of ancient heroes. He talked about the ones who had gone before in the struggle, Blacks, Chicanos, and Indians, "a lot of brave warriors." His male military metaphor continued: The early days were like when his father had hit the beach at Iwo Jima. The first ones had established the beachhead (and here he mentioned the name of Saul Nevarez specifically) and while they dug in, the planes and ships and foot soldiers came in behind to reinforce them.

During this part of the speech, I looked casually over at my husband and saw to my surprise that he had tears in his eyes. I felt them well up in me, and looked around. The man had everyone's rapt attention. He was telling the Movement story.

Toward the end of the speech, like an evangelical preacher winding up his sermon with a call to redemption, he offered a warning and a call to arms: "There are those who don't want to help because they've forgotten how they got here." To illustrate what he meant, he cited the example of Indians who had "benefited from all the struggles of those that have gone before them," and then when they get out of medical school, or dental school, they did not want to go back to their communities because they wanted to have comfortable middle-class lives. He urged the audience to remember where they came from, summing up the entire thrust of the evening by saying, "Now you have your union cards. . . . I feel that you were born today because your people need you."

At that point, as he quietly stepped back from the podium, the audience sprang to its feet and burst into a sustained, fervent standing ovation. This is when I realized that everyone else had been feeling similarly to the way Beto and I were feeling. The speeches had built up to this moment. A Chicano nationalist, symbol of the Movement in its most specific form; a Black government bureaucrat, a member of a fellow minority group who was now in a powerful position; and then a Native American, a representative of that quintessential disenfranchised minority, and one of the revered elders of medical affirmative action, all of them invoking a shared history of struggle rooted in the sixties Civil Rights experience. Skepticism, rivalries, jealousy, bitterness were swept aside in the intensity of feeling that somehow we were all part of something profound and important and bigger than all of us.

A few other announcements were made after that but they were anti-climactic. Still, when it was all wrapped up, no one wanted to leave. We lingered around the tables, listening to the last strains of the trio as the waiters began to clean up. A rumor circulated that one of the doctors was hosting a reception in his suite in honor of Chicanos for Creative Medicine, a pre-medical undergraduate organization of which he had been an organizer. The trio was transferred downstairs to the rooms, and cartloads of icy beer and soft drinks wheeled in, compliments of the host.

This turned out to be a marvelous party with booze and spirits flowing freely in an out of the room, out into the halls and the patio outside. The mood was happy and intimate. I ran into Ignacio Garcia, the president of C.M.A.C., and he hugged me uncharacteristically, a relaxed, perfectly happy smile stretched across his usually more serious face. Beto and I lingered and talked until we were exhausted and then we were ready to go home, though the party was still going. We floated back to our car, hand in hand. It couldn't get any better than this.[5]

SECOND ANNUAL SUMMER ASSOCIATES RECEPTION

It was a night of stars, a glittering reception on the top floor of the Los Angeles City Hall tower with Chicano celebrities of the L.A. law circuit clinking glasses and mingling furiously in a room of windows flung open to the night sky and the sparkling city below. Attorneys, law students, judges, city commissioners, assorted politicians and curious friends—most of them visibly Latino, a crowd of dark heads and Hispanic features decked out in suits and ties, silk dresses and heels—buzzed eagerly around each other and a set of tables heaped to the ceiling with gorgeously prepared southwestern hors d'oeuvres. This mountain of food, sculpted of baskets, earthen platters, pastel table cloths and exotic, richly colored flowers, and rising magnificently up out of the middle of a room on the top of a tower overlooking Los Angeles, set the tone for the evening—high drama and Chicano yuppie perfection. Every morsel of food was beautiful and ethnically correct: tiny finger sized chicken *empanadas*, (no beef or pork for this cholesterol and calorie conscious crowd), miniature vegetarian *tamales* accompanied by bowls of green and red chile salsas, heaps of careful little squares of fruit (not just watermelon and strawberries, but *jicama*, *papaya* and *membrillo*), tortilla chips with bean dip and *guacamole*, and an enormous corn salad molded elegantly in the shape of an ear of corn.

The event was hosted by a group of Latino (mostly Mexican American) predominantly corporate lawyers in their first few years of law practice in major firms. They had recently formed an organization called the Latino Lawyers' Association which stated as its goal to "ensure greater access and opportunity for Latinos in the legal community and to be a force for the political, educational, social and economic enhancement of the Latino community." This included promotion of Latinos in the public political sphere and corporate law firms, fostering education for Latino high school students, and networking socially and politically with each other. Most of the members of the group had gone to law school at prestigious universities like Stanford or the Ivy League schools, and several of them had worked together in various "Latino" organizations and projects while in school. They had hosted a reception the year before, a modest affair. This year their ambitions and resources were far greater and they had planned an elegant, impressive evening.

While the official purpose of the event was a reception to welcome Latino law students working for the summer in major law firms in Los Angeles, the less formal purpose of the evening was voiced by one of the reception committee members as she showed me around before the event began. "It's our coming out party," she chimed, waving her hand around the beautiful, window-wrapped room. By "coming out" I took her to mean the group's public assertion of its presence on the Los Angeles law scene. It took the rest of the evening's events to reveal to me not only some of the dimensions this "coming out" took, but to identify the "coming out" as a kind of challenge on many levels, to the status quo of the Chicano Movement culture and its strongest adherents in the Mexican American law community, the leadership of the Mexican American Bar Association.

I had felt intimations of the multi-leveled purposes of the event when I attended one of the early planning sessions of the reception committee. The overwhelming concern at this early stage was to host an event that would impress their own law firms with its professionalism and attention to detail and to include on the invitation list a large enough number of students, lawyers, and public dignitaries that they could count on at least three hundred people attending. Exposure was clearly a key concern; everyone racked their brains for ideas about how to get the media to cover the event.

The planning was careful, with minute attention to detail. First, they raised money by soliciting $500.00 donations from all the law firms they represented, eventually soliciting seventeen law firms to contribute. They hired a catering company which specialized in southwestern cuisine and would handle the invitations and other details for them. They invited not only the Latino students who were working in corporate firms that summer but other Latino students from all the local law schools. They made special invitations to various dignitaries, including all the local Latino politicians and judges, as well as lawyers from various organizations and firms like M.A.B.A. (Mexican American Bar Association) and M.A.L.D.E.F. (Mexican American Legal Defense and Education Fund). And they wrestled over the issue of who would speak and about what they would speak, balancing out a concern with having women, prominent politicians, and representatives of M.A.B.A. represented.

While they invited over 1,000 people and expected no more than 300, well over 300 people attended that night. The large room was packed for more than four hours as people came and stayed and went.

Their Master of Ceremonies that night was the Principal Administrative Coordinator from the L.A. mayor's office and their speakers were the Assistant Presiding Judge of the Los Angeles Superior Court (Mexican American), the Los Angeles City Attorney (non-Hispanic), the President of the Los Angeles City Planning Commission, who was a past president of M.A.B.A. and a partner in a large law firm (Mexican American), and the current president of M.A.B.A. (Mexican American).

The speakers talked about serving the community, becoming involved in government, and the various programs that M.A.B.A. offered. Unfortunately, it was very difficult to hear them. Indeed, several of the speakers expressed frustration at the lack of attention and the noise level because they were not set on a raised platform, the amplification was not adequate, and the room was packed with people (more perhaps than the committee had anticipated) who were busy mingling, talking, eating, and being impressed by the festivity and/or the political ramifications of the event.

For that, really, was the less official purpose of the evening, to impress the Mexican American establishment and the law firms which had sent their money and their representatives. This purpose, which was understood at some level by all the members of the organization but not fully endorsed by all of them, made the evening truly a "coming out" party of a small cadre of ambitious, primarily young (under 35) lawyers, who wanted to send a message to what many of them considered the "old guard" of the Mexican American Bar Association. The message was that they wanted to be included in the power structure and that they had big money and lots of political savvy behind them.

The message was received loud and clear and the M.A.B.A. elite, many of whom were there that evening, appeared to be upset by the challenge. I became aware of just how riled they were about an hour into the evening, when I ran into one of the former M.A.B.A. presidents, a man I had interviewed a few weeks earlier. I asked him, "So, what do you think of all this?" and he said, "I don't like it at all," and frankly proceeded to tell me exactly why he was not pleased.

After that conversation and a few others, some careful eavesdropping, and a bit of detective-style deduction, I gathered that the M.A.B.A. crowd who was there that evening, which included several past presidents and current officers, was upset because they felt that the Latino Lawyer's Association was setting itself up as a young rival to their own organization which was over thirty years old. Furthermore, some felt that it was a deliberate political move designed to maneuver some of its members into leadership positions in M.A.B.A. or in the wider political community without going through the channels that had already been established. Said one M.A.B.A. member, "I'm not going to let these young upstarts just come in and get everything without paying their dues." . . ."We have paved the way for them. The path has been greased by us. They have to remember their roots. Part of the reason they're here is because of us."

From this M.A.B.A. member's perspective this group of young corporate lawyers from Ivy league schools calling themselves "Latino" and refusing to make the obligatory gestures of obeisance to the power structure, were openly challenging their elders and breaking the code of the Movement, which was to acknowledge and respect "those who had gone before in the struggle."

First, the event itself appeared to be sending confused messages to the students and lawyers who attended. The L.L.A. was not well known, for it was a new organization. As far as I knew, only one of its members was highly active in M.A.B.A., the established Mexican American Bar Association with its origins going back even before the Chicano Movement generation of the sixties. Furthermore, the L.L.A.'s precise relationship to M.A.B.A. had never been spelled out, although its members had discussed the problem. Thus, when guests were greeted at the bottom of the elevator to the tower, they were asked to fill out a card asking whether they would like to receive information about 1) the Latino Lawyers Association, 2) The Mexican American Bar Association, or 3) both the above organizations, without any clear explanations of what the organizations were nor what relationship they had to each other. M.A.B.A. members surely felt this was an upstart move, to be claiming some affiliation with their organization and yet at the same time, to be soliciting members out from under their noses.

Even more significantly, however, was what I knew from talking to the members of the Latino Lawyers Association myself. Several of them stated that they had political ambitions and that their organization was in some ways a "springboard" to help them gain political reputations without having to "play the institutional game" as they would have to by going through M.A.B.A. or the local Democratic committee. Furthermore, as another member of the group characterized it to me, some of the group members intended to "infiltrate" M.A.B.A. and eventually "take it over."

The way that the group legitimated their challenge to M.A.B.A. was by characterizing what they perceived as the differences between the two groups. These were generational and educational. One lawyer explained the generational difference in this way:

> They used to be solo practitioners and people who did political kinds of work or worked for the Public Defenders or District Attorney's offices... And those were the first wave of Latino lawyers. From what people have told us, the old group of people were mostly men who had a lot of bad attitudes toward women, sort of chauvinistic, and people claim that there was this old boy's network and you had to be with the right people.

Another perceived generational difference was that M.A.B.A. continued to focus on a Mexican nationalist identity, as witnessed by its name Mexican American Bar Association, and that although it included other Latinos in its ranks, it was not recognizing the potential of embracing a wider Latino lawyer membership as well as political constituency. Most of the L.L.A. members tended to couple this observation with their perception of the educational differences between the two groups. As one L.L.A. member explained, because of their members' education in East Coast establishment schools, they felt they were "better suited for the type of politicking and economic development that our community is gonna be developing in the near future." This member explained how the exploding Latino population due to increased immigration from Central and Latin America and the high birthrate would require a new kind of leadership adding that, "I don't think that these old line Latinos, Latino attorneys and Latino public figures are prepared to be leaders of that movement."

From my point of view, this was classic politicking. Certain L.L.A members were fabricating differences where there weren't any major differences in order to launch their group politically. I had observed M.A.B.A. fairly closely. Although it was still dominated by Chicano Movement culture, including a leaning toward patriarchal style and male control, women were active, if not dominant, in the leadership. The current M.A.B.A. president and president-elect were both women, and women had in the last several years staged a coup of their own within the M.A.B.A. ranks, organizing themselves to challenge the "good old boy" system. Furthermore, all the M.A.B.A. elites that I talked to were fully comfortable with the inclusive term "Latino," and were moving in the direction of coming to terms with the new "Latino" political realities of Los Angeles, whether or not they fully advocated abandoning any form of Mexican American nationalism.

Thus, the L.L.A., by casting M.A.B.A. members as an old cadre of male chauvinist, government lawyers who were insensitive to women and incapable of handling the complexities of the new "Latino" reality, were setting themselves up as the new leadership wave (Ivy League trained and comfortable in the corporate halls of America) of the Latino future in Los Angeles. This was a quintessential example of the classic challenge that every up-and-coming generation gives to the older generation in the struggle over how (and how soon) they will wrest the scepter from those that wield it.

And they seemed to be succeeding at their plan to speed up the process of their own grasp at power. That very night, one of their members was appointed to the L.A. Human Relations Commission. A representative from the Mayor's office who was also acting as Master of Ceremonies, made what appeared to be a surprise announcement. As he explained the story to the crowd, I found the circumstances surrounding this appointment intriguing.

He described how he had recently been invited to an. L.L.A. meeting to talk to the group about how one became an L.A. commissioner. When he told the group that the process required money as well as influence, he noted that several members expressed disappointed because they were all young in their careers. What resulted from the meeting, however, was that several of the members nevertheless sent him resumes, and the speaker proceeded to recommended to the mayor that he appoint a young person who didn't necessarily have any money to one of the commissions. The result was that one of the L.L.A. members gained an appointment. Clearly the group had already been making political moves and succeeding to a certain extent. The announcement at the reception (which I believe was a surprise to all concerned) was an obviously successful maneuver to outflank the M.A.B.A. establishment.

After the announcement was made, I began to wonder if everyone on the committee would be equally pleased that the unofficial purpose of the evening, i.e. political exposure, was superseding the official purpose to welcome the new law students. What I suspected was that a few of the women from the organization, many of whom I had interviewed, might be feeling that the politically ambitious males (for it was only males whom I had heard openly expressing political ambitions) had hijacked the reception and turned the Latino Lawyers Association strictly into a vehicle for their own political purposes. Frankly, although I did pick up some displeased growling from one woman, I was unable to substantiate this intuition, although it seemed perfectly apparent to me that these males were the most obvious beneficiaries of the event. In fact, not only did one of them become a City Commissioner, but a year later I noticed another of them being installed as a Board Member of M.A.B.A.)[6]

In short, the evening's events produced several different results. The confrontation between the L.L.A. and M.A.B.A. was resolved through several meetings of their respective leadership members. It was negotiated that the L.L.A. should become a subcommittee within M.A.B.A. Also, several of its members would be promoted to the Board as soon as possible. As to the L.L.A itself, from what I could gather, the intense social networking and support group aspect of the organization had broken down substantially, perhaps due to the now more openly visible differences within the group.

While these young upstarts ultimately managed to gain a toe-hold in the establishment by hosting a ritual challenge to those in power, these political gains were almost lost that night through one small but highly significant incident.

About a half an hour into the festivities, I noticed several of the reception planners huddled intensely in a corner. Then one of them scurried off as though to accomplish an unpleasant errand quickly. I sidled over in their direction, professional curiosity propelling me towards what I was sure was a tasty bit of cultural detail.

Soon I was able to discreetly approach one of the committee members and ask him what was up. He told me candidly that a few moments earlier, a compatriot of Cesar Chavez who was attending the festivities that night had discovered grapes on the hors d'oeuvre table and was extremely upset. At that very moment, the committee member reminded me, Cesar was fasting to protest the use of pesticides on grapes, and the grape boycott was definitely still "on." He moaned that it had been a major political faux pas to allow grapes to be served that evening.

The irony (you must forgive my anthropological glee) was delicious. A star studded event sparkling with innumerable members of the L.A. Chicano Who's Who, a coming out party of eager, politically ambitious Chicano corporate attorneys, a gathering of many former Chicano Movement activists, and someone had forgotten the meaning of "grapes."

Grapes, like Coors beer, head lettuce, and Gallo wine had once been forbidden foods for Chicano movement activists because of United Farmworker boycotts in the sixties and seventies. Grapes continued to be on the forbidden list, because the United Farmworkers Union (U.F.W.) was still boycotting their sale.[7] By serving grapes at such a publicly Mexican American event,[8] and getting "caught" by a friend of the Movement hero Chavez (who at that very moment was fasting to publicize the ongoing boycott) the young "Latino lawyers" were risking everything that they had been fighting that evening to gain: i.e. political credibility. Cesar Chavez and the U.F.W. were central symbols of the Chicano Movement of the sixties and seventies, a direct tie for students to their blue-collar "roots" as farm workers and disenfranchised working-class members. Members of the Chicano Movement cohort who were now successful lawyers, no matter how influential or powerful they might become, would never forget the symbolism of grapes. It would be like admitting that you forgot who you represented, that you had lost your concern for the Mexican masses, that your allegiances were now strictly with your own class.

It was one thing to be able to host a glitzy, glamorous, high stakes evening to impress members of the professional class, but to forget the meaning of grapes in such a public political forum was a direct challenge to the Chicano Movement ideology of solidarity with the blue-collar worker, an ideology which was still the dominant political discourse of the Chicano politician. As a M.A.L.D.E.F.[9] lawyer who was there that night said to me when I told him what had happened, "We (meaning the Chicano Movement cohort) know better than that."

The immediate result of this event that evening was that the grapes were taken off the table, and Chavez's friend was asked to make a little speech about the boycott toward the end of the evening. The speech was a mild chastisement, a reminder not to go and sin again.

What is crucial here is that this grapes incident threw the conflict of the cohorts into high relief, making it clear that what ultimately was being challenged on this glitzy turf beyond a changing of the guard was the Chicano Movement culture itself. The Latino Lawyers had not thought about the grapes because the issue of "grapes" and farm workers had not been an integral part of the formative period of their youth. They had not spent their college years on the picket line in front of grocery and liquor stores, nor spent their weekends and summers in Delano working with the Union, nor plastered their dorm walls with original murals and posters of Cesar and the U.F.W. eagle. This was the generational experience of the average M.A.B.A. member, but not of the Latino Lawyers. Their political consciousness was shaped by different forces, and they were frankly proud of this fact. They had not experienced the intense baptism into Movement values which saturated the souls of the Movement generation, making their every move into the higher strata of professional status a careful dance of justification in relation to the blue-collar Mexican American whose ultimate incarnation was the farm worker. Rather, they promoted themselves as the first generation who would move easily in the corporate world, who would call themselves "Latino, " who would serve their people with the smooth sophistication of an accustomed elite.

I must admit that it was difficult for me to reserve my judgements about the events of this evening. I had followed this group of pleasant, intelligent young people in the L.L.A. for several months, enjoying their company and feeling grateful for their openness to my fieldwork inquiries. And I had experienced excitement about the reception, largely because I was swept up in the momentum of the group and also because it was a beautifully organized, wonderfully situated, and historically significant event, not to mention a great party.

However, as I gradually began unraveling the various meanings of the events I had witnessed and tried to write about them, I found that my Movement values kept swelling up from the depths, overwhelming my careful attempts at neutral analysis. I found myself tapping sweeping, sarcastic condemnations of the reception organizers into my computer. For example:

> In all their concern for creating the perfect impression that evening, they perhaps ended up saying what they really were about more clearly than they intended: a room high above Los Angeles, above the crowds, people dressed in silk, heels, and Italian suits, and food that paid homage to "Latino" roots without descending to plebeian cholesterol laden, greasy stereotype. And then there were the grapes. The working-class Chicano had been forgotten that evening, and the new professional Latino, with a token nod in the direction of the Chicano Movement, was challenging the old way of doing politics.[10]

I was not the only one with ambivalent feelings about that evening. While in many ways, the evening could be called successful (a lot of people came, and it generated much excitement) it left several of its planners feeling ambivalent, if not worried. As one of them put it to me as he slipped out the door toward the end of the evening, he had "mixed feelings". He was trying to leave before he was collared by a partially inebriated and very angry M.A.B.A. old-timer who wanted to give him a piece of his mind. He was obviously worried about this M.A.B.A. response to the reception, yet he said to me, with total ingenuousness, that when he concentrated on "the real purpose of the evening", which was to make the new summer associates feel comfortable and to give them an opportunity to meet people, he realized the whole thing had been a success.

All judgements about their sincerity aside, perhaps what the L.L.A. lawyers had miscalculated was how swift and angry the reaction of M.A.B.A. members would be to their challenge. This may have been because they underestimated the political savvy of these "old timers," not realizing that its leadership was already intensely aware of the changing realities of Los Angeles ethnic politics, including not only the increasing Central American demographics and "Latino" political landscape, but also the emerging power of women professionals. The Chicano Movement culture as practiced by the M.A.B.A. "in crowd" was already being challenged from within. What must have angered them greatly was that this group of young people had made their challenge from the outside, without first immersing themselves in the organizational discourse which had been churning among members and between new generations for thirty years.

COMING OUT PARTIES: AN EMERGING ELITE

While the Latino Lawyer's reception was more obviously a "coming out" party, it shared another sense of "coming out" with the C.M.A.C. reception. These two rituals were only two of many such parties hosted by upwardly mobile, politically ambitious professional Chicanos in Los Angeles over the last several years. Like all these other events—festive M.A.L.D.E.F. fundraiser picnics, elegant M.A.B.A. installation banquets, informal Latinas in Health barbecues—these two events were joyous celebrations of the Los Angeles Mexican American success story, quintessential class rituals, ripe with quivering (and controversial) new cultural meanings. And their creators and participants were intensely aware of the impact these events could be having on the wider social and political scene—a challenge to the status quo, and a portent of ethnic realities to come.

For as U.C.L.A. Public Health professor David Hayes-Bautista[11] was saying as a popular speaker on the L.A. Chicano professional organization circuit, the demographics were changing rapidly in California, so that within the next fifty years or less, the majority population would be Latino. Professional Chicanos were gearing themselves up for this exciting future of potential leadership.

Of course, within those Chicano professional ranks, controversies were intense about what form that leadership would take, and at the center of the conflict was the role of Chicano Movement culture. In the late 1980's, the Chicano Movement cohort dominated professional politics, and in order to be successful in these professional organizations, it was necessary to have mastered the discourse, if not genuinely feel a part of the culture itself. But that culture was coming under attack from several angles, including an increasingly organized and sophisticated women's movement, and the new, post-Movement "Latino" generation, as exemplified by the Latino Lawyers Association.

As the C.M.A.C. "Circles of the Past" reunion illustrated, however, it is perhaps easier to orchestrate a ritual which reinforces the dominant hegemony—in this case, *Chicanismo*—than to host one which challenges that same hegemony. The C.M.A.C. conference organizers simply had to carefully organize their event around the shared themes of the Movement, with attention to the particular manifestations these took in terms of the medical experience. Thus, even though several of us felt that women had been peripheralized in the patriarchal history telling that night, and that the essential "unity" of these actually quite fractious groups was exaggerated for the sake of boosting this new physicians organization, we were perfectly willing to forget all this and bask in the familiar and elevating myths, forged in the fire of the Chicano Movement, which had sustained us all through the rigors and traumas of pre-med, medical, and residency training.[12]

The L.L.A. reception committee was up against a far more difficult task in hosting a ritual which was essentially a challenge to the prevailing Chicano law establishment. First, they simply were not thoroughly familiar with the political arena upon which they were throwing down their gauntlet. Most of them were young, or had been trained in East Coast schools and were therefore inexperienced in the intricacies of California Chicano pre-professional and professional politics.

And perhaps even more importantly, they were proposing a new ideology, which was not yet fully articulated, even within the private discourse of any one of them. Its basis was essentially that since they had been trained in Ivy league "Anglo establishment" schools, they were better-educated and more in touch with national and international events. An essential part of this claim, which challenged a central tenet of Chicano Movement ideology, was that they had no interest in promoting the narrative of *academic* struggle which so dominated the current Chicano professional discourse. One of them actually urged at a planning committee meeting, and was not opposed, that they should tell the speakers to avoid the usual cliches congratulating the crowd on having made it and assuring them that they were just as successful and smart as the Anglos. "I know I'm good. I don't need anyone to tell me that," he quipped, and everyone nodded in agreement.

By so establishing their credentials primarily through a claim of superiority, the L.L.A. was subtly challenging another dimension of the Chicano struggle myth. This was the way that an emphasis on having "struggled" through school allowed increased identification with other Chicanos who had not successfully made it through the educational system. This kind of interpretation of one's educational achievements—"We might not have made it," "We got here by the skin of our teeth and the help of all these other Chicanos"—de-emphasized the differences between those in the blue-collar class and those in the professional class. The L.L.A. was perhaps unwittingly making claims for their own uniqueness in terms which ultimately threatened the way that Chicano professionals had for the last twenty years explained and justified their superior class position. Those in power were not going to let this challenge off easily. It threatened not only their political positions, but also the very basis of their identities as ethnic professionals.

NOTES

1. These rituals include monthly organizational meetings, annual conferences, receptions and dinners to welcome newcomers and honor achievement and service, small planning committees, officer installation banquets, and various kinds of fundraising events.

2. While I have chosen a lawyers' event to represent a more culturally conflictive ritual, and a doctors' event to represent a more culturally cohesive ritual, I do not mean to imply that one professional group is more deeply steeped in the Chicano Movement than another. I chose these two rituals because I simply had more access to the complexities of their planning and execution, and knew more about the planners and participants than for any other rituals I attended, so was able to collect richer data.

3. All names in this work are pseudonyms unless otherwise noted.

4. These were N.C.H.O. (National Chicano Health Organization), C.C.M. (Chicanos for Creative Medicine), Los Curanderos, B.A.R.C.H.(Bay Area Coalition for Health), C.H.E. (Chicanos in Health Education), La RaMA (La Raza Medical Association), La Raza C.M.A. (Chicano Medical Association), and P.M.A. (Pacific Medical Association). The Pacific Medical Association had been the first attempt at a physician organization. All the rest were either pre-medical or medical school student organizations.

5. Three years later I learned from some of its organizers another crucial aspect of this conference. While it was indeed a celebration of unity, it was also a coming-of-age party and a coup of sorts. The organizers had purposefully organized the event to send a message to one particular doctor who had been politically influential in early medical school affirmative action struggles and who now was perceived by many as trying to keep Chicano medical organizations under his own individual control. This doctor had been a role model for many of these younger (by ten years plus or minus) but they were now wary of what they perceived as his unwillingness to share power with them now that they were professionals themselves. The organizers of the conference felt that his leadership style was not democratic or grassroots enough. This doctor was made the official honoree of the conference, mentioned in almost all of the speeches and thanked for his role, and given an award luncheon in his honor. In one sense this could be seen as a generational coup, but it is in situations like this that the problem of reifying generations becomes apparent. This doctor was about ten years older than most of the organizing doctors; however, he appeared to identify with many Movement values and had been active in affirmative action struggles in the sixties. The CMAC faction was at one level overthrowing an elder, but it was not challenging the Chicano Movement ideology. Even within the Movement generation there were "mini-generations" which divided people into those that had started their education and careers in the early affirmative action years, and those that had followed them several years later. In this case, the younger Movement members felt that they were challenging the "Sixties" way of doing politics which was autocratic and patriarchal, developed in the years when

there were few Chicanos in medicine and each person carved out his own individual kingdom. Their own politics, they felt, was more egalitarian and democratic and had been developed in the collective struggles of the first relatively large number of Chicano medical student and physician organizations.

6. Interestingly enough, it turned out that I had overlooked one particular woman in the group, who was actually a few years older than most of the other members and was not from an Ivy League school nor presently working in a prestigious law firm. She was, however, quite a politician. Only a few years after my research, I learned that both she and one of the other (male)members of the committee had run for and gained City or State political offices.

7. However, many Chicano professionals who identify with the Chicano Movement cohort are still uneasy about buying or drinking anything with a Gallo or Coors label, and jokes about this may surface at parties or events where someone brings or serves either of these brands. Interestingly enough, however, I often encountered grapes being served at professional Chicano events, and never once heard anything said about it. When I asked a friend once about it, he said that somehow, in the L.A. urban setting, the grape boycotts seemed a remote issue.

8. Although the invitations had called this a "Latino" event, most of the participants were of Mexican American descent, which reflects the city's demographics.

9. Mexican American Legal Defense and Education Fund, a national legal advocacy organization.

10. While I interpret this particular ritual as a challenge to Chicano Movement culture and to the M.A.B.A. establishment, I am not claiming that the L.L.A. was in no way committed to certain goals associated with the Chicano Movement, particularly to helping advance the blue-collar masses. Many of the L.L.A. members privately expressed strong feelings about their own commitment to bettering the "community," feelings which were clearly more than political posturing. In fact, several L.L.A. members were committed to a mentoring program of Latino high school students in barrio high schools, and in fact, a few years later (after my official fieldwork period), one of them organized the "Hispanic Professional Roundtable" organization to sponsor Latinos from diverse professions in mentoring such students.

11. This is his real name. His book dealing with the subject is *No Longer A Minority: Latinos and Social Policy in California*, Los Angeles: U.C.L.A. Chicano Studies Research Center Publications, 1992.

12. I say "we" here deliberately, because I had experienced this narrative by living with my husband and perhaps being overly-identified with his struggles through medical school and residency.

CHAPTER 2

The *Familia*:
Cohesion And Conflict

The Movement generation owes its cultural strength to its dense networks. These networks originated primarily in the 1960's and early 1970's when Chicanos first entered California universities and colleges in large numbers. This network community is to a degree typical of ethnic, class, or mutual interest networking groups where key relationships are created through college friendships and associations [Ehrenreich 1989:13-14]. However, it's density and cohesiveness are unique, the product of a vital Chicano student Movement culture transformed by its creators into the professional context.

It bears the marks of this history in several distinct ways. First, individual Chicanos experience these networks through friendships reaching back into their undergraduate years, friendships often begun within Chicano student organizations and classes, all of which were created by student Movement activism. These friendships form the basis of a network "community" in Los Angeles today, a dense tangle of overlapping personal, work, and political relationships.

In order to enrich the sense of how these networks work, I draw on my own experiences as an intimate participant observer, showing how I followed my own networks to find a community where I could participate and observe.

The friendship networks forged in undergraduate years often center around undergraduate organizations like the Chicano pre-med and pre-law associations of each school. In fact, the leadership cadres developed in these undergraduate contexts often go on to form the leadership pool of current Los Angeles Chicano professional organizations. In order to illustrate just how undergraduate organizations evolved into Chicano professional organizations, I describe a specific organization, the Chicano/Latino Medical Association of California (C.M.A.C.). The leadership of this group derives from undergraduate networks forged in the heart of the Chicano Movement.

Perhaps where Chicano professional networks are the mos⁺ similar to other professional networks is in how they are employed for multiple purposes and with varying motivations, ranging from cultivating business partners and jobs, to finding housemates, fiancées, babysitters and tennis partners. However, one reason for networking which is probably unique among Chicanos, particularly in its intensity, is a sense of obligation to attend Mexican American functions in order to demonstrate support for the Chicano professional community.

What is most interesting about Chicano professional networks, however, is the way that Chicanos themselves think and talk about their networks, the meanings that sustain and nurture them. These meanings are rooted in the Chicano Movement. The Movement metaphor of *"familia"* is a key symbol for unlocking the way that Chicano professionals feel about themselves collectively. This metaphor has been stretched and adapted from the home/family context of pre-college years to fit the friendships forged in college years. It is then carried into the professional context where it continues to enrich and complicate the relationships between Chicano doctors and lawyers. This metaphor of family fosters a sense of unity within the Chicano professional community, and at the same time may gloss over conflict and power relationships within that same community.

THE NETWORK EXPERIENCE

Most Chicanos educated during the Movement years were involved in multiple organizations and activities revolving around their ethnicity. During this time they developed dense networks of relationships. What follows is a description of the life of a hypothetical Chicana, just out of law school, demonstrating how an individual can follow his/her undergraduate and graduate school networks into professional life.[1]

Bianca Castillos graduates from a northern California law school and moves to Los Angeles, taking a job in the City District Attorney's office. She had heard about the job opening from a

Chicana friend who works there. Bianca knows a few other people, and as she begins to network with friends, former classmates, and colleagues, she discovers that she knows a lot more L.A. people than she realized.

One of her Chicano colleagues at work tells her about the Mexican American Bar Association and she goes to a meeting. She discovers that the president of the organization is a woman she used to know from MEChA, a Chicano undergraduate organization (Movimiento Estudiantíl Chicano de Aztlán). She also runs into some old friends from her undergraduate days at Irvine, and they invite her to a party. At the party, Bianca meets a guy who is the brother of a guy she knew in law school. It turns out that his wife, who is a doctor also attending the party, is a woman Bianca grew up with in the Central Valley. The two of them end up sharing stories all night of what happened to various friends and family members back home.

They plan that night to form a reading group with other professional Chicanas and begin meeting once a month to discuss various fictional works, particularly books by minorities and women. One of the women Bianca meets in the group is a physician who becomes her gynecologist.

Bianca eventually marries a Chicano she meets on a special committee of M.A.B.A., and when they have children she asks one of her old M.E.Ch.A. friends and her husband to be "padrinos," or godparents.

While it is a composite scenario, this pattern is typical of college educated, professional Chicanos who network among themselves in Los Angeles. It is experienced similarly by both men and women.[2] In many ways, the Chicano professional community in Los Angeles is like a small town in the midst of a vast metropolis; everybody knows everybody. Most organization meetings and professional ceremonies are also mini reunions where people catch up with old acquaintances and mingle with friends.

The easy camaraderie of these networks has much to do with the fact that many of the relationships have endured years of friendship and political interactions going back to undergraduate and graduate school connections. However, although they are so central to the lives of many Chicano professionals, Chicanos for the most part take the small town nature of their network-laced lives for granted. They are too busy enlarging and enjoying the networks to reflect much on their significance.

This was where being a participant observer in the classic anthropological tradition was an advantage. It also helped that I was not only married to a Chicano professional, but had my own connections to Chicanos going back to undergraduate relationships. I was in a unique position to experience and reflect on these networks. In one sense, my perceptions were probably very different from those of Chicanos, because I was constantly astonished and pleased at the density of the community, and how I was always running into old friends or people I had interviewed everywhere I went. I perceived this as radically different from my own Anglo anonymity living in Los Angeles, but my Chicano acquaintances on the other hand, as I mentioned, seemed to take such small town life in the big town as a given.

However, in another sense I was able to experience these networks in many ways exactly as might a "native." Like the fictional Bianca Castillo, I entered Los Angeles with a few connections, began networking, and soon stumbled onto organizations.[3] In this way, I did not start with organizations, but rather with individuals whose networks led me to these organizations. I followed these networks somewhat randomly, led by the subjects themselves, in the same way that most social scientists bumble into the social networks which they hope to study. As people introduced me to other people, I gradually followed relational routes that looked promising, following my intuition and eventually focusing on several central organizations where I had come to know people fairly well.

The most important of these were the Mexican American Bar Association (M.A.B.A.), the Chicano/Latino Medical Association of California (C.M.A.C.), the Stanford Chicano/Latino Club of Southern California, and the Young Latino Lawyers Association.[4,5]

I discovered in these organizations a rich setting for further fieldwork contacts, since they gather a large number of people in their respective embraces. For example, M.A.B.A. in 1989 had a membership of approximately seven hundred members. At its monthly meetings there might be at the minimum fifty people, but often more than a hundred. Approximately five hundred people attended the annual officer installation banquet in 1989. Furthermore, the M.A.B.A. leadership represents men and women lawyers from diverse educational institutions, the monopoly perhaps exercised only by those graduating from major California law schools and a few Ivy League schools.

While significantly smaller than M.A.B.A., at C.M.A.C.'s first organizational meeting in December 1989, at least 34 physicians attended. Monthly weeknight meetings bring in anywhere from five to thirty people. At the second annual statewide conference there were approximately 250 physicians. The current core leadership predominantly originated in University of California at Davis networks; however, it also includes physicians with undergraduate and graduate affiliations at Stanford, U.C. Los Angeles, U.C. San Diego, U.C. Santa Barbara, U.C. Berkeley and other schools.

Following network tributaries to organizations like these shaped my research methods and the way that I viewed the community which I had planned to study. Before I started fieldwork, I had envisioned myself doing sort of an ethnographic sampling of various individuals throughout the Los Angeles area. I viewed networks as a means to the end of meeting people, not as something to be studied in themselves. When I finally realized that the networks were more than just connections between atomized individuals, that they were a "community" whose whole was greater than the sum of its parts, I began to focus my energies on a relatively narrow range of people and organizations. This allowed me not only to mimic the experiences of Chicanos themselves (entering into the stream of relationships just as did the fictional Bianca Castillo) but also allowed me to get to know several people well under a variety of circumstances. It also gave me the opportunity to watch the historical unfolding of particular groups and institutions from a fairly intimate vantage point.

I launched into fieldwork from three main network sources. The first was a Stanford Chicano law professor who gave me the name and number of a former Stanford student who was currently working for a corporate law firm in Los Angeles. This lawyer had written a study for the Stanford Bar Review about the experiences of Chicanos in corporate law firms, and was eager to introduce me to a cluster of primarily young (under 30) corporate lawyers from various (primarily Ivy League) law schools who had recently formed a group they called the "Young Latino Lawyers Association," later changed to the "Latino Lawyers' Association." This is the group described in the first chapter which hosted the reception and challenged MABA. I eventually got to know several of the group members and followed the organization for over a year, until it ultimately became a subcommittee within the

Mexican American Bar Association, where it was at the end of the 1980's called "The Latino Lawyers Committee."

My second primary set of network sources were my own undergraduate relationships with Chicanos from Casa Zapata, the Chicano Theme House and dormitory at Stanford University. These included Chicanos that I actually knew between the years 1972 and 1976, and Chicanos I met during fieldwork in Los Angeles who had gone to Stanford either before or after I did, but who had also participated in the undergraduate networks clustering around Casa Zapata.

So, for example, when early in my fieldwork I contacted an old Zapata friend who worked as a lawyer for M.A.L.D.E.F. (Mexican American Legal Defense and Education Fund) in Los Angeles, he introduced me to several M.A.L.D.E.F. attorneys, to M.A.B.A. (Mexican American Bar Association) about which I knew nothing at the time, and to the Stanford Chicano Alumni Association. It was one of his M.A.L.D.E.F. friends who invited me to my first M.A.B.A. meeting and introduced me to her best friend, the then current president elect of M.A.B.A., who sat next to me at dinner and discreetly answered all my questions about who was there that night and the history of the organization.

Soon afterward, when I attended my first Stanford Chicano Alumni Association meeting on the urging of this same Zapata friend, I met a pediatrician who, it turned out, worked for the same hospital that my husband did. I also met a judge who was a former M.A.B.A. president. I subsequently met several lawyers and doctors at these Alumni meetings who became good sources for interviews and candid insights into Chicano professional life.

My third primary source was my husband's vast Chicano physician network. This network originated, like mine, in Stanford and Casa Zapata, but spilled beyond into the Stanford Chicano Pre-med club and then on into the medical school networks of the University of California at Davis and the University of California at Los Angeles.

During my fieldwork period between January 1988 and April 1990, many of these network connections from various sources began coalescing into a politically vital Los Angeles Chicano physicians network. Out of this network, two important health organizations actually formed in 1988 while I was in Los Angeles: 1) C.M.A.C., the Chicano/Latino Medical Association of California, an organization composed of primarily Mexican American physicians and 2) the Hispanic Women's Health Alliance, an organization of Latina women with careers in various health fields, including physicians and public health professionals.

I had particularly close access to C.M.A.C., since its first president was my husband's close friend going back to the Stanford Pre-med club, who later went to medical school with my husband at Davis. Along with this friend, a cluster of other Chicanos with network connections through Davis and U.C.L.A. medical schools (most of whom I had known over at least a ten year period) formed the nexus of this organization. Moreover, many of the members of this same network inaugurated the first primarily Chicano Residency Training program at White Memorial Hospital in East L.A. in June 1988.

No less important, although not described in this book, two or three of the women physicians from this network helped found the Hispanic Women's Health Alliance in 1988.

While my initial contacts all stemmed from Stanford associations in one way or another, I certainly did not limit myself to following Stanford networks nor interviewing Stanford graduates. Like the typical Chicano professional, I began with my own college networks, then branched out from these through the available Los Angeles networks to a wide range of people from diverse backgrounds. In fact, the organizations and networks I followed included people from all the University of California campuses, as well as University of Southern California, Pomona, several state universities, Columbia, Harvard, Yale, University of Texas at Austin and other out-of-state universities. Less than a fourth of the forty people that I formally interviewed had any association with Stanford.

FROM UNDERGRADUATE CLUBS TO PROFESSIONAL ORGANIZATIONS

While Chicano Movement undergraduates organized classes on Chicano literature, mural painting, and ballet folklórico (to name only a few cultural activities) even more crucial to their lives as future professionals, they created the pre-professional support groups which form the basis of today's professional organizations. At both the undergraduate and graduate levels, Chicano organizations were central to the lives of many Chicanos. Through these groups, they studied together, passed on information about the ins and outs of advancement into professional schools and jobs, and supported each other emotionally through the rigors and trials of professional education.

Chicano pre-law and law students have been organized since at least the 1960's and many leaders of the student groups from those years are now politically active in M.A.B.A. One M.A.B.A. Board member in his late thirties helped found the Organization for the Legal Advancement of Raza, Inc. (O.L.A.Inc.) while a law student . This organization in the late 1970's conducted L.S.A.T. preparation courses for Chicanos across campuses in California and Arizona and offered a summer legal studies institute.

C.M.A.C. [Chicano/Latino Medical Association of California], the current Chicano physician's association in the city has its roots in multiple Chicano pre-med and medical school organizations. One C.M.A.C. physician described its history as an evolution from undergraduate "pre-med organizations" to the current professional organization in the following way:

> At Santa Cruz they called themselves "Chicanos for Creative Medicine. In the Southwest it was "C.H.I.S.P.A." At Stanford it was the "Stanford Chicano Pre-medical Society." At Santa Barbara it was "Los Curanderos." Those groups became "La R.A.M.A." [Raza Medical Association] and N.C.H.O. [National Chicano Health Organization] which are the medical school organizations which helped people get through medical school. Now they are called "C.M.S.A.," the Chicano Medical Student Association. And those groups led to physician's organizations, the Pacific Medical Association which has now evolved into C.M.A.C. [Chicano/Latino Medical Assoc. of California].

This physician describes an evolution of medical organizations since the mid-sixties when Chicanos began to enter institutions of higher education in significant numbers due to affirmative action. Undergraduate pre-medical students organized themselves to help each other and often worked with Chicano undergraduates from other schools. Eventually enough of these students entered medical school to form organizations which shared information and support. In turn, by the 1980's, enough students had become physicians to begin to form a Chicano physicians' organization. The first attempt at such an organization was the Pacific Medical Association, which in November 1988 was reinvigorated and renamed the Chicano/Latino Medical Association, or C.M.A.C.

How C.M.A.C. actually coalesced into an organization which now has statewide and national connections and political influence, is a fascinating story about the evolution of an undergraduate network. The leadership of today's C.M.A.C. developed primarily out of a University of California at Davis group of Chicano pre-meds and medical students, in school together in the mid 1970's. These students formed an unusually tight network, enhanced by their involvement in two unique political projects.

The first, and perhaps most important, was *Clinica Tepati*, a free clinic established by Chicano medical students in a Mexican American neighborhood in Sacramento. Affiliated with U.C. Davis Medical School, Chicano pre-medical students and medical students ran and staffed the clinic every Saturday with the assistance of volunteer physicians. The clinic was maintained in those years amidst substantial controversy at the medical school. It was founded by Chicano nationalists who considered it an exclusively Chicano project, designed according to the Movement value of responsibility to their barrio communities, to help the nearby under-served Mexican American community. Chicano students fought bitterly with U.C. Davis administrators in order to keep it as a legitimate school affiliated clinic.

The other unifying factor, pertaining more to the medical students than to the undergraduate pre-meds, was the political organizing which Chicanos developed to cope with the campus upheaval caused by the 1978 United States Supreme Court case of University of California Regents vs. Bakke. Chicano medical students worked with African-American students to develop strategies of how, in particular, to deal with the case's intrusive and intense media coverage at the medical school.[6]

The politics surrounding both Clinica Tepati and the "Bakke" case served as training grounds for leadership and intense networks which, transported to Los Angeles in the 1980's, formed a core group of prepared physician leaders. This group, once paired up with a critical mass of Chicano professionals, would have a tremendous impact on Chicano physician politics.

MULTIPLE NETWORK USES

Networking is not simply a function of the desire to advance politically, as the popular use of the term among professional circles might suggest. It is actually a form of urban community life which flows out of friendship, work, and organizational networks. These networks are held together, however elastically, by the multiple forces which motivate Chicanos to socialize with other Chicano professionals. These forces include the fact that networks enable people to make connections and gain knowledge which enhance their chances at career success. This is particularly true for lawyers who participate in M.A.B.A., since networking among fellow Chicano attorneys may enhance chances of advancing in one's career, particularly if one is interested in public offices like judge, city commissioner or state representative. With physicians, the benefits of belonging to an organization like C.M.A.C. are less obviously beneficial politically, but no less useful in terms of networking for information about jobs and other useful professional information.

Both Chicano lawyers and doctors often find jobs through friends and acquaintances in their Chicano networks. A Chicana who worked for a progressive corporate law firm told me how she helped a Chicano friend from the Latino Lawyer's Association, who was unhappy with his law firm. She set up a meeting with her firm's personnel director, and her friend eventually moved firms to join her. Similarly, many of the members of the Davis network of Chicano physicians have followed each other into the Residency program at Kaiser Permanente hospital and stayed on as staff physicians.

However, Chicano professional networking cannot be understood in strictly utilitarian or functional terms. People network with each other for multiple reasons, many of them overlapping. Some reasons are consciously strategic, others more unconscious and taken for granted. The reason most often cited for attending Chicano functions is a desire to support an organization which is committed to promoting the betterment of the Chicano community. Chicanos who are deeply ingrained in Movement values tend to feel motivated to participate actively in as many Chicano fundraisers, banquets, and organization barbecues as they can, often simply as a matter of showing "support." I would be amazed at how often I would run into the same people at the many functions I attended during fieldwork. For example, I met one couple at a M.A.L.D.E.F. barbecue, at two different Stanford Chicano

Alumni functions, at two different M.A.B.A. banquets, and at a Sunday afternoon barbecue at the home of a Chicano physician couple all in the space of a few months. This couple, a family practice doctor and a public defender, had full-time professional lives and two young children at home. When I asked them about why they attended so many events, they said that they thought it was vital to show that they "supported" these organizations.

In fact, showing one's "support" can become very expensive in Los Angeles for the zealous Chicano professional. Black tie fundraisers and formal installation dinners staged at the best downtown hotels are becoming quite common. One active and conscientiously networking lawyer friend of ours laughingly warned us that if we lived in Los Angeles much longer, my husband would have to invest in a tuxedo.

The other reason most Chicanos network is simply a desire to meet with friends and other people like themselves. Said one Chicana physician to me enthusiastically after a cocktail party of U.C.L.A. Chicano medical school graduates: "I love going to Chicano social things! I just walk into the room and feel instantly comfortable. . . All those brown faces! People that look just like my *tias* and *tios* and *primos!*"[7] Another Chicana physician said that she was active in several Chicano organizations and often took her children along with her because she wanted them to be exposed to a variety of Chicano professional role models. Almost all Chicanos who actively network admit that they often attend events simply to see their friends, particularly since in their busy professional lives within this geographically immense city these functions are the most efficient way to keep track of people socially. In fact, M.A.B.A. has actually formalized several opportunities for combining organization business with socializing and leisure through its annual Dodger game picnics, Christmas parties, and summer seminars at beach resorts in Mexico.

People also keep in touch with each other through more private networking. This includes dinner parties, backyard barbecues and hurried meetings over lunch, calling each other regularly on the telephone, and going to favorite bars and restaurants together. This kind of networking overlaps with the more formal networking, because often the people with whom Chicanos work in organizations are the same people with whom they go out on Saturday night to a salsa club, or with whom they gather up children and hold a Saturday afternoon picnic.

In any given week, for example, my husband the family practice resident might talk on Monday night on the phone to a medical student to give advice about the upcoming Chicano graduation ceremony at U.C.L.A., on Tuesday be on the phone with his friend Luis chatting about mutual problems with their respective residency programs, on Wednesday night attend a C.M.A.C. meeting (and probably run into that same friend and possibly the medical student as well) on Thursday night go to U.C.L.A. to lecture U.C.L.A. students on the significance of the Bakke case, on Friday night attend a C.M.S.A. (Chicano Medical Students Association) awards banquet, on Saturday morning play tennis with a fellow Chicano physician, Saturday night have Chicano friends from Stanford over for dinner, and on Sunday attend a H.I.S.M.E.T. barbecue for fourth year medical students looking for advice on residency programs. This schedule is perhaps a slight exaggeration, but was generally the pattern of our life, as well as of the lives of many active Chicano physicians we knew.[8]

There are also certain places where Chicano professionals know that they can drop by after work in the evening and almost always find someone they know. The bar at Tamayo's, a Mexican restaurant in the heart of East L.A. is a favorite hang out of this kind. As an extension of its popularity among professionals, the C.M.A.C. and the Stanford Chicano Alumni Club regularly held brunch and dinner meetings at Tamayo's.

Women seemed particularly loyal in their long term friendships sustained through networking. I observed one group of Stanford Chicanas, all successful professionals, who had maintained strong ties to each other since their undergraduate years in the early seventies, living and studying together as students, and then politically and socially networking together as professionals.

Besides career boosting and friendship, networking provides other benefits. People find their pediatricians, real estate lawyers, financial planners etc. through their networks. One Chicana physician involved in C.M.A.C. was obstetrician to half a dozen Chicana doctors that she knew through long term networks. A Chicano lawyer I knew met a Chicano investment banker at a party and found a new business partner and housemate.

People also find dates and mates through their networks, and sometimes the intrigue that results from such small town connections is worthy of a soap opera. People constantly exchange information about events of mutual interest, like the upcoming Linda Ronstadt concert, the Chicano art exhibit at the L.A. County Museum, or the *Cinco de Mayo* festival on Olvera Street. Women exchange advice about their (Latina) maids and child care providers. People crack jokes and talk about the "old days" when they were student activists, reliving their youth among compatriots.

In short, Chicano networks are where people not only forge serious career alliances, but where they let their hair down and have fun with people who share their background, interests, and perspective on the world.

"FAMILY:" THE CULTURAL CONSTRUCTION OF THE NETWORK COMMUNITY

The way that people talk about their communities, both the wider Mexican American community and the more specific Chicano professional communities, is usually in terms of "family." The metaphor serves as both a unifying theme which enhances a sense of belonging to a unique community, as well as a symbol which masks underlying tensions and power struggles which strain network connections.

When people talk about how they feel about the other members of their organizations and friendship networks—indeed, about any group about which they are speaking inclusively—it is in terms of "family." The idea of *"familia"* captures the spirit of group identity experienced and expressed by the Chicano professional community. A few lines from a speech given in February 1990 by the incoming president of M.A.B.A., Norah Olguin, in which she thanks her family for coming that night to the annual installation banquet, demonstrate this simply:

> It's just incredible that my family came out from New Mexico. And
> that's what the Latino community is all about—family support.

In these few lines symbolically linking her family and their support of her with the larger Latino community, Nora Olguin captures the essence of how Chicano professionals culturally construct their ethnic/professional community. This conception is rooted in the Chicano Movement culture of the sixties and seventies, where the idealized notion of extended *familia* gave shape to the Chicano community. Another quote from a Chicana obstetrician, Nina Hurtado, develops this concept more fully. Notice how she weaves her ideas about her own biological family together with her conception of how the relationships between other Chicano medical professionals should be arranged:

> I think where we are right now [i.e. Chicano doctors] we're moving into the middle-class, progressing, but we're not moving individually. We're moving as a body. And I think we've had that sense of *familia*, that was always important to us growing up. And I think it's also important that we maintain that. And it's so easy to lose in a society that has so many divorces, doesn't have extended families, has nannies and baby sitters that are paid for instead of other extended family members coming in and taking care of children. Losing that community spirit kind of destroys that part of us that is so essential. And I think that's why as medical students we gravitate to each other when we have problems, or when we don't have problems, when we're just celebrating, because we know we're succeeding together as a *familia*, for a purpose, for our community. And it makes us feel good.
>
> . . . I think we can't succeed except as a group. Have you seen that movie "Stand and Deliver"? All those students succeeded as a group. They all studied together; they went to all those sessions together. That's what we all need to do. We can't expect our people to do it without everybody assisting. I know I didn't get through medical school by myself. My friends, my family, even my nieces and nephews, I would look at their picture and say, "For them, I have to succeed, I have to go on." It's still there. It still works to reinforce why I went into medicine. Not for my own individual gain, but for my people. And that's what makes it all worthwhile, all the pain and agony, all the secluded time studying. It makes it worth doing.
>
> But that's what's happening now. We're starting to succeed, and as we do, we're kind of marching forward as a group. And as we go on, we're proud to see our colleagues in certain positions, while we're still battling in the early stages. We still feel some *envidia*[9] but now when I see someone succeeding, I'm proud. I want to see more of us succeed. Because the further they go on, the further I know I can go on, building upon each other's success. That's the thing that sets us apart from . . .the Anglo way of doing things. They will succeed at all costs no matter who.

> ... I disagree with Richard Rodriguez[10] that we have to lose this *familia*, this kind of innocence, this *corazón*,[11] spirit, to assimilate and succeed in an Anglo environment ... especially if we do it as a group and don't become isolated. I don't feel that you have to lose your Chicanoism, your Latinoism, your spirit in becoming this quote, "Professional."

In this quote, the Chicana physician movingly articulates one of the essential ways that Movement Chicanos shape the way that they see themselves as different from the dominant Anglo society. On one level, Chicano genetic families are different from Anglos families: Chicano families maintain extended family ties whereas Anglo families live truncated nuclear arrangements. Chicano mothers, grandmothers and aunts take care of Chicana professionals' babies, while Anglos use non-family members like baby sitters and nannies. Chicanos stay married while Anglos divorce. This is what this physician calls "that community spirit."

She then attributes that sense of "community spirit" to keeping another level of "*familia* " together, that of her fellow Chicano physicians and medical students. They gather with each other like a family with their problems and their celebrations. More significantly, they act as a family unit in the way that they advance in their careers, not competing as isolated individuals succeeding "at all costs no matter who" but as a unit, banded together, helping each other like the students in the Luis Valdez film "Stand and Deliver." Even in the face of "*envidia* " (envy) about how someone else may be doing better than herself, the spirit of community compels this physician and other Chicanos to realize their interdependence, not only with each other as fellow struggling students and professionals, but with the wider community of aunts, uncles, and cousins, for whom, and because of whom, they continue to strive to succeed: "My friends, my family, even my nieces and nephews, I would look at their picture and say, 'For them, I have to succeed. I have to go on.'"

This Chicana conjures up another important way that the image of family works to construct a unified cultural identity for Chicano professionals. This is revealed in her line about "building upon each other's successes." Family imagery, particularly in terms of generations succeeding and helping each other, is central to the way that Chicanos describe relationships between Chicanos on various rungs of the success ladder toward professionalism. The image revealed when people talk about their responsibilities to Chicanos who are "behind" them on the path to "success," is that of older siblings helping their younger brothers and sisters; again, *familia*.

When I was first struggling to find a way to talk about Chicano networks, I asked my husband how he would convey the concept. He immediately launched into an enthusiastic description, using the metaphor of family generations. Here he describes his own experience with the U.C. Davis network:

> Show it in generations, cause that's the way it works. Start with Abram Zapata and Gary Naranjo and those guys at Davis [medical school]. They helped me and Victor when we came in. And we helped the undergrads, Nora and Zoila and Luis. And then I recruited Nora to U.C.L.A. [medical school] and then to Kaiser [residency program]. And Zoila came to U.C.L.A. And then Victor recruited Zoila and Luis to White Memorial [residency program].
>
> The issue is: how can I get into medical school? And they go to people already in medical school for that, people they know. Then the issue is: how do I get into a good internship program? And then the issue is, how do I get a job? Knowledge is passed down. And it's like waves. More people are coming and coming. It starts with one or two, and then the next year four and five and so on.

While this describes how Chicano pre-meds seek help from those that have already successfully mastered the steps to professionalism, the relationships work not only from the bottom up, but also from the top down. Chicanos at each level of professional training feel a tremendous obligation to help those that are behind them on the educational ladder. One Chicana physician told me that she wouldn't dream of not "keeping an eye out" for the Chicanos and Chicanas who were behind her in the residency program. Another Chicana described how she loved to go to high schools and colleges to inspire and recruit young Chicanas and Chicanos to enter the health field. Many Chicano medical students and physicians take time from their already heavy schedules to individually counsel students and to speak at Chicano pre-med conferences about getting into medical school and the jobs that are waiting for them in the "Chicano community" when they get out.

It is not only physicians, of course, who feel this responsibility toward the family of Chicanos struggling toward professional success.

Chicano attorneys similarly express and demonstrate concern for those behind them on the career ladder. One of the standing committees of the Mexican American Bar Association is called the "Law Students Relations/Youth Outreach Committee" which coordinates relations with both Los Angeles Latino law students as well as Latino students in the elementary through high school grades. Speakers from M.A.B.A. give advice at local law schools about getting through law school, passing the Bar exam, and finding jobs. In the "First Monday of October" program, M.A.B.A. speakers go to dozens of high schools throughout Los Angeles to speak to high school students about higher education opportunities.

One of the sources of the family metaphor is in the life experiences of Chicanos as they become educated, moving from blue-collar families and communities, into elite educational institutions and then on into white collar professional life.[12] When telling the stories of how they became professionals, many Chicanos describe leaving their families and finding another "family" in the Chicano community of their particular university or graduate school. While the word "family" is not often used explicitly, they describe leaving home and a familiar community, arriving in an alien environment, and finding a supportive and close network of friends with whom they felt much in common. Said one lawyer about some of the Chicanos she met when she first went to law school:

> That was my first away-from-home experience and I kind of felt like this was family or something. They understood what I was going through.

Another Chicana put a similar experience this way:

> When I first applied to law school, I was contacted by La Raza Law Students Association. . . . They had an orientation program a week before school started, so it was a real supportive network. And being that I was completely away from Fresno I didn't know a soul there I latched onto that. And I really needed that—in the sense that I had come from Fresno—I had come from a Cal State University and here I meet these people who had gone to Harvard, had gone to Stanford, to Berkeley, and I was going, 'What am I doing here? I don't belong here.' And I really needed that support.

In her study of Chicano students, Alice Reich [1989] describes how this notion of "*familia*" developed within late sixties Chicano student culture as a challenge to perceived Anglo ideas about assimilation. Chicanos defied the negative stereotype of the extended family as a hindrance to social mobility by portraying extended families as resources rather than detriments to their educational achievements. The metaphor was extended to the university Chicano community; friends were "*carnales*" and "*carnalas*," brothers and sisters.[13]

But the metaphor had its uses beyond helping Chicanos survive the transition between social classes. It also served to keep certain groups within power even within the Chicano Movement generation itself. The Movement was not only a form of resistance to the culture of the dominant Anglo university, but was a type of political hegemony of its own. Just as within biological families, notions of "family" unity serve both to nurture and include people, but also to mask relations of power and the subsequent tensions between individuals and subgroups.

It's a simple fact of the "family" metaphor that, while some are included within the "family," others are not. The struggle over naming which I discuss in the third chapter demonstrates how powerful this tool of inclusiveness/exclusiveness can be. Are Hispanics not born of Mexican parentage included in the family? Are Chicanos who never participated in the Movement and who never networked in Chicano undergraduate and graduate organizations in the family? Often, the "family" is intended to mean members of the Chicano Movement cohort and those who identify with its culture. One Mexican American physician who described his relationship to Chicano organizations as peripheral explained to me that he felt he was not "remembered" when organizations made their mailing lists because he had never been active in "all that Chicano stuff" when he was a student. He felt that he was being excluded from events and organizations that he might otherwise enjoy attending.

Three other contradictory tensions stand out with the use of the "*familia*" metaphor. First is the problem of individual rivalries and differences within networks, many of which reach back into earlier undergraduate struggles. In a speech given at the annual C.M.A.C. conference, one physician summed up the political in-fights which had characterized pre-professional and physician organizing since the sixties as mere "family squabbles." However, as another Chicano physician active in C.M.A.C. explained to me, these "domestic" altercations can seriously impact the cohesion of Chicano organizations and continued political organizing. I met many people who feel bitterness about former undergraduate struggles and limit their interactions with current professional networks accordingly. For example, one former student activist physician refused to associate with C.M.A.C. because he said he knew most of the parties involved and didn't "want to have anything to do with them" because he didn't want to get "burned" again. Another ex-activist said that he was wary of Chicano organizations because as an undergraduate he felt he had been ostracized by the Chicano nationalists for his middle-class background. This doctor was proud that he worked in a community clinic in East Los Angeles, contending that his work in such an under-served area demonstrated a solidarity with the Chicano community in a way that defied those nationalists who had as students once questioned his loyalty to "the *gente*," the people.

Another source of conflict and/or tension is that of gender. One of the legacies of the Chicano movement which was perhaps carried on into professional life along with the "*familia*" metaphor, was that of patriarchy. M.A.B.A.'s leadership provides an interesting example (although this problem is not unique to lawyers). The organization was dominated by male lawyers from its inception until the early eighties when the women organized themselves and elected the first woman president. A couple of M.A.B.A. Chicanas explained to me that the women had debated about forming their own organization ("like the Blacks did") instead of continuing to "put up with the male chauvinism" of the M.A.B.A. old guard. Rather than separating themselves, they chose to "basically take over the whole thing." They now have their own standing committee within M.A.B.A., called "Latina Lawyers" and this group, among other things, organizes the annual Hispanic Woman of the Year Award banquet. More importantly, they also lobby and organize for female representation as Board members and officers. Since 1981 there have been three women presidents.

However, I noticed that despite the fact that women are formally running the monthly meetings, males tend to dominate the social space through humor and other forms of disruption. Furthermore, while one woman claimed that things were run much more efficiently now that women were doing things, she did concede that, so far, men appeared to be benefiting more from the organization professionally than women in terms of getting political positions like judgeships and city commissioner appointments.

In the case of physicians, the only president of C.M.A.C. was a male until the elections in Fall 1991, when a woman was elected. Several women serve on the Board of Directors and women in the central network have been active in leadership roles of the pre-medical and medical school organizations. But interestingly, some Chicana physicians have chosen to affiliate more actively with the Hispanic Women's Health Alliance which is primarily made up of public health professionals rather than physicians. In fact, one C.M.A.C. board member resigned soon after the formation of the group in order to put more time into the women's organization as president.

The last area where conflict and tension are generated within networks is that of differences between generations or cohorts [Ryder 1965]. As discussed in another context in Chapter 1, three generations of Chicanos, or three cohorts, participate in professional networks in Los Angeles. These divisions cannot be understood strictly in terms of chronological generations, i.e. how old people are and during which years they went to medical school, since individuals occasionally may identify with a cohort group which is chronologically not their own. However, such a generational division is helpful in mapping out certain tensions between groups and subcultures within the Chicano professional network community.

The oldest cohort includes those who had their undergraduate and graduate training before the Sixties, before affirmative action and nationalist ethnic activism began to shape the experience of upwardly mobile Chicanos. This generation is few in number because it is pre-affirmative action. However, many of its members have networked among themselves; in fact, M.A.B.A. was founded in the late 1950's by members of this generation and C.H.A.M.A. (California Hispanic American Medical Association)[14] was similarly founded by members of that cohort.

The next generation, the Chicano Movement cohort, includes those Chicanos who had their upper level schooling during the 1960's and 1970's, their larger numbers the direct result of affirmative action and Chicano activism. Members of this cohort networked intensely among themselves both as undergraduates and graduate students, and created a unique university Chicano culture. The continuation of these networks and the legacy of that Chicano culture currently dominate the network culture of Chicano professionals in Los Angeles.

The most recent cohort includes those Chicanos educated in the 1980's.[15] These are the inheritors of the legacy of Chicano nationalist student culture and the academic affirmative activism of their cohort predecessor. This is the "post-Movement cohort," the one that is beginning to challenge the Movement generation in struggles like the one described in Chapter 1.

Of course, the whole concept of "cohorts" is based on generalizations. These are simply structural models meant strictly as tools which should not be reified. Not everyone educated between a particular set of historical dates is necessarily part of a particular cohort; many individuals do not fit neatly into one cohort category, and as I mentioned, some actually identify with a cohort culture different from their own.

For example, the only Chicano full professor of Medicine in Los Angeles or in California, a man in his seventies, networks comfortably with two cohorts. He works with young Chicanos through his involvement with the U.C.L.A. admissions committee and Chicano recruitment and retention at the university. He is fully comfortable with many aspects of Chicano nationalism, and identifies strongly with the affirmative action values of this cohort generation. However, this doctor also mixes socially and networks with members of his own Mexican American generation, whose members are not usually as nationalistic or as activist as the Movement cohort.

Another example is a young Chicano corporate lawyer, a chronological member of the post-movement cohort, who strongly identifies with certain aspects of the Movement cohort nationalist culture. He is comfortable moving in M.A.B.A. leadership circles which are controlled by the "older" cohort. However, he also networks with his own generation of Chicano lawyers, and has certain political ideas which differ from the classic nationalist positions of the Movement cohort.

This kind of cross-cutting identification between cohorts is a key to what binds the Chicano professional network community as a *"familia"* beyond the tensions and conflicts generated by divisions of individual personality, gender, and cohort. Both the elderly medical professor and the young corporate lawyer of my examples, identify with the goal of helping other Chicanos achieve success in American society. While this goal has been espoused by many Mexican American activists since the nineteenth century, the goal had its strongest and widest public articulation by the Chicano Movement generation. The essence of this goal was summed up neatly in the second half of the conversation I had with my husband about medical school networks, in which he characterized the networks as waves, each generation helping the one behind it, within the wider cause of a shared Movement cause and history:

> *Beto*: And the wave is a metaphor for their romantic ideas about the whole process.

> *Anthropologist*: A metaphor? How?

> *Beto*: Passing it onto the next generation. They see themselves as pioneers, the ones from the sixties who started everything.

> *Anthropologist*: Like who are you talking about?

> *Beto*: Like Gary Naranjo. He sees himself as passing it on to Victor and me.

> *Anthropologist*: And you see yourself sort of like that too, don't you?

> *Beto*: Yeah, we all do. It's part of the myth. Because we see ourselves as part of something bigger that's happening to society. That, yes, we do belong to something that matters. So if you're a wave working up in San Francisco and someone else is in Los Angeles, you feel like you're part of the same ocean, the same cause.

> *Anthropologist*: And what is that cause? Now don't get mad. I think I know, but I want to hear it explicitly from you.

> *Beto*: Well, help our people, try to change society, make it better. It makes us part of the Civil Rights Movement. . . . It ties us all together!"

NOTES

1. I chose a hypothetical case instead of a real one in order to preserve the anonymity promised to my informants.

2. Although women may also know each other through specialized Chicana women's interest groups.

3. This experience is undoubtedly similar to that of most anthropological fieldworkers who begin with a few names and introductions, and work from there to larger networks.

4. For a brief description of these organizations, see the Appendix.

5. While these were the organizations with which I had the most extensive contact, my fieldwork also included the following organizations and institutions: The Chicano/Latino Medical Students Association (C.M.S.A.), the Hispanic Medical Education Training Program (H.I.S.M.E.T.), the Mexican American Legal Defense and Education Fund (M.A.L.D.E.F.), the White Memorial Residency Training Program, the Kaiser Permanente Residency Training Program. Chicanos with whom I did interviews and with whom I interacted in various settings were involved in a much wider range of institutions and ethnic organizations including some of the following, but certainly not limited to these: Comisión Femeníl Mexicana Nacional, California Area Health Education Center (A.H.E.C.), Hispanic Public Defenders Association, Hispanic Professional Roundtable, Aztlán Track Association, and the Mexican American alumni groups of both Pomona and University of Southern California.

6. Bakke challenged the University of California Medical School at Davis's admissions policy as a Title VI violation. The university at that time had an admissions policy which reserved sixteen slots out of one-hundred for minority applicants, and which rejected him, a white student, twice although his qualifications were allegedly higher than some of those minority students who were admitted. The Supreme Court ruled that quota systems were inadmissible but that state universities had a right to use race as a factor in admissions decisions.

Bakke entered the university as a student in 1977 and the press followed him onto campus, hounding minority students and hanging around outside of classrooms. Minority students—Chicanos and African-Americans (who were then calling themselves "Blacks")—chose spokespeople and coached each other on what to say to the press when asked questions.

Furthermore, several of the Chicano students had been involved in campus politics and admission's committees, and were convinced that Bakke had been tipped off by an administration insider who wanted the quota system to be challenged. Many Chicanos and African-American students did not agree with the quota system and argued that certain administrators and/or faculty at U.C. Davis were setting the university up for a law suit on purpose. The students felt that a quota system set a ceiling on the number of minority students that could be admitted each year.

7. Translation: "aunts, uncles, and cousins."

8. Actually, my husband's networking life was more complicated than this scenario suggests because during the years of my fieldwork, I was constantly using him as an escort to attend functions in which he would otherwise have had little interest. In fact, his duties as a network assistant even once included parking cars for an expensive M.A.L.D.E.F. benefit so that we could get in free.

9. "Envy."

10. Richard Rodriguez is a journalist and spokesperson for the California "Hispanic" community whose views on assimilation are often challenged by Chicanos with Movement backgrounds and is widely identified by Movement Chicanos as an apologist for a non-Movement oriented Mexican American viewpoint. His book, *Hunger of Memory*, published in 1982, is still widely read by Chicano students and professionals and its issues debated. Discussions about Richard Rodriguez came spontaneously up several times in my fieldwork (I did not generate them). Interestingly, during my fieldwork period, Rodriguez did an article for the Los Angeles Times on Chicano professionals, and interviewed several people with whom I was acquainted through fieldwork, "Success Stories: Voices from an Emerging Elite," in *The Los Angeles Times Magazine*, November 6, 1988, pp. 8-19, 55-56.

11. "Heart."

12. The relationship between the concept of biologically-related "familia" and that of the larger Chicano "familia" can be understood as a kind of synechdoche rooted in actual historical experience, the biological family standing in metaphorically for the "imagined community" of Chicanos in general.

13. The Chicano nationalist metaphor of "familia" corresponds with Benedict Anderson's [1983] observation that nationalist groups imagine themselves as community because "regardless of the actual inequality and exploitation that may prevail in each, the nation is always conceived as a deep horizontal comradeship."

14. I discuss C.H.A.M.A. in Chapter 3, where I describe its conflict with the Movement cohort organization C.M.A.C.

15. By the time of publication, this would include Chicanos educated in the early 1990's.

What's in a Name?
Chicanos, Latinos, Mexican
Americans and Hispanics

Ethnic labeling is an emotionally-charged issue within the contemporary Chicano professional community. This has to do with the changing dynamics of both this community as well as the wider arena of Los Angeles ethnicity. In terms of internal dynamics, the Chicano Movement with its allegiance to the term "Chicano" is challenged by a new generation of Chicanos with a more third-world, "Latino" perspective. But this new generation is in turn responding to the demographic fact that Spanish-speaking immigrant populations from numerous countries other than Mexico are flooding the ethnic scene, challenging the traditional "Mexican" flavor of L.A. "Hispanic" ethnicity.

While ethnic labeling is most controversial among Movement Chicanos, it effects the entire Chicano professional community. In fact, in order to move effectively within Chicano elite circles, it is crucial to understand the importance and sensitivity of naming. What you call someone is not a matter of finding the right term and using it thereafter referentially, but rather an intuitive understanding of when and where and with whom to use certain terms contextually.

As a starting point, there are certain general patterns of use which are helpful to know. In situations where Chicanos professionals want to employ a term which denotes their or another's specific ethnicity (i.e. country of origin), they use either "Chicano," "Mexican American," or "Mexican." When desiring a broader term which embraces all Spanish-speaking peoples, the terms "Hispanic,"

"Latino," or even at times "Latin" may be used. More obviously
metaphorical language may also come into play at times. One such
term is *"raza"*, or "race" which can refer specifically to people of
Mexican origin or more inclusively to all Spanish-speaking peoples.
Two other commonly used terms are *"la comunidad,"* (the community)
or *"la gente,"* (the people) which can refer to whatever group the
speaker wishes to include.

The more nuanced and contextualized uses of these terms is the
subject of the following discussion.

AN EVENING DISCUSSION

The intense feelings that people have about ethnic labels and the
intimate way that names are woven into the web of Chicano elite
culture came home to me early in my fieldwork. In January 1988 I
invited some friends over for a dinner party. Of the three invited
couples, all were Chicano professionals or pre-professionals, and most
were either lawyers or doctors. They were all between the ages of 28
and 35 and were people my husband and I knew either through
Chicano undergraduate or medical school networks.

Around the dinner table we talked about personal things like
college experiences and how we had met our respective spouses.
People laughed and joked, recalling and disclosing semi-intimate
details of each other's lives, making everyone gradually very
comfortable and relaxed. After dinner, however, when we moved into
the living room for coffee, the conversation heated up and waxed
political. A discussion began about the terms "Latino," "Hispanic,"
and "Chicano." While everyone in the group was comfortable with
calling themselves "Chicano," the issue was whether "Latino" or
"Hispanic" should be used as well. The discussion became so intense
that at one point one of the guests raised his voice in a long diatribe,
blocking all polite discourse. His outburst angered another guest so
much that he refused to speak for the rest of the evening.

Although the argument sputtered, fumed and shot up erratically,
the issues and their advocates clustered roughly into two camps. Leo
and Maria Limón[1] argued that the use of the term "Latino" lumps
Chicanos in with immigrant groups from Latin America, thereby
glossing over the historic uniqueness of Chicanos as a colonized rather
than immigrant people. The term "Hispanic," for them, was a

necessary evil to be used politically and professionally when referring to or working with communities of diverse Spanish-speaking groups.

Dorotea and Lázaro, on the other hand, argued that Chicanos' political consciousness should expand to include other Spanish-speaking groups and their issues and that "Latino" was an inclusive term preferable to the term "Hispanic" which they perceived as government imposed.

These two positions represent two different ends of the spectrum of the Chicano discourse about naming. At one end is the exclusive Chicano nationalism of Leo and Maria which typifies the Movement generation. They are concerned that the issues and perspectives of Chicanos not be obfuscated by a rising flood of political interest in immigrants from various Latin American countries. They feel that Chicanos have a different claim on the United States, as a people whose land—the Southwest, formerly Mexico—was stolen by the Anglo Americans. Leo views his profession as a lawyer as a lifetime commitment to helping the Chicano community. As he said to me in an interview:

> The Chicano community is to me the Mexican American community in the sense of United States citizens of Mexican descent, in addition to those recent immigrants from Mexico, who in my view taking a historical perspective are coming to Aztlán, to a part of the United States that was once a part of Mexico, and so therefore we have a different claim. This was never a part of Cuba. Cubans who come here are guests. We are not. . . .
>
> My motivation is to help the Chicano community. It's a very provincial attitude. Again, it is tied back to my identity of who I am, and the need for me to reinforce that in fact, from my perception, that anyone who is "Latino" is an immigrant, and whatever we deign, we the American populace deign to give them, they should be grateful for, because immigrants are guests here. I am not a guest here. Chicanos are not guests here. I refuse to be lumped in with those who are guests here.

Leo said this with vehemence. It was central to his view of himself and of his community that "Chicano" not be lost in the broader term "Latino" and that the Chicano community not be confused with immigrant Latin-Americans. Throughout his interview, as he talked about his personal history and his professional life, he emphasized a deep involvement with and commitment to this Chicano community.

This kind of nationalist position on Chicano issues, exemplified by Leo and Maria's suspicion of the term "Latino," is typical of the more extreme position taken by many members of the Chicano Movement cohort. In fact, Leo and Maria are two or three years older than Dorotea and Lázaro, and were undergraduates in the early 1970's when the Chicano movement was still influential on California campuses. Thus Leo and Maria may have been more deeply influenced by the more nationalistic forms of Chicano Movement culture than Dorotea and Lázaro.

The other end of the continuum is exemplified by Dorotea and Lázaro's perspective. While they call themselves "Chicano" and participated actively in Chicano university cultural life as undergraduates, they are more third-world oriented and less nationalist in their political perspective. As Chicanos, they feel an affinity with citizens of Latin America and immigrants to this country. This more inclusive kind of position is more typical of the post-Chicano movement cohort. While its members may identify positively as "Mexican American", or "Chicano," they tend to see themselves as part of a widening "Latino," or "Hispanic" political arena in California.

Both Dorotea and Lázaro have been involved in California politics since their undergraduate training and intend to be active in the future. When asked about what she calls herself ethnically, Dorotea answered that she calls herself "Chicana." She sees it as both a descriptive term, meaning being of Mexican descent, and a political term, meaning a certain perspective about ethnic identity between two cultures. However, she feels that "Latina" is more inclusive:

> I guess I do use the word "Latina" a lot, and again, I think it broadens my definition a lot because it encompasses many other cultural groups with the same issues that I also feel, same sort of ethnic issues. . . .
>
> I think that my whole definition of community when it comes to my cultural background is a sort of more third-world perspective, and I think that's why I readily accept the term "Latina" because I identify with "Latino" issues.

Later in her interview it became clear that Dorotea was deeply committed to this idea of being politically committed to a larger "Latina" community, and that this issue shaped the way she told the story of her life and the nature of her professional aspirations as a doctor.

For both these couples, their opinions on what terminology to use are rooted in their senses of who they are individually as members of an ethnic community and what that ethnic community encompasses. These views are deeply felt, empowering them with a sense of professional and political mission. All four of these people are active in Chicano and/or Latino networks, both within their professional callings and in their outside social and political commitments. The tense dynamics of their differing positions is typical of the wider Chicano professional community in Los Angeles. These tensions, so easily stirred by the issue of ethnic labeling, reflect a deeper hegemonic struggle within this community between a Chicano/Mexican American centered cultural identification and political orientation, usually represented by members of the Chicano Movement Cohort, and a "Latino", or "Hispanic" oriented cultural identification and political orientation, typically represented by the post-sixties cohort, and in some instances, the older pre-sixties cohort as well.

THE POLITICS OF NAMING

This ideological contest, wrapped in the issue of ethnic labeling, is at the heart of current internal political struggles within Chicano professional organizations. Within these professional groups the question of naming is often the language through which issues of power are discussed and shaped. I was witness to such a discussion in June 1989, when I attended a meeting of the Board of Directors of C.M.A.C., the Chicano/Latino Medical Association of California. As I described in Chapter 1, C.M.A.C. is an organization of Chicano physicians almost all of whom have been educated in the United States since the late sixties. They qualify, therefore, as members of the Chicano Movement cohort.

The meeting was held in the upscale Spanish-style Pasadena home of one of the Board members. The main issue that night was whether or not this organization should merge with another organization, called C.H.A.M.A., the California Hispanic American Medical

Association. This latter group was started in the 1950's and consisted primarily of Mexican American and other Latin American doctors many of whom were educated and trained in Latin America. The physicians in C.H.A.M.A.'s leadership were predominantly over the age of 45, while those of C.M.A.C. were primarily under 45. Interestingly enough, though, C.H.A.M.A. had recently recruited three prominent C.M.A.C. members onto their Board of Directors. It was two of these doctors who now brought the issue of merging to the C.M.A.C. Board.

The problems inherent in combining the two groups emerged gradually around a discussion of a name change. The C.H.A.M.A. board had indicated that it would not relinquish its name, and the question put to the C.M.A.C. leadership was whether or not they were willing to give up the name "Chicano," and identify the group as "Hispanic." The C.M.A.C. doctor who introduced the question, Rudolfo Villalobos—also one of the C.H.A.M.A. members—said in his preliminary statement that for him the name was not important: "I don't care. I know who I am." He also added that according to certain statistics, only 4% of the Mexican American population used the term "Chicano."

In response to Rudolfo, Luís Durán, a family practice resident, launched an emotionally charged plea for keeping the name "Chicano." He talked about its important political implications. He was joined by another resident, Cruz Santoyo, who said that "Chicano" was an indication of a particular political perspective, and he didn't care if only 4% of the population used it. He urged that they needed to keep this term because of what it meant in terms of a political history. He then described how it disturbed him that already, when he talked to pre-med undergraduates, they were so politically unaware that they didn't even know who "Bakke" was.

The fact that this doctor brought up the issue of "knowing who Bakke was" was particularly apt for this group. Three of the nine Board members had been medical students at the University of California at Davis during the 1978 United States Supreme Court case of University of California Regents vs. Bakke.[2] Two others had been undergraduates at Davis at the same time. The former Davis medical students shared a common memory of suffering intense media coverage as minority students the year that Bakke was granted admission into the medical school. These memories included being hounded from class to class by reporters who shot questions at them like "Do you feel qualified to be in medical school?"

All the board members—even those who had not been in Davis during the Bakke years—would recognize the historical significance of the event that this word "Bakke" was meant to convey. This was a direct appeal to the sense of collective history of the group. Being "Chicano" meant remembering the Bakke case.

At this point, some of the other members who had remained quiet during the first part of the discussion, broke in. Gary Naranjo, another family practice doctor, said vehemently that he did not want anything to do with the C.H.A.M.A. organization. He was angry, he said, that he had recently discovered they had put his name on a membership list sent out for publicity of their organization, without his permission. He said that C.H.A.M.A. did not reflect his views, and that for him the name "Chicano" was central. He didn't like the term, "Hispanic:" "What's 'Hispanic'? A government invention! And 'Latino.' That's even worse! What's 'Latino'? Italians are 'Latino'. I don't relate to that."

Another doctor, Valeria Molina, chimed in, saying to Rudolfo that she didn't understand how he could deny the importance of the term "Chicano" when he wouldn't even "be here" [i.e. be a doctor] if it weren't for Chicano activism. He nodded, and said, "I know, I know. You're right." But still, he felt that the name was no longer important. Valeria was alluding to the Chicano Movement's active role in affirmative action struggles, and the fact that Rudolfo, like the rest of them, owed his getting into medical school to diligent political work by other Chicanos. Being "Chicano" meant remembering that history.

As the discussion went on, people began offering their opinions of C.H.A.M.A. as an organization. They contrasted it with what they envisioned their young organization doing. It was interesting that as they discussed what they felt were the problems of C.H.A.M.A., they began to more sharply define their own goals for C.M.A.C. As one of the members characterized the meeting to me afterwards, the group had gradually defined C.H.A.M.A. as "old time, foreign medical graduates, conservative, Republican, entrepreneurs (in it for the money) not our ideal, but they are working in the community." By contrast, he said, C.M.A.C. had "U.S. MD's and our ideology will win out eventually anyway." While not making it explicit, he implied to me that C.M.A.C. in contrast to C.H.A.M.A. was an organization of United States trained MD's, progressive, Democrats (as opposed to

Republicans), and committed to helping their communities without exploiting them. For him and for other Chicanos at the meeting, being "Chicano" had to do with advocating this kind of political agenda.

There was actually no disagreement from any of the Board members about the nature of C.H.A.M.A., but rather a disagreement about whether or not it would be useful to merge the organizations. Rudolfo Villalobos emphasized that he felt they could merge and eventually turn the organization in the political direction that suited them. He pointed out that C.H.A.M.A. had money and connections that might be helpful. The group was already aware that C.H.A.M.A. had gained recognition as a physicians group representing the "Hispanic community" in California from Governor Deukmejian and the California State Assembly. A glossy-colored photo brochure from C.H.A.M.A. which was passed around that evening testified to that. Responding to this, Gary Naranjo argued that C.M.A.C. members had the know-how and connections to secure funding without C.H.A.M.A. help. Someone else pointed out that all they needed to do was make their own claim to represent the Hispanic community, and they would be recognized as a more legitimate group, since all of them were U.S. trained physicians, while the majority of C.H.A.M.A. doctors were not.

People intermittently tossed in more casual remarks about how they felt about the members of C.H.A.M.A. "It's just a social club. They want their daughters to meet Spanish-speaking doctor husbands at their yearly banquets!" This was a reference to what was perceived as C.H.A.M.A. members' snobbish, status and money-oriented ethnicity. And, "they just think we're a bunch of Indios anyway!" This comment elicited laughter, and referred subtly to the perception that C.H.A.M.A. members were Latin American elites who identified with European Spanish roots and who looked down on Chicanos because of their low status and Indian origins. Being "Chicano" here meant recognizing a sense of solidarity with blue-collar Mexican Americans, and an ethnic identity rooted in being "Indian" in contrast to "Spaniard."

Summing up the general tone of the meeting towards the end, Cruz Santoyo exclaimed that although the C.H.A.M.A. organization had been around since the fifties, and many of the individual members since the thirties, they had never helped any of them [Chicanos] get into medical school. "So what does that tell you? Being Chicano and all that activism *did* make a goddam difference!"

As the minutes of the meeting later recorded, it was agreed by a majority of the Board members by the end of the discussion, that

> C.M.A.C. will remain a separate organization. C.M.A.C. has a strong, young, U.S.-trained membership of physicians, strong affiliations with other organizations, political and health policy issues to address, and are more community-oriented. Our goals and objectives for the most part, follow a different focus. C.M.A.C. will address this via our committees and will work toward being recognized as the vehicle by which Chicano health issues and policies are addressed.

Several aspects of the importance of naming stand out from this board meeting. The first is that the name "Chicano" carries tremendous emotional weight for many of these Chicano Movement cohort doctors. This is rooted both in how they perceive their own personal history struggling to become physicians and how they conceive of their collective history as post-Civil Rights activism Chicanos. The majority decision to retain their name and a separate organization reflects a distinct sense of historical identity, that of being "Chicano" and being part of an ongoing movement. As Cruz Santoyo emphasized in his summarizing statement, for this cohort the meaning of being "Chicano" embraces a strong sense of being part of a historic struggle towards affirmative action in higher education, or more specifically, the struggle to get more Chicanos into the health professions, particularly as physicians. It is implied that Latinos and Mexican Americans who do not identify with this struggle, or the name that symbolizes that identification "Chicano," are outside of the group.

An incident which occurred a few months later at a joint C.H.A.M.A. and C.M.A.C. function illustrates the way many C.M.A.C. members feel about the depth of difference between the groups. This was a reception for "Latino" residents and prospective employers at the home of two physicians. I learned about the incident from my husband, who as a member of C.M.A.C. knew about the naming controversy. As we were driving home, discussing the reception, he exclaimed, "I've got to tell you something that happened! This is classic! You'll love it! It crystallizes the whole reason why we [C.M.A.C.] can't get together with C.H.A.M.A.!"

As he told it, he had been talking to the President of C.H.A.M.A., Elias Monguia and his wife about families and children. He was holding our six-month-old baby at the time. Mrs. Monguia turned to him and said, "Your baby has all the advantages of both worlds. He can take advantage of being Latino in order to get into a good college!" Beto said he was momentarily stunned. He murmured back to her, somewhat chagrined, that he hoped it wouldn't come to that: "I hope he'll be able to get in on his own." This is how he described his assessment of the incident:

> It was classic. That attitude plays into what the Whites' idea of affirmative action is. They [meaning C.H.A.M.A. people] see being Latino as something to use in the current political climate in order to get into prestigious universities. And it was so hard not to laugh or to say something stupid. It was so ironic. It was, you know, sort of an awkward thing since I've been on those [medical school] admissions committees working just to keep people like that from getting into medical school!

There are several important elements in this statement. From Beto's perspective, as it would be from the perspective of many Movement generation Chicanos, this woman's comment demonstrated her ignorance of "Chicano" Movement culture and therefore represented the collective ignorance of all the C.H.A.M.A. members about this culture. Within this culture, affirmative action is not something to take advantage of, a loop hole that middle and upper-class Latinos can manipulate—as she implied in relationship to our son—in order to "get into medical school." Rather, affirmative action is an opportunity for poor, disadvantaged, and/or politically committed (i.e. to the Chicano movement's goals) Chicanos or Latinos to enter the highly competitive medical education track which had been virtually closed to Mexican Americans before the Civil Rights and affirmative action struggles of the sixties and seventies.

In fact, Beto, like many movement Chicanos sees himself as a participant in this evolving struggle, doing his part on medical school admissions committees by trying to screen out minority applicants who want to use their ethnicity as a means to "get in" without truly being disadvantaged or interested in their ethnic culture or in benefiting the blue-collar Mexican community.

Thus, one aspect of being "Chicano" for movement Chicanos like those who dominated the C.M.A.C. Board meeting is identifying with this sense of commitment to struggle for affirmative action. Cruz

Santoyo's comment about how he was worried that Chicano pre-meds didn't know anything about the Bakke case was a reflection of this attitude. If upcoming Chicano health students didn't know about Bakke, it meant they had no knowledge of the movement history, and thus no appropriate ethnic awareness.

Another aspect of being "Chicano" for this cohort, as demonstrated only briefly from some of the more casual comments during the meeting, is a sense of unique cultural identity as Mexican Americans. This student culture, born and bred in various California towns and barrios, was nurtured in colleges and universities across California during the sixties and seventies, (and to some extent currently) among students who were primarily the first generation to attain higher education in their blue-collar Mexican origin families. This student culture emphasized solidarity, both political and cultural, with their blue-collar backgrounds, and celebrated Mexican as well as Chicano foods, history, literature, and art. As exemplified by Corky Gonzalez' poem, "Yo Soy Joaquin" which became a movement classic, it projected a positive ethnic identity through the use of racial metaphors idealizing *mestizo* (mixed Spaniard and Indian) and Indian (primarily Aztec and Mayan) heritage.

In contrast to their own Chicano movement culture, C.M.A.C. members characterized C.H.A.M.A. members as outsiders, upper-class snobs, concerned only about money and prestige, and like the Spanish in Mexico, identifying with a "European" heritage and looking down on their poor "Indian" cousins, the Chicanos.

For the Movement cohort, these two central aspects of "Chicano" culture—identifying oneself as being part of 1) a common history of affirmative action and civil rights struggle in the United States, and 2) a common history of cultural heritage reaching into an idealized Indian past and rooted in blue-collar, Mexican American communities—is an essential element of their sense of ethnic uniqueness. The word "Chicano" connotes this common culture for the group.

Another aspect of the importance of naming to Chicano ethnicity is more directly political. C.M.A.C. members shape their identity as an organization partially in terms of being leaders in the health field for the wider Chicano population in California. They understand this leadership as a mediating role between the wider Chicano community and local, state and federal government bodies and agencies. As their brochures states, one of the goals of the organization is "to promote

Chicano/Latino health policy issues at state and local government levels." The C.M.A.C. board members feel that they are an emerging powerful ethnic group that can have more political clout as health oriented representatives of the Chicano community than C.H.A.M.A. with its older, Latin-trained physicians. As one C.M.A.C. member said:

> They need us; we don't need them. They are foreign medical grads. In the first place, they're not as strong as they present themselves to be. They've got a lot of money, but they don't really represent the Chicano/ Latino community in California. And they need us, the U.S. medical school grad doctors for credibility with the AMA [American Medical Association] and the C.M.A. [Calif. Medical Association], because it is extremely important here in the U.S. to have the prestige of coming from a U.S. school.

The differences between C.M.A.C. and C.H.A.M.A. as characterized by C.M.A.C. board members are essentially the differences between cohort cultures. This does not mean that the two organizations have completely different goals; from the evidence of their brochures and publicity literature, they have many overlapping aims, particularly that of helping the Latino population gain better access to health care. What C.H.A.M.A. does not share with C.M.A.C. is the Chicano pre-med and medical school network culture, a Chicano Movement cohort culture.[3]

MORE COHORT STRUGGLES OVER NAMING

This kind of naming and the struggle between cohort hegemonies is not exclusive to Chicano physician organizations. As the immigrant population from varied Latin American countries increases in the United States, Chicanos in most of the professions are being called on to deal with a wide variety of Spanish-speaking people and issues in their professional practices, and are positioning themselves for leadership of this wider Latino community. Doctors and lawyers, as some of the more visible members of this elite professional class, are in particularly strong positions for such leadership. Among Chicano lawyers, who by the very nature of their profession are in the public eye and who often are politically ambitious, the issue of naming is as controversial a topic as among physicians.

In Autumn 1988 the Mexican American Bar Association entertained a motion to change the name of the organization. An ad hoc committee was organized to conduct a survey, and a questionnaire was sent out to over 750 attorneys on the M.A.B.A. mailing list. According to the November M.A.B.A. newsletter, the questionnaire had four purposes: 1) to determine what percentage of the membership wanted a name change; 2) to determine the ethnic breakdown of the organization; 3) to determine what name the members would choose if they chose to change the current one and; 4) to determine if changing the name would attract new members or alienate current members.

263, or 33% of the questionnaires were returned. 78.5% of the respondents were Chicano and the other included some other Latin Americans, a sprinkling of Anglos, Spanish Americans, and other ethnic groups. Out of those questionnaires, 49.4% favored a name change and 41.5 % opposed it.

This response was strong enough to prompt the leadership to set up a meeting in December of that year to vote on the issue. The question was whether or not the bylaws should be amended to change the name of the association. The names chosen for this possible change were the following, all more inclusive than the current name, "Mexican American Bar Association:"

Hispanic Bar Association
Latino Bar Association
Latin American Bar Association
Mexican American and Latino Bar Association

The debate at that night's meeting was heated, with various members of the organization giving speeches about their points of view. Again, like the C.M.A.C./C.H.A.M.A. conflict, the split appeared to fall between cohort generations. The Chicano Movement cohort of those 35 and over favored retaining the name "Mexican American," while the younger cohort supported some of the more inclusive names. In the end the members present at the meeting voted to retain the name "Mexican American Bar Association."

OUTSIDE INFLUENCES

Such reevaluation of names and jockeying of ethnic political positions within Chicano professional organizations is part of a larger confluence of events and forces in contemporary Los Angeles. On the one hand, the group with the most influence and power is the Chicano Movement cohort, a first generation of professionals now firmly established in their jobs, their organizations, and networks. The culture that informs and sustains their ethnic cohesiveness is rooted in the Chicano Movement. It is a culture that affirms the specific history and experience of blue-collar Americans of Mexican descent.

However, these professionals are finding that in their capacities as professionals and community leaders they are being confronted with multiple challenges to the ethnic exclusivity of their Chicano culture, challenges from both outside and inside the Chicano professional class. In the first place, they are finding that in their jobs or their positions as political leaders they are increasingly being called on to work with, or represent, all "Hispanics," particularly due to the increasing immigration of people from various Latin American countries into Los Angeles. In the second place, many members of the Movement cohort, as well as most of those from the other two cohorts, are pressuring their organizations to form alliances with other "Latinos," in order to be more effective in their goals of establishing equality of education and opportunity for underrepresented minorities of Spanish-speaking descent. Furthermore, some of this pressure may in turn be the result of state and national government tendencies to lump all "Hispanics" into one category. This may pressure the organizations who negotiate with these government bodies to identify themselves as "Hispanic" in order to gain the benefits of money and political influence for their groups.

These pressures on the Chicano Movement cohort culture, and the responding resistance to such pressures, has generated an ethnic field of relations charged with tension. At the heart of this tension is the issue of ethnic labeling. Every decision about such naming, from that of what to call an organization, to that of what to call oneself or the person sitting next to you at a dinner party, requires a subtle and sensitive dexterity with labeling language. Every Chicano, whether active in ethnic networks or not, or from whichever cohort, has some awareness of this need for careful labeling.

STRATEGIES OF ETHNIC LABELING

People use different strategies for dealing with ethnic labeling, but almost everyone changes the terms they use according to the situation or person to whom they are speaking. As one lawyer put it when asked what ethnic label he used to call himself: "I think it's really a matter of who you're talking to and what you're talking about." Another lawyer said something similar in an interview, indicating some of his own preferences and opinions about various labels:

> *Anthropologist*: What do you call yourself in terms of your ethnicity?

> *Lawyer*: I use different terms at different times. . . . I'm Mexican. And I guess I'm "*Mexicano*" in that sense. I identify very much with Mexico. When I'm with Mexicans, they don't know that I'm actually a Chicano, but that's because I'm so familiar with the Mexican culture. . . . But I call myself different things different times. Everybody does. I never call myself "Hispanic." I do call myself "Latino."

> *Anthropologist:* Why not Hispanic?

> *Lawyer:* It's just a term I don't like. It's not a Spanish name, we'll say. "Latino" is a Spanish name, and that's the term that I use when I'm with other Latinos. I call myself "Latino." When I'm with other Chicanos, well, then I'm a "Chicano" as well. When I'm with Mexicans from Mexico, then I'm a Mexicano with them also.

While this lawyer seems comfortable with his personal label switching, the choice about when and where and for whom one should choose particular ethnic names can be tricky and complicated. Most of people's choices seem effortless and unconscious. However, many indicated that they deliberately used certain terms in certain contexts. For example, sometimes the name shifting can be in terms of home vs. other places, as with several Chicanos who said either they would never use the term "Chicano" at home with their parents or had spent time convincing their parents that it was a legitimate term. This problem often occurs in families where parents are first-generation immigrants and cannot understand the binational and often politically charged ethnic identity embraced by the term "Chicano."

Or the shifting can be in terms of work place vs. social places. One obstetrician told me that she used "Chicana" in most social situations, but switched to "Hispanic," or "Latino" at the hospital where she worked since that was the language used by the predominantly non-Hispanic staff. This kind of name-switching between private and professional life was shared by many Chicanos of various cohorts.

In informal conversation, people may range through many terms, sometimes using them interchangeably with no easily discernible pattern. I noticed that in their interviews with me, several people switched terms depending on what or who or when in their lives they were talking about. For example, a professional who said she called herself exclusively "Hispanic," referred to herself (apparently unconsciously) as "Chicana" when talking about her college days. This was fairly typical of interviews.

I myself, particularly in unambiguously ethnographic situations like formal interviews, carefully chose my ethnic terms according to intuitions and information about the person with whom I was speaking. Later, as I read over my field notes, I noticed that there was a subtle interpersonal power dynamic involved in these interactions over terminology. I generally tried to match their choice of terminology, although I slipped at times, since I wanted to make them comfortable and I was in the position of needing something from them, rather than the other way around. The interviewees, however, varied in whether or not they chose their terminology in relationship to mine. Some maintained their own use of terminology no matter what I said, and others shifted when I did. Still others seemed to become self conscious about terminology after I had brought up the subject, and began to stumble over the labels when trying to describe someone: e.g. "My roommate from B_____ was Chicana, or Latina, or Mexican American."

It appeared to be a matter of power and deference within the interview relationship. Those who I felt were most comfortable with me were the most casual and fluid about their uses of terms, particularly people that I knew within other contexts. Those who appeared to remain more formal with me tended to keep to their own terminology, and those who appeared to feel a little intimidated by me as a researcher (there were only a few of those) were the ones who expressed awkwardness about their usage.

When I asked Chicano friends about this interpersonal power dynamic surrounding the use of terminology, several indicated that they felt much the same thing went on between any two Chicano or

Latino strangers, particularly in cases where it was difficult to establish the background of the persons or person to whom they were speaking.

An additional problem in deciding what labels to choose in what situations, is that the terms have multiple meanings, and not everyone uses the terms to mean the same things. In order to successfully negotiate ones' way as a Chicano professional, it is necessary to understand nuances beyond the simple meanings that I gave to certain labels at the beginning of this chapter. For example, the term "Chicano" has at least four different meanings, and the same people may employ all the meanings of these terms in different contexts:

1) Any people of Mexican origin living in the United States.

2) Any people of Mexican origin living in the United States who have been here beyond one generation. For example, a Chicana doctor from the Imperial Valley and a Chicano lawyer from San Bernardino both said that they grew up thinking of themselves as part of a "Chicano" community, meaning non-immigrants of Mexican descent.

3) Any people of Mexican origin who embrace a particular (i.e. nationalist) political perspective. This can have a positive or negative connotation, depending on whether or not the person has ever identified him or herself this way. Many Chicanos indicate that they grew up calling themselves "Mexican American," or "Mexican," but in college due to the influence of the Chicano movement began to call themselves "Chicano" as part of their assertion of a new sense of ethnic identity. The more negative connotation of this term, often carried by members of either the pre or post Chicano movement cohort generation, is expressed by a 26 year old corporate lawyer:

> It seems that the word "Chicano" comes out of a particular political upheaval and maybe I don't necessarily identify with that movement, although I know it's helped me a great deal. But, so I just consider myself "Mexican American."

4) A hybrid cultural identity, neither American nor Mexican, but something unique, or as an obstetrician put it: "being raised, or

caught between two cultures." This interpretation of the term is more typical of Chicanos influenced by Movement culture. Another obstetrician described it this way in her interview:

Anthropologist: What do you call yourself in terms of your ethnicity?

Doctor: . . . When people ask me what I am, I say, "I'm Chicana," And then I attempt to explain to them what that means.

Anthropologist: And what do you say?

Doctor: I basically say that my parents were raised in Mexico, that I'm of Mexican descent, but I was born here and I think that there's a political connotation to that. It's a term that you can [use to] say, "we're not really accepted as American, but then we're not *Mexicanos.*"

Much of the other terminology has similarly complex, historically positioned meanings. Labeling them "Mexican American," during their student years would have insulted members of the Chicano Movement cohort. The term was associated with a conservative and unenlightened ethnicity, what they called themselves *before* they went to college and became "Chicanos." Ironically, for the most part, these same cohort members have become comfortable with the term and may use it now interchangeably with "Chicano" to refer to themselves or others. Members of the older and younger cohorts for the most part use this term exclusively (although some may refer to themselves occasionally as "Mexican" or *"Mexicano"*) when describing themselves and others of specific Mexican descent.

The labels "Latino" and "Hispanic" are used by members of all three cohorts, both as more ethnically inclusive terms and sometimes in place of a more specific ethnic term, in spite of the fact that they may be referring only to Americans of Mexican descent. However, many members of the Chicano Movement Cohort have strong feelings about these terms, particularly "Hispanic." [4] One Chicana physician explained to me that while she preferred to call herself "Chicana," for a more inclusive term, or the term she used at work in the hospital, she preferred "Latino" over "Hispanic:"

Anthropologist: Do you ever use "Hispanic" or "Latina," or pretty much "Chicana?"

Doctor: Pretty much "Chicana." "Latina" when I'm in the hospital. For me "Hispanic" connotes negative things... old world concepts of Spaniard and whatever Spaniard connotes... For me "Hispanic" is a negative term. Something about cultural denial, and it's historically a negative term, you know, Spaniard and European dominance. "Latino" still doesn't specify. "Chicano" is a very specific term for a specific identity. "Latino" is more of a unity term, which I accept also.

This doctor's position on "Hispanic" is firmly rooted in the culture of the Chicano Movement cohort. For her, "Hispanic" connotes "Spaniard" and the European subjugation of the indigenous Mexican people with whom Chicano Movement culture identifies. Furthermore, it is widely understood by Chicano professionals that "Hispanic" was a term selected by the federal government to classify citizens of "Spanish-speaking descent," and that many Chicanos reject it for the term "Latino." "Latino" is more widely accepted because it was adopted by Chicanos themselves when creating ties with people from other Latin American countries.

Almost everyone I interviewed from all three cohorts was aware that "Hispanic" was more controversial than "Latino." Nevertheless, many were comfortable using it, particularly in work or other professional situations which required a broader term than that of Mexican American or "Chicano." A public prosecutor, who although a chronological member of the Chicano Movement Cohort did not strongly reflect Movement culture, put it this way:

It seems that the two terms of the day are "Latino" and "Hispanic" and I'm comfortable with either of those. I don't really have any preference. I know about the arguments about "Hispanic" being very anglicized and the fact that the government has sort of given us that label, or whatever, and therefore we shouldn't adopt it. I don't feel uncomfortable with that label. I feel very comfortable with "Latina" also.

This lawyer seems to be typical of the growing consensus among many professional Chicanos, that both "Hispanic" and "Latino" are useful terms for the emerging reality of Los Angeles demographics and politics.

A CULTURAL SHIFT

The current controversies about terminology that simmer within the Chicano professional community reflect a growing cultural shift. The Chicano Movement Cohort as the generation in power has begun to open its formerly exclusively Mexican identity to include "Latinos" or "Hispanics." For many this is simply a matter of personal evolution, corresponding to broader historical trends. Said one Chicano judge in his late thirties:

> Growing up we would call ourselves Mexican Americans. In college the term switched to "Chicano." In law school it was the same thing. And I'll still use that term periodically, but more often now I think I use the term "Hispanic," or "Latino." And I use it primarily because the ethnic make up of California's changing. One time it was predominantly Mexican, and it still is. There are just a lot of Hispanic non-Mexican groups. I believe in unifying with those groups. I prefer the broader term of "Hispanic." . . . Personally, I still feel like a Mexican, or a Chicano.

A lawyer in his mid thirties, active in the M.A.B.A. leadership, described several of the historical dynamics merging to create a shift in the use of terms:

> In college during the early and mid seventies it was ""Chicano" which was, as it turned out, a somewhat narrow view of ethnicity to the extent that it did not take into account the fact that there are Cubans, and Puerto Ricans on the East Coast and an increasing number of folks coming from Honduras and Nicaragua and El Salvador into the western region of the United States, which I think caused an evolution of the language, such that "Chicano" is still used, but the same people who were "Chicano" are still "Chicanos;" however the people who use the word "Chicano" now are probably sprinkling their vocabulary more with references to "Latino" and to the extent that they're dealing in any professional capacity, I think

the professions have now gravitated towards adopting "Hispanic" as a common reference.

At one point in my life I was convinced that "Hispanic" was used predominantly by conservative Republicans, but, if that was ever true it's becoming less true just because, as the different people coming into the country increase in numbers, I think folks are just trying to find a comfortable handle, and I think "Hispanic" has become the favorite as a result of the media adopting it. The newspapers and the television commentators use "Hispanic" and therefore the rest of the country, including more liberal, left-wing activists are adopting "Hispanic."

This attorney succinctly identifies at least four historical influences on the change in naming patterns. One is the broadening of "Chicano" consciousness to recognize the existence of Cubans and Puerto Ricans as fellow Spanish-speaking minorities in the United States. Another is the fact of increasing immigration of groups from Latin American countries other than Mexico. Both of these factors have led to more use of inclusive terms like "Latino" and "Hispanic." Furthermore, Chicanos as professionals have gravitated increasingly toward the use of "Hispanic," because it is the predominant term used in the professions. And finally, the term "Hispanic" was itself adopted by the professions, he suggests, because the media have adopted it.

The pressures for such changes in labeling and in ethnic consciousness can be broken down further into more specific factors. Many Chicanos have found Latin American political allies and friends through pre-professional training, at work, and in rallying support for particular political projects. Also, they are often called on to work with Latin American clients or patients, simply because they are Spanish-speaking. Additionally, as Chicanos become more active politically on a national level, their awareness of mutual problems and potential allies broadens to include other Latin American minorities.

Thus, at one level, many Chicanos accept without great controversy this shift to include "Latinos" in their networks and organizations and labels. This kind of attitude was reflected in the recent name change of the Stanford Chicano Alumni Club of Los Angeles. An informal poll and discussion was generated by the leadership, and it was decided without dissent to rename it the "Stanford Chicano/Latino Alumni Club." The fact that the majority of the membership were Chicanos who had known each other at Stanford during the late 1960's and early 1970's may indicate why there was so little discussion. There was no fear that the organization would be inundated with the concerns and cultural interests of other "Latinos."

Similarly, even C.M.A.C. (Chicano/Latino Medical Association of California), the medical organization which rejected merging with C.H.A.M.A. (California Hispanic American Medical Association), voted to add the term "Latino," to their name. But as one member joked with me when I questioned him about it one night on the telephone: "Yeah, it's Chicano/Latino, but you notice that in the acronym, C.M.A.C., the "L" is silent!" As long as "Chicano" was the dominant orientation of the organization, he didn't mind "Latinos" being included.

So, while many Chicanos appear to accept this change as a matter of opportunity rather than a threat to Chicano ethnicity, other Chicano professionals are more uneasy with the shift in labeling and ethnic consciousness. One could cynically say that it is simply a matter of power dynamics; one group wants to make political claims in the name of "Chicanos" and another in the name of "Latinos." The cultural differences are mere trappings. However, as I have discussed and described at length, many Chicanos believe that there are more substantive matters at stake in this question of naming.

To put it plainly, there is simply the matter of to what constituency, or community, one is politically responsible as a professional and a community leader. Part of that consideration includes the question of whether or not by working on behalf of "Latinos," or making political claims on various local, state, and national governments in the name of "Latinos," the actual resources and benefits available to Mexican Americans specifically will be lessened. Leo Limón, one of those at my dinner party who also worked as a lawyer for M.A.L.D.E.F. (Mexican American Legal Defense Fund) was concerned that this organization was beginning to lean in the direction of helping "Hispanics" more than "Chicanos." As I quoted him earlier, he felt that Chicanos had a different claim on national resources from other Latin Americans since the southwest United States had once belonged to Mexico. He said that while he didn't mind helping Latinos, or other minorities for that matter, he had not dedicated himself as a lawyer to work for the benefit of any group but his own.

This nationalist perspective is shared by many Chicanos nurtured in the Chicano Movement culture, and it is rooted in a particular historical claim about being a colonized rather than immigrant people in the United States. Chicanos who would argue with Leo, like Dorotea and Lázaro who were also at my dinner party, do not necessarily disagree that Mexican land was stolen by the United States in the Mexican American War and that therefore Chicanos have a unique position. However, they feel that the basic issues of racism and discrimination are present for all American Latinos, and that people from Mexico as well as other Latin American third-world countries share a common claim for justice and equality in the face of United States cultural, political and economic hegemony.

It appears that the decision to use the term "Hispanic," or even "Latino" for that matter, is not likely to arise out of deep feelings of ethnic belonging or pride in a collective history. It is usually more of a politically strategic decision, like that made by the leadership of the Hispanic Professional Round Table Association, a new umbrella organization created to pool the resources of multiple Hispanic professional organizations to promote education at the pre-college level. As one of the founding members of that organization said to me when I asked him about the name of the organization:

> First and foremost, I consider myself Chicano, but I often won't even
> bring the term up, because if I can get someone to work in a school
> and help some Latino kids, I don't care what we call ourselves.

Although it seems that the inclusion of "Latinos" in Chicano dominated organizations may at one level broaden political resources, the question arises as to whether or not an allegiance to a broad "third world" Latino identity can truly mobilize people to a common and enduring sense of ethnic difference in the face of dominant American institutions and culture. In other words is it possible for such inclusive terms as "Latino" and "Hispanic" to inspire allegiance and participation in particular ethnic organizations with the same potency that the terms "Mexican American," and even more so, "Chicano" can?

For those who claim these names, usually members of the Chicano Movement cohort, these labels serve as powerful symbols capable of conjuring up a strong, deeply-felt sense of a very specific shared history. This history is constructed in the form of a story of triumph through struggle against a dominant American hegemonic. It is a historical narrative shared by those who identity with Movement culture. Because the Chicano Movement cohort currently dominates Chicano professional ethnic organizations, this counter-hegemony, summed up in the terms "Mexican American" and "Chicano," is the symbol which binds Chicano professional culture in Los Angeles. It remains to be seen what cultural key, if any, will replace it as the basis for ethnic collective organization once this cohort has been usurped by the post-Movement generation. [5]

NOTES

1. All names used in this dissertation, unless stated otherwise, are pseudonyms.

2. See footnote 6, Chapter 2.

3. However, not all members of C.H.A.M.A. are ignorant or untouched by the Chicano Movement culture, nor do they necessarily see their goals as different from C.M.A.C. in terms of helping the Chicano community gain access to better health care. One distinguished C.H.A.M.A. member, a professor of Medicine at U.C.L.A. Medical School, is a hero for former U.C.L.A. medical students due to his success in getting more Chicanos and other minority students into U.C.L.A. Medical School. Another member, a recent president of C.H.A.M.A., retired a few years ago from his successful private practice to head up a community clinic in East L.A., a community primarily of Mexican Americans. He is deeply involved in that community's health politics and sees his membership in C.H.A.M.A. as part of that commitment to improving "the quality of life specifically through the delivery of health care to the underprivileged people of our society." [Quote from a speech delivered to the Chicano pre-med society, "Chicanos for Creative Medicine."] He is comfortable and proud of being Mexican American and calls himself "Mexican" or "American of Mexican descent," but says he cannot identity with "nationalist" organizations like those pertaining to 'Chicanos' since he is more comfortable identifying with all Spanish-speaking immigrants.

4. The position that Leo and Maria Limón took at my dinner party, preferring "Hispanic" to "Latino," was unusual, and by their own observation is probably due to Leo's growing up in Texas and Maria's subsequent living there for several years, where "Latino" is not a term used.

5. When my husband Beto first read my conclusion here, he argued that an inclusive "Latino" identity would probably eventually have the same power as that of "Chicano" to mobilize people. This was because of what he identified as the upcoming struggles in California between Mexicans allied

with other Spanish-speaking "Latino" immigrants against the dominant Anglo culture, conflicts bound to emerge due to the increased numbers of Latinos in California and the threat that would pose to the status-quo.

CHAPTER 4

Race and Gender:
The Body Language of Ethnic
Identity

In the dining room of the Chicano Theme House dormitory at Stanford University during the early seventies, a visiting Chicano artist named Zarco Guerrero[1] painted a mural depicting three enormous heads. On the left he painted the face of a young Chicana, brown, dark-eyed and smiling. On the right he painted the toothless, wizened face of an old woman, also brown and dark-eyed. In the center he placed a completely blank, pale pink face surrounded by a mass of blonde hair.

The mural created controversy campus wide. And for good reason. Zarco had captured the raw, defiant essence of the Chicano Movement message in this simple scene: Brown was beautiful. And he meant this both literally and figuratively. Mexican darkness and Mexican features were desired and cherished in the figures of Mexican womanhood. Mexican culture was alive and vital in its Chicano youth, symbolized by the young woman, and in its Mexican roots, symbolized by the elderly woman. As for the blank, female, blonde face, the message declared that Anglo beauty and American Anglo culture were empty and meaningless for Chicanos.

Almost twenty years after Zarco painted his mural at Stanford, the Los Angeles Theater Center presented a piece called "Latinos Anonymous" for its Spring 1990 season. The play was written and acted by four Latinos, two of whom were Chicanos, and one of whom at least, had been active in the Chicano Movement in the seventies. The play's premise was that audience and cast members were present at a "Latinos Anonymous" meeting where recovering "Latinos" were trying to overcome their addiction to "Angloness."

I attended the play one Sunday afternoon with a few Chicano physician friends, all of whom identified strongly with the Chicano Movement. We all thoroughly enjoyed the play's commentary on and celebration of "Latino" identity in the late 1980's.

On the way home from the theater, we discussed two of the sketches in particular. Both depicted addictive "Angloness" using the symbol of the white, blonde female. In the first, a Chicano actor muses about why he is attracted to Angla women as on-stage a high heeled, slicked up, vamp-of-a-blonde seductively slithers around him. The tone of the piece is light and humorous until the actor suddenly shifts the mood from seductiveness to anger with an abrupt change in his voice. "Perhaps you remind me of the American dream. The one I'm not a part of." He spews the words out bitterly, then wheels and walks away.

In the second sketch, the "Mayan Defense League" comes to the rescue of a Latina who is about to peroxide her hair blonde. The three Mayan priests in full-robed regalia thoroughly search the woman's house and discover white bread and blue contacts, other sure signs of her defective "Anglo" leanings. After scolding her, they perform a "ritualotomy," complete with incense, hand motions, and drum, to exorcise her desire to be an Angla. The message they leave her as they fly off to the next ethnic emergency is "Just be who you are!"

Both these skits exhorted Latinos to reject the Anglo image of beauty and cultural value symbolized by the Blonde, and to discover their own cultural identity as Latin Americans with indigenous, Indian roots symbolized by the Mayan priests. Like Zarco's mural, both employed the language of bodies, particularly women's bodies, to symbolize cultural differences.

It is no coincidence that the same symbolic language used in a mural painted in the midst of the Movement in a Chicano dining hall, language which caused an outraged uproar from many non-Chicanos on the Stanford campus in the early 1970's, should be employed by artists at least sixteen years later in a major Los Angeles theater and enjoy great popularity among highly mixed audiences of Chicanos, Latinos, and Anglos, as well as other ethnic groups. The long arm of the Chicano Movement was stretching out across the years, influencing the use of Movement symbolism into the 1980's and beyond. The Movement cohort's experience was so culturally cogent that it continues to reach out and touch both members of the Chicano generation who have now grown older, and a new group of "Latinos" who are increasingly embraced with Mexican Americans in a collective "Latino" identity.

However, while the play, "Latinos Anonymous" and these skits about the Blonde distinctly bear resemblance to themes of the Movement, they also show the marks of the particular historical experience of the 1980's, including changes in both the lives of the Chicano Movement generation and in the ethnic politics of California and Los Angeles today.

MOVEMENT SYMBOLISM

The use of body language in both the 70's mural and the 80's play is ripe material for historical and cultural analysis. Such biological metaphors of the human body have been used since at least the nineteenth-century, particularly in the United States, to construct notions of immutable ethnic difference. Movement Chicanos have both adopted and amended this language of race, gender, and bodies in their own struggle for ethnic and class identity.

Zarco's Movement mural relied on the body language of both gender and race by clothing his message about cultural differences in metaphors of female bodies (heads) with noticeably different ("racially") skin color, hair color, and facial features. The Latinos Anonymous sketches drew similarly on the body language of gender and race. In one sketch a Chicana (female body) tries to change her racial appearance by bleaching her hair. In another, a blonde Angla (female body of one race) tries to seduce a Chicano (male body of another race). The messages of these body codes are multi-leveled. They are at one level about physical appearance and attraction, what one should look like and what kind of bodies one should desire. At another level they are about competing cultures, about powerful forces compelling people in a battle about different ways of constructing social reality.

This symbolic linking of the body language of gender with that of race creates a jungle of metaphors which are difficult to untangle, being so rooted in western empiricist thinking. The body is understood within this cultural tradition as a basic touchstone of empirical reality. It is perceived as something immediate, touchable, obvious to anyone as a verifiable reality. What is not often recognized is that this empirically verifiable body is perceived through a particular veil of cultural meanings which have been ascribed to it. These meanings are actually culturally relative and constructed within particular historical struggles.

The roots of Chicano Movement symbolism about race language employed in the struggle over ethnic identity are multiple. Using the mural and play as examples, a good place to begin is with the symbol of the Blonde. The Blonde, who represented all Anglo women, was a potent Movement symbol used to represent the enemy Anglo culture. The Blonde incorporated a host of attitudes with a dense historical past. She symbolized the American dream of success, of moving up the ladder from blue-collar immigrant to white collar American. The desire to look like the Blonde, like the woman in the sketch who was about to peroxide her hair, or to possess the Blonde, like the man in the sketch who felt attracted to the vamp, became central symbols of the seduction of Chicanos away from their "native" Mexican culture and blue-collar class identification. To possess a Blonde, or to be oneself the possessed Blonde, conjured up images of the "Good Life," White Anglo Saxon Protestant middle-class style.

One of the sources of this imagery for the Chicano Movement was the writing of contemporary Black intellectuals like Franz Fanon.[2] Fanon offered a subtle, eloquent analysis of the relationship between racism, gender, culture, and desire:

> "Out of the blackest part of my soul, across the zebra striping of my mind, surges this desire to be suddenly *white*.
>
> I wish to be acknowledged not as *black* but as *white*.
>
> Now. . . who but a white woman can do this for me? By loving me she proves that I am worthy of white love. I am loved like a white man.
>
> I am a white man.
>
> Her love takes me onto the noble road that leads to total realization. . .
>
> I marry white culture, white beauty, white whiteness.
>
> When my restless hands caress those white breasts, they grasp white civilization and dignity and make them mine.[3]

Fanon's image of the black male body caressing the breasts of a white female body and in this way "grasping" white culture is graphically powerful precisely because it conjures up images of bodies clutched together in the heat of sexual passion and the fever of racial tension, black and white, male and female, the one grappling to caress/possess/master the other in the fantasy of a black male who longs for acceptance in the dominant society.

These issues were similarly arousing within the Chicano student Movement. What bodies one desired became a cultural issue. To date an Anglo woman, especially a blonde, became a symbol of betraying your own culture, of wanting to be White, or Anglo, of desiring upper-class status, privilege, and "dignity" at the expense of one's allegiance to one's own people. Poet Ricardo Sanchez captures the Movement equation of the Anglo female with assimilation in the following:

> The Chicano, in the main, never did—and still does not—want assimilation; there is no sexualized compulsion for making love to a blue-eyed, blonde gringa. [1973: 37]

Of course, a Chicana female dating an Anglo male was also frowned upon. In fact, intermarriage of any kind was equated with "losing one's culture," and becoming more "Anglo" by "diluting the blood." Often, Chicanos who were the children of mixed (Anglo and Mexican) marriages were suspected as somehow "less" Chicano because of their "mixed blood", regardless of their cultural orientation or commitment to the Movement [Reich 87-88].

The dominant symbolic image employed to symbolize the relationship between Anglo and Chicano "races" and cultures was that of the male/Chicano and female/Angla. In this tendency to make the male experience of oppression and resistance normative, the Chicano Movement was consistent with other nationalist movements.[4] "Woman" was the symbol upon which Chicano ideas about both "White" culture and "Brown" culture were projected, just as Zarco depicted in his mural and the Latinos Anonymous players depicted in their sketches.[5]

Another source of the imagery of bodies and race for the Movement was that of the culture/power dynamics within Mexico. In Mexico, attractiveness is often associated with European rather than Indian physiognomy. Advertising billboards in Mexico regularly depict upper-class looking, blue-eyed blondes curled around various products (liquor, perfume, dishwashers) thus symbolically linking the consuming of certain goods with social mobility, status, and European and/or "Anglo" looking women. The "*novelas* " or soap operas produced in Latin American countries (and viewed daily in many Chicano households in the United States) feature light skinned, European looking, often blond heroes and heroines, occasionally depicting maids and country bumpkins with more "mestizo" or "Indian" features. Closer to home, in many Chicano students' families, children were classified as attractive or not according to how light skinned or light-haired they were, and whether or not they had green or blue eyes instead of brown.

Chicanos in the Movement were highly aware that this Mexican tendency to base status and beauty on a hierarchy of physiognomy was rooted in the colonial history of Latin America and European Spain, a history in which the "Indian" was relegated to the lower rungs of society. Movement culture went further in recognizing that for Chicanos the crucial racial hierarchy was that created by the centuries long relationship of the United States to Mexico, and more particularly in the relationship of Mexicans and Chicanos to Anglo American cultural and economic hegemony since the nineteenth century. Chicanos recognized that there was a link between European features and social class status in the United States, and they identified this as racist. They further recognized that their access to the American dream of social mobility was blocked by racist institutions and the ethnocentric cultural values of the dominant Anglo society.

The racism of American Anglo society has strong historical roots. While early ideas about "racial" difference had been developed in Europe in the early nineteenth century, they were fed and strengthened in the United States as its population expanded westward and searched for ways to justify its subsequent ruthless exploitation of Blacks, Indians, and Mexicans.[6] By the mid-nineteenth century, when the United States was itching to get its hands on Mexican territories, theories which justified "manifest destiny" in terms of "Anglo Saxon" "racial" superiority were fanned to spread like wildfire into the general public by politicians yearning to provoke a Mexican American confrontation.[7] Mexicans were characterized as a "colored mongrel race" of "barbarous tyranny" and "superstition" by such prominent politicians as Robert Walker, a Mississippi senator and leader of the Democratic party who became President Polk's Secretary of the Treasury. By thus using the language of race—inherent biological, genetic difference—to characterize all differences between Mexicans and Americans, and linking this to cultural practices like government forms ("barbarous tyranny") and religious practices ("superstition," also called "papism"), Walker and his compatriots began a tradition which justified exploitation of Mexican Americans in terms of alleged "racial/cultural" superiority, and contributed to the now widespread belief that social inequalities in America are due to cultural differences which are inherently "racial."[8]

What Movement Chicanos did in the 1960's and 70's, much like the Black/African-American nationalists of the same era, was to simply turn that language on its head by claiming that their "race" or "*raza* " was superior to that of the Anglos. Anglos since the nineteenth century had constructed their own sense of ethnic and cultural superiority out of the language of race, and now Chicano nationalists chose to do the same. They did this in two distinct ways. One was to elevate the Indian side of their heritage which had been rejected by their parents' generation and denigrated by "Europeans," both Spaniards and Anglo Saxons. Aztecs and Mayans were enlisted as noble ancestors who passed their culture down through the bloodlines to the new "Chicano" generation. This was deliberately posed to contrast with Anglo claims to having inherited the "Western" tradition from Greece and Europe through their racial lines. As part of this claim to be descended from an ancient line of heroic, culturally superior indigenous people, Chicanos developed the idea that the Southwestern regions of the United States had originally been the land of the Aztecs before they journeyed south to the Mexico City area. This was the land of "Aztlán" named in Aztec legend, which Chicanos claimed as their rightful inheritance as descendents of the Indian peoples.

The other way that Chicanos held up their racial superiority was to celebrate the racial inheritance which had been treated with disgust by Anglos, their "mestizaje," the mix of Indian and Spaniard [Muñoz 12-15; Reich: 87-88]. In one of the popular Chicano journals of the time, *El Cuaderno*, E.A. Mares explained that Chicano "Cultural Nationalism" was:

> . . . totally unlike the cultural awareness of other American ethnic
> groups, in that it is based on the concept of Mestizaje—group pride
> in multiple genetic and cultural origins exhibiting pluralism rather
> than seeking purity [1973: 41].

In this quote, Mares argues to reject classic Anglo doctrines of racial purity which had been used to discriminate against Mexicans since the nineteenth century, and instead suggests the celebration of racial mixing. Of course, he was not advocating the mixing of Anglos and Chicanos, but rather posing an attitude of pride in the racial mix of Spanish and Indian which Anglo Americans had so despised as "mongrel." A few lines from the poet Ricardo Sanchez, from his poem "Juan," capture the spirit of this Chicano pride in being of a "Brown," "Bronze," "*Bronce*" race, or "*raza*":

we are mestizo   chicano
                THE BIRTH OF CHICANISMO,
                        born in fire and hurt,
                        living soul,
                        singing out our liberation

                        love personified
                        we are the people of the sun

LA BELLA RAZA DE BRONCE ... we are more than being,

                        we are past, present, future

                HUMANITY ON THE MOVE ...
                                        MENT.
                                        [1973:90]

Here the poet Sanchez conjures up the image of a *mestizo* (mixed) and "*bronce*," (bronze skinned) race, beautiful and struggling "in fire and in hurt" toward liberation. In both identifying themselves with their "pure" Indian past and their mixed "mestizo" past, Chicanos linked biological with cultural inheritance in the same way that Anglos had done. They did not reject the language of race but instead turned the dominant culture's racist language around and transformed it into a critique of the "White" race and its culture. In effect, Chicanos were saying, "We are a people united by a race different from the Anglo race, superior because of its unique [mixture of] blood." When Zarco painted his mural with two distinctly "brown" female faces, he was drawing on this symbolism of "racial" pride.

Ironically, while at the same time challenging the dominant culture by shaping its own set of values based on Mexican, Indian, and

Spanish racial inheritance, Movement culture accepted the Anglo American equation of race with culture. In this way Chicano culture stayed within the Western discourse in which the language of bodies, in this case of race, are employed to explain and construct cultural differences between peoples. Chicanos were not challenging racial politics per se, but rather using racial politics to make their own claims in the name of race. They were challenging Anglo America on its own ground. If they were to be marginalized, disenfranchised, and locked out of dominant institutions based on their race, then they would create their own racial mythology and their own institutions.

This was the organizing principle of Chicano nationalism and the centerpiece in the culture of the Movement. This was the message of Zarco's mural, in which race and culture were intimately linked through the language of gender in the symbol of "The Woman:" *We are a beautiful, brown people with a unique and superior culture. We (symbolized by the male who is the painter, the Subject) protect and promote our culture (symbolized by the female, who is the Object). The culture (female) which the Anglo (the male) possesses—that is, the Blonde who despises us for our color and who tries to seduce us to intermarry, shed our culture, become professionals and forget our blue-collar, ethnic roots and assimilate culturally and genetically— offers us nothing because she is herself a pale, empty, anonymous face/culture/race.*

This is the same message conveyed by the Latino in the "Latinos Anonymous" skit who is almost seduced by the Blonde and then rejects her because she "reminds him" of the American Dream, the one he's not a part of. In a perhaps more heavy-handed way, the skit reiterates the Movement message that rejects Anglo American hegemony, drawing on the symbolism which was first cogently expressed by Chicanos of the Movement cohort.

RACIAL METAPHORS AND THE MOVEMENT COHORT TODAY

Movement claims to ethnic uniqueness in the name of racial difference and within the language of biology and bodies continue to affect the ways that members of the Chicano Movement cohort construct their own sense of ethnicity as middle-aged professionals. Changes in the language are due to both life cycle shifts in attitude and to changes in the social-historical context.

First, because racism is still prevalent in American society, Movement Chicanos continue to shape their own sense of ethnic uniqueness in terms of "racial" language and to express their bonding in terms of a mutual "racial" inheritance. Chicanos who deny that racial heritage are still suspect in their Chicano loyalties. In this spirit, Chicano professionals who continue to be strongly Movement oriented often enjoy using racial language to identify other Chicanos politically. For example, in Chapter 3 in my description of a C.M.A.C. meeting, I talked about how people classified their rival group, C.H.A.M.A., as "European-oriented" Latinos who saw Chicanos as "a bunch of Indians," i.e. *inferiors*. This was a Movement dismissal of Mexican Americans and other Latinos perceived as "out of touch" with their Indian heritage, in contrast to the classic Movement identification with that racial/cultural inheritance. In the same vein, a favorite story told by various U.C.L.A. graduate Chicanos was about the way that one of the Mexican American professors would criticize Chicanos who seemed to deny their Mexican heritage by saying, *"No mas le falta la pluma ."* This meant literally, "All he lacks is the feather," and was meant to imply that they look so Indian—and it was funnier when applied to someone dark—all they lack are the feathers, and yet they are trying to put on airs and pretend they aren't Mexican.[9]

The popularity of identifying with Indians is so strong in Movement culture that it affects other cohorts as well. At one of the Young Latino Lawyers' committee meetings the group spent several minutes one night clowning around with each other about who had, or did not have, a "Mayan" nose in the group. One of the members was perplexed as to just what a "Mayan" nose looked like, and I later sent him a postcard showing a number of Mayans in profile.

Chicanos continue to engage the language of race/body/blood to describe who is included in the embrace of their ethnic identity by the use of the term *"raza,"* or "race." Race is considered a matter of shared "blood" or *"sangre."* The *"familia"* metaphor which organizes much of the thinking about the Chicano community, as I talked about in Chapter 2, is similarly rooted in ideas about relationships defined by blood and generated by bodies [Reich: 123].

What is different in the use of racial body language today is that Chicano professionals are broadening their concept of who belongs in this "racial" *familia*. The specifically Chicano nationalism of their youth is at times giving away to include Latinos in the *"raza."* The Latinos Anonymous play demonstrates this historical shift in the way it employs Chicano Nationalist symbolism to talk about a broader "Latino" resistance to Anglo culture.

Racial categories also permeate the way that Chicanos perceive the physical appearance of others and categorize them either as "One of us" or "Other." Here too, the line is blurred between "Mexican/Chicano" and "Latino." One Chicano lawyer described how he would often approach strangers and introduce himself at the health club he attended simply because they *looked* "Latino" and he felt a bond with them.

While Movement racial metaphors for ethnic identity still prevail in the culture of Chicano professionals, the passionate, sharply defined, nationalist body language of race is no longer openly fashionable among most Chicano professionals. This is due to numerous factors. First, the burning sexual issues concerning who it is legitimate to date and mate are no longer so crucial to middle-aged, usually married or mated Chicano professionals of the Movement generation. While many Chicanos say that they prefer to marry within their own "culture" or "race," this appears to be more out of a concern for compatibility than out of fear of "diluting" the blood. Also, it is apparent that whether or not someone is married to an Anglo or Angla does not have a bearing on whether or not they are active in ethnic politics or in "serving the community." More than a few Chicanos and Chicanas active in major professional organizations in Los Angeles are married to non-Chicanos. In a similar vein, many of the Chicanos who had been suspect during Movement years because they were genetically mixed Anglo/Mexicans have proven themselves loyal Movement Chicanos over the years. Of course, occasional private mumbling about people who marry outside of the "raza" or about "halfers," does occur, but these are not publicly acknowledged sentiments.

Second, Movement generation Chicanos are now in their middle years and firmly entrenched in their careers, mixing daily with Anglos, in many cases in the workplace as well as socially, and feeling less alienation and anger toward a system in which they have proven successful. Their anger at racism is often now a matter of vicarious concern for the Chicanos who still live in barrios and continue to experience the brunt of racism in a way that most of them no longer do, at least in most aspects of their lives.

Third, the historical milieu has changed since the sixties when Blacks and Chicanos were part of a larger cultural upheaval in which young people across the ethnic board challenged the System. Shouting about "racist pigs" was no more socially conspicuous in those years than yelling "Hell No, We Won't Go" about the Vietnam Draft. Not so in the 1980's. While young, Movement Chicanos identified and talked about racism easily; as professionals, they are now more discrete about using this language.

It appears that it is no longer accepted in the wider arenas of public or even academic discourse to talk about "racism." Patricia Williams suggests this in her book, *The Alchemy of Race and Rights: Diary of a Law Professor*[1991]. She talks about how she was told by law school colleagues not to make trouble when she confronts them about sexist and racist stereotypes often employed in supposedly neutral law exams:

> . . . in so directly turning students' attention away from precisely what is most provocative and significant in these problems, [it] reiterates exactly what is so difficult about raising these issues in any kind of social setting; the feeling of impropriety, the sheer discourtesy of talking about what has been, by our teachers at every stage of life, explicitly tabooed: It's okay to purvey these unchallenged images as gratuity, but not to talk about them in a way that matters, that changes outcomes." [pp.86-87][10]

While as Williams points out, even to *identify* problems of racism and sexism is largely taboo in everyday parlance, among Chicano professionals, a subdued, indirect allusion to "discrimination" is less threatening, although not always acceptable. They often avoid the word "racism" as though it conjures up images of raw feelings expressed rashly by over-emotional youth. Chicano professionals do not want to be identified with "children" or "emotionalism," ideas which contribute to the stereotype of childlike Mexicans unable to function in an "adult" professional world.

Moreover, using the word "racism," is to identify the problem at its source, that is, discrimination based on metaphors of the body, and such metaphors are perceived as unchangeable, immutable, "real." Many people do not want to feel that discrimination is practiced on them for attributes over which they have no control—their genetic inheritance. Still others recognize, however instinctively, that "racism" is a "dirty word" in American culture, precisely because it describes the actual reasons that people of "color" have proportionately higher percentages of poor, incarcerated, homeless, and working-class people in a way that contradicts the classic American success story of which they are a part.

Perhaps most fundamentally, Chicano professionals no longer see themselves—nor are they—powerless students hollering at the System for change and recognition. They are now professionals with jobs, responsibilities, power, and public images to maintain. Even those who actively work towards transforming the ravages of racism have opted to do so "within the System." They are unlikely to bring up the volatile charge of "racism," except in intimate circumstances among close Movement-oriented friends.

GENDER IN PROFESSIONAL CHICANO ETHNICITY

Probably the most blatant challenge to the Movement language of race is the complication which current gender realities pose to the classic nationalist, gendered language of racial solidarity and resistance. While Movement Chicanas (females) even in their student years challenged the patriarchal legacy of blue-collar culture in the Movement, they subordinated that challenge for the most part out of concern for the "*raza*" and in their belief that the most important struggle was against racism in the wider society, rather than sexism within their own Movement.

However, what happens to the smiling Chicana pictured in Zarco's mural as the "essence" of *Chicanismo* when she comes of age and is no longer willing to be the projection of male ideas about nationalism and the guardian of the ethnic home fires?

Actually, Movement Chicanas were never content with ethnic resistance framed exclusively from the male perspective. Even as students, they struggled with the Movement tendency to model itself after an idealized blue-collar, Mexican traditional lifestyle where women were subordinated at home taking care of the "*cultura*" by patting out tortillas and stirring up beans. In an article in the Stanford Chicano newspaper in 1972 called "Machismo vs. Revolution," a female student chastised her male compatriots:

> The dudes here at Stanford M.E.Ch.A. have a lot to learn, not only
> on issues of Machismo (some don't even recognize it when they do
> it) but also on the issues of Chicana liberation. Just because we say
> that we want to be liberated doesn't mean we've decided to go on a

"white" trip. We just mean that in order for us to work with each other, we have to understand each other to the point where the dudes will stop treating and thinking of us as second class Chicanos. Most of the dudes will say that they do see us as equals, but you know the old phrase, "easier said than done." You can see it in our elections, men for chairman, women for secretaries. Then of course, when any function comes up, the Chicanas always end up doing the cooking. If the dudes happen to feel the kindness to wash the dishes, they act all proud as if they did us a favor. So, there's the excuse that girls know shorthand, and girls can cook; well, all the dudes need to do is ask the girls to teach them how to cook, and the next time around we have new cooks."

. . . Chicanas are oppressed on three levels: 1) as members of a third world group 2) as women in society in general 3) and as Chicanas by the Chicanos. As Chicanas we must first liberate ourselves before we can stand by our men; we must stop oppressing each other. But, we must work together; so it depends on both Chicanos and Chicanas.

Irene Rodarte, [pp.3,8]

This student begins by pointing out that Stanford men need to learn not only about their own tendencies toward *Machismo*, i.e. the classic "Mexican" role of the dominating, protective male, but also about "Chicana liberation." By this, she assures her readers, she does not mean the "white" trip of the Anglo feminist liberation movement. What she means has to do with specific male behaviors at M.E.Ch.A. functions on campus. She urges that men should learn to wash dishes and cook, and that women should be voted into leadership roles for the "revolution", doing it together as "Chicanos" with the same cause, not in antagonism across gender lines.

This student goes on to outline just what the three dimensions of Chicana oppression are: 1) as third world women, 2) as women in society at large, and 3) as women within the culture. The consciousness of these elements remains strong among Movement as well as non-Movement Chicana professionals today, although the talk about "revolution" has dimmed. Professional Chicanas are not so much interested in winning a revolution as in achieving equality and success in their jobs and in their professional lives, as well as seeing more Chicanos and Chicanas achieving the same in their own lives.

When discussing their personal struggles, Movement women often bring up the subject of having had to work against sexism as well as racism in their schooling, training, and workplaces. For some, it is clear when they are being treated differently as women or as members of a "racial" group. For many others, they are unable to distinguish for which, or both, they are being slighted, since such discrimination manifests similarly (if not voiced overtly) in belittlement, patronization, and exclusion. This experience reflects the fact that racism and sexism, as I discussed earlier, are discourses which have traditionally been intertwined within dominant European culture. Both are rooted in body language, and both tend to shape an "Other" by ascribing child-likeness, or nature/savage/body primitiveness to both women and minority peoples.[11]

However, identifying and talking about sexism within the Chicano professional community itself is more problematic. In the first place, within public forums the discourse of equality and feminism has had enough influence that blatant sexism is seldom displayed. Women participate equally as officers and spokespersons for all the professional organizations, and there is often a conscious effort by some men in leadership positions to make sure that women are equally represented. This is not simply a matter of male *noblesse oblige*, but a result of the fact that Chicanas are increasingly visible and successful in their professions, and are demanding equal time.

For example, in the early 1980's, as reported to me by a female officer of M.A.B.A., a group of Chicana lawyers who felt disenfranchised by the association, decided that instead of forming their own association for women, they would create a caucus and push for women in leadership positions. Their organizing was successful, and several women presidents and officers have been elected since that time. This solution allowed them to stay within the majority association, which was in keeping with Movement traditions of loyalty to *Raza* over loyalty to gender.

However, despite the fact that women are now intimately involved in the workings of the organization, it remains to be seen whether or not they benefit from the organization as much as the men historically have through their "old boy networks" which supported each other in quests for political positions like judge and commissioner. Furthermore, at the several M.A.B.A. functions I attended, men still control social space through joking, talking over speakers, and other disruptive behaviors, in spite of the fact that women were running the meetings. For me, much of this disruption had a certain reminiscent ring of the strutting, Macho displays of Chicano Movement days, most of which derived from blue-collar Mexican practices; and in truth, most of this behavior was displayed by men from the Movement cohort.

However, whatever my observations, female leaders of M.A.B.A. tended to brush off any implications that the organization might stil[1] be dominated in some ways by the men. In this reluctance to probe the questions posed by an outsider anthropologist about possible persistent sexism, these Chicanas are proving loyal to the Movement notion that loyalty to "Raza" or the race, is more important than loyalty to one's gender group.[12]

What this acceptance of Movement attitudes about the greater inequality of race over gender ignores, however, is the fact that racism and sexism are closely intertwined within any power structure. The Chicano Movement culture was created from a male perspective as Chicanos identified with colonized peoples around the world and countered this "emasculation" of their cultural identity by Anglo culture with a masculine counter figure, the Macho, street fighting L.A. gang member. The bodies of women became the symbols of the contested cultural ground between these two masculine images. Brown Chicanas were comfort, strength, and biologically-rooted resistance to Anglo culture. Blonde Anglas were dangerous, the temptation incarnate of "selling out." But in both cases, women were symbols, possessions.

These tensions are still alive within Chicano professional culture, although less obviously, and less publicly. While the Movement Macho still appears to strut his stuff at least in the margins of M.A.B.A. social life, in the medical community, male-dominated attitudes are less obvious, but nevertheless displayed within forms like the official patriarchal history of C.M.A.C. given at the reunion I described in Chapter One.

Where the real problems of sexism lie, however, are in the ways that professionalism is shaped in relationship to family and other arenas of relationship typically associated with women. Here the question of working together toward social change becomes working together in professional organizations which help our people and boost our own careers while at the same time achieving success in our jobs. The problem of the student movement years remains, however: who does the dishes?. This is partially "resolved" by hiring help, but it is still the women for the most part who hire, fire, and supervise servants and baby-sitters and who wrestle with the question of whether or not they should take time off from their jobs to stay home with the children.[13]

It appears, then, as I will discuss in Chapter 7, that while Movement Chicanos question "professionalism" in the name of a different kind of social awareness and sensitivity, this seldom extends itself to questioning the way that professional lifestyles must be sustained by the subordinate help of women. This includes not only the working-class mothers and immigrant nannies and housekeepers, but also the career Chicana who must often handle the double responsibilities of work and home, including hiring and supervision of housework and childcare and whose status as a serious professional is often questioned when she elects to work part time in order to fulfill her family responsibilities.[14]

The protectiveness of their organizations that many Chicanas displayed when questioned by me about the ongoing problem of sexism is a legacy from the Movement. These women were protecting their "raza" from the outside Anglo society, represented by me, the Angla researcher. And perhaps they are right to be careful. Perhaps the gendered language of resistance to the dominant culture, however sexist it may be, and whatever sexism it may protect within ethnic organizations, is necessary in the face of the struggle against the racism of the dominant Other. Perhaps the strutting Macho, whether the street gang version or the cultured professional, is necessary to shaping ethnicity, the "Male" ethnic hero protecting the "Female" culture and underclass, and the "Female" hearth tender protecting the reputation of her hero man, in the name of the patriarchal *"Familia"* of the Movement.

A PERSONAL NOTE OF CONCLUSION

This issue of race, gender and the construction of ethnicity using body metaphors has had particular resonance for me since the first day I walked into the Chicano dormitory in 1972 at Stanford and felt my WASP, blonde, female body observed and assessed as distinctively and threateningly "Other." It has taken me twenty years of interacting with Movement Chicanos, a nineteen-year marriage to a Movement Chicano, the birth of my two ("racially" and culturally) "halfer" sons, and the work on this book, to come fully to terms with this ethnic war of identities. Because I am inescapably clothed in my very Anglo and female body it is often impossible to live my bicultural life without being called on to explain or defend myself to one group or another.

Of course, Chicanos live with this bicultural identity struggle every day as well; I can make no claims to unique suffering. We are all trapped in the language of bodies. Biological metaphors dominate Western life because they are the most convenient and compelling language for constructing social differences and creating hierarchy. Chicanos continue to use the language of race because people in power continue to discriminate, exclude, and horde power in the name of race. It is the same with other culturally distinct groups who are treated as racially different. Their claims to power are likewise in the name of race, because race is one of the dominant languages of power. Women similarly must make claims in the name of gender within the confines of body language, because the world is carved up in gendered categories and they are excluded on the basis of their gender.

A story told to me by a Chicana pediatrician with two young daughters speaks deeply about the violence done to human beings through the language of bodies. Her eldest, a rosy-brown, black-haired, dark-eyed beauty, had insisted on having a blonde Barbie doll over her mother's gentle protests. Later, that same daughter burst into tears one day, telling her mother that she wished she could be blonde like her Barbie. She was convinced that her dark hair made her ugly. Her mother was understandably disturbed. What more could she do to convince her daughter that she, in all her dark splendor, was beautiful? She pledged to herself that she would surround her children with Chicano role models, taking them to as many Chicano events as possible to show her that women of her own color were not only beautiful, but successful role models. And in fact, this woman did cart her daughters to many Chicano professional occasions.

As long as such internalized racism, imposed by the cultural force of the dominant culture, is possible among little Chicanas like these, Chicanos will have to shape their alternative identities in the language of race. It is impossible to throw out racial and gender politics in order to produce equality, as some have suggested,[15] until body metaphors which reduce cultural choice, human creativity, and individual ingenuity to biological determinants, have been abandoned as the culturally arbitrary and inherently divisive categories which they are.

NOTES

1. This is his real name. I recently learned that Zarco was asked by a former Zapatista to do a large sculpture of the virgin and child for the lobby of an obstetrics office in Arizona.

2. Franz Fanon in *Black Skin, White Masks* discusses how the white woman represents "white," upper-class culture and status to the black male.

3. Fanon, p. 63. I was first given this book to read by a Chicano friend with whom I wrestled out many of these issues of blondes and Chicanos, "The Blonde" and "The Chicano," when I was an undergraduate at Stanford.

4. Why nationalism as counter-hegemony is usually associated with masculine imagery is an area that beckons to be analyzed, but which is beyond the scope of this project. Cynthia Enloe in *Bananas, Beaches, and Bases: Making Feminist Sense of International Politics* says, ". . . [N]ationalist movements have rarely taken women's experiences as the starting point for an understanding of how a people becomes colonized or how it throws off the shackles of that material and psychological domination. Rather, nationalism typically has sprung from masculinized memory, masculinized humiliation and masculinized hope. Anger at being "emasculated"—or turned into a nation of busboys—has been presumed to be the natural fuel for igniting a nationalist movement." p. 44.

5. The Latinos Anonymous playwrights also played around with male body/culture images in a sketch about competing Latin styles of machismo and I believe in a few other sketches as well.

6. The following books deal with 19th-century relationships between Mexico and the United States in terms of racism: Mario Barrera, *Race and Class in the Southwest: A Theory of Racial Inequality*, 1979; Robert Blauner, *Racial Oppression in America*, 1972; Thomas R. Hietala, *Manifest Design: Anxious Aggrandizement in Late Jacksonian America*, 1985; Reginald Horsman, *Race and Manifest Destiny: The Origins of American Racial Anglo-Saxonism*, 1981; Philip W.Powell, *Tree of Hate: Propaganda and Prejudices Affecting United States Relations with the Hispanic World*, 1971.

7. Horsman, *Race and Manifest Destiny: The Origins of American Racial Anglo-Saxonism*. This is a carefully-constructed, fascinating history of the multiple intellectual and political-economic influences which went into shaping the theory of Anglo-Saxon superiority based on "race" in the mid nineteenth century.

8. Horsman 1981, Chapter 11, "Anglo-Saxons and Mexicans" and Chapter 12 "Race, Expansion, and the Mexican War," pp. 208-248.

9. My husband urged me to point out that this is an expression used often by working-class Mexican people.

10. Copyright c 1991 by the President and Fellows of Harvard College. Reprinted by permission of Harvard University Press.

11. For a fascinating analysis of how 19th-century European racist scientific theories (including those of Freud) about "the Jew" intertwined racist and gender categories in relationship to notions about the body, see Sander Gilman's *The Jew's Body*, New York & London: Routledge, 1991. I suspect that "racial" theories which later developed in the United States in relation to African-Americans and Mexicans, were first shaped in terms of the Jew as "Other."

12. In contrast, several Chicana doctors dealt with the sexism issue by joining an all female Health Issues organization which embraced Chicanos in various health fields—nurses, administrators, etc—and was not exclusive to doctors.

13. And of course, it is blue-collar women who they are taking advantage of as servants and babysitters (whether strangers or family-members) which may pose some tensions in their Movement ideology as well as sense of gender solidarity.

14. This is beyond the scope of my work here, but deserves a rich exploration by other researchers.

15. I am thinking specifically of the popular book by Shelby Steele, *The Content of Our Character: A New Vision of Race in America*, 1990.

CHAPTER 5

Race, Racism and the Power of Stories

At the hub of Movement generation culture, holding the multiple spokes of Chicano identity together, was the idea that all Mexican Americans had experienced racism, either individually or as part of a people. While this belief was certainly not original with these campus youth, it was within the Movement that it gained its most compelling form as resistance ideology. It became central to Chicano Movement culture primarily through the telling and sharing of what I call "The Experienced Racism story." This kind of story generated a particular belief about racism during Movement years, and continues to spread its influence in the culture of Chicano professionals.

AN EXPLOSION OF STORIES

During the Movement years a discourse about racism exploded on college and university campuses across California and the Southwest among Chicano students. Both formal discussion groups (classes, "rap groups") and informal discussion groups (talks between friends and acquaintances) encouraged solidarity through the sharing of stories about experienced or observed racism. For many, this was the first opportunity to share feelings of rejection, confusion, anger, and defiance about experiences with Anglos and the dominant society. For others, who had not experienced such overt racism, or had not identified certain experiences as racist, this was the first time they had confronted the idea that they belonged to a minority group which experienced discrimination. Discussions about the relationships of racism to class and culture issues, some passionate and personal, others reasoned and academic, broke out in classes, meetings, and informal discussion groups all over campuses.

I participated in many such discussions between 1972 and 1976 at Stanford University, including two student-designed and led classes, a weekly Chicano Theme House "rap group," and innumerable informal discussions in which Chicanos (and on occasion, Anglos) discussed these issues and reflected on their own experiences of racism. Since then I have met Chicanos from all over the Southwest who have told me about a similar proliferation of discourse about racism and Chicano nationalism across campuses before, during, and after these same years of my own intimate participation.[1]

My husband had also participated in many such discussion groups and classes. As I was shaping this chapter I asked him about how he remembered the dynamics of these experienced racism stories and the discussions surrounding them. He reminded me of an incident which happened to him while he was a student.

While in college at Stanford he lived off campus with another Chicano friend in the adjacent town of East Palo Alto, an area populated primarily by African-Americans and Hispanics. He was a scholarship student, scraping by on a meager allowance, and drove a beat up old Toyota that his father had given him.

It turned out that the direct route from his neighborhood in East Palo Alto to the campus passed through a wealthy section of Palo Alto. One day on the way to school he and his friend were pulled over by the police in the middle of this neighborhood. When the officer approached them, Beto, assuming he had inadvertently committed some relatively innocent traffic violation, asked the officer what they had done. The officer refused to answer, telling him curtly to hand over his license. He then directed the two students to stay in their car and not to go anywhere, returning to the squad car, presumably to obtain information about their licenses through the radio.

He kept them waiting for at least twenty minutes, and then returned with their licenses and no explanation. By that time Beto and his friend were upset, and asked him again what they had done. He said simply, "There was a robbery in this area. You fit the description."

What was important about this event, said Beto, was the discussion it generated between himself and his roommate. Beto was a dark-complected Mexican farm worker immigrant who had experienced substantial discrimination since he had migrated with his family to the United States at the age of seven. Beto's roommate, however, while also dark complected, was a second or third-generation Chicano from the heart of the urban barrio in Denver. When the two of them discussed the incident, they at first had completely different interpretations. Beto, who had grown up believing that discrimination was simply something that happened to immigrants because they didn't understand the culture and were considered outsiders, was upset by the incident, but dismissed it as "one of those crazy things" that happens sometimes. His roommate, however, immediately identified the incident as "racist" and described how in his own barrio not only were Chicanos routinely stopped by police, but that city helicopters nightly scanned the streets with their searchlights, creating an atmosphere of siege in the Mexican community.

It was episodes and discussions like this, said Beto, that taught him to think differently about all the things that had happened to him growing up, and then later to see other incidents in a new light. He was pulled over by police several times in his student career, simply because he was in the wrong neighborhood at the wrong time with suspect physiognomy and skin color. He had begun to understand his own experience as part of widespread racism in American society.

This kind of mixing and sharing of experiences, interpretations, and stories about racism among Chicanos during Movement years created a discourse about racism which underlies Chicano Movement ideology and which continues to exert its influence on the culture of the Chicano professional in Los Angeles today. However, not all Chicano professionals share this discourse to the same extent, because not all Chicanos participated in or identify with Movement culture.

First, while many Chicanos on college campuses in the sixties and seventies found this process and language liberating and exciting, to discover their own "racial"/cultural identity and to bond through mutual recognition of similar racist experiences, others never learned to speak the language of *Chicanismo* nor to tell these stories about experienced racism.

Second, Chicano professionals who never experienced the Movement, either because they were educated before or after its peak, and then never connected with Movement networks or culture, often do not speak in this language of *Chicanismo* and experienced racism.

Whether or not all Chicanos share this discourse, it is the *Chicanismo* speakers of the Movement generation who form the solid core of the Chicano professional class, perpetuated through their dense networks and shared cultural attitudes. With them from their Movement youth years came this cultural form of the Experienced Racism story and the discourse surrounding it. This group is the one that dominates the Chicano physician and attorney professional organizations in Los Angeles, and has dedicated these organizations to the goals of improving the opportunities of both fellow Chicano professionals and of the wider community of Chicano small business and the working-class.

Most Chicanos from whatever generation or cultural identification can embrace this reason for organizing, because it is universally accepted that Chicanos are underrepresented in the middle and upper-classes, in the professions, in politics etc. However, what the Chicano Movement generation shares is a student movement culture which attributed this under representation to "racism." This contrasts with other recurring explanations; for example, 1) the idea that there is an expected lag time for any particular immigrant to assimilate and succeed into the professions and that Mexican Americans are just beginning to make it, or 2) the idea that the community, due to cultural attitudes, lacks initiative to become upwardly mobile.

But the Chicano generation unequivocally attributed their under representation in the professions to racism. Nevertheless, since acquiring professional status, they use the term "racism" sparingly. They have replaced their student radical language and tactics for more subtle, less confrontational rhetoric and strategies. Yet beneath the polite discourse, the language of race and racism, with all its power to conjure up the language of "Truth" rooted in bodies, blood, and genetic inheritance (as I discussed in Chapter 4) still plays the dominant, pulsing theme which gives meaning to their professional lives. A shared perception of belonging to the same "race" and therefore of belonging to a group against which "racism" is used to discriminate, binds Chicano professionals of this cohort deeply both on a very personally-felt level, and on the level of more public rhetoric. Because of the power of this cohort group in Los Angeles today, any Chicano professional who networks with other professional Chicanos, even if they are one of those Chicanos who never related strongly to the Movement, must be acquainted with this language of race and particularly of racism. Whether or not they accept this discourse and integrate it into their own sense of ethnic identity and public political responsibility varies considerably, as reflected in the stories they tell about themselves.

SUCCESS STORIES AND RACISM

What I discovered through asking people to tell me their "success" stories is that while certain classic elements reoccur, the question of racism is dealt with differently by people depending on whether or not, or how strongly, they identity with Movement culture. Everyone's life stories tend to shape the narrative as an explicit or implicit struggle for success in the spirit of the classic American success story, "rags to riches", blue-collar to professional, powerless childhood to fulfilled adulthood. They move from descriptions of early family support or discouragement, on to school life from elementary through graduate school, and then to tales of working up the ladder in the work setting. However, what sets the Chicano Movement stories apart from the classic American narrative is that all of them at some level describe their lives in relationship to the question of racism.

People that I knew well, who understood that I shared the Movement culture, freely wove the subject of racism into their stories. For others, who knew me only vaguely through Chicano connections, or did not know me at all, I deliberately asked questions which indicated my interest in and sympathy for this kind of story telling. In most cases people swiftly responded to these indications of my position, either by talking about racism or by deflecting my inquiries. In a few cases, usually of Movement generation males who did not know me, I had to work very hard to elicit any kind of open talk about racism.

While it is possible that in some cases people shaped their stories to "please" me, adding what they perceived as the appropriate genuflection in the direction of the "experienced racism" canon, there were several cases where people frankly told me that racism had little or nothing to do with their stories, despite what they may have perceived my opinion was on the subject. Furthermore, I saw most of my interviewees in many different settings, so I could corroborate my own interpretation of how they related to the Chicano Movement culture and thus to the language of racism from other sources besides the formal interview.

I encountered roughly four ways in which people talked about racism in their lives. The first two are typical of those who identify strongly with the Chicano Movement generation and its culture. The third and fourth types are more typical of those who either identify peripherally or do not identify at all.

In the first, the tellers indicate from the first that their life stories are bound up with a struggle against racism, particularly but not exclusively in the context of schooling and academic achievement.

In the second, the tellers describe how they progressively do better in school, unperturbed by the forces of racism, until they reach college or a work setting and "discover" that they had been encountering racism all along, or that the only reason they didn't experience racism was because they were light-skinned, light-eyed, and/or light-haired.

In the third kind of story, the tellers relate the classic American success story of struggle and success in school, and when asked directly about racism, say something about experiencing "discrimination" and wanting to be sensitive to other Mexican Americans who similarly experience "discrimination." However, they deny any shared sense of experienced racism.

In the last kind of story, the tellers describe academic and professional success but blatantly deny that they or any other Mexican has experienced discrimination, let alone racism.

A typical story of the first type was told to me by a lawyer from an immigrant family. Here he explicitly describes his motivation to succeed as a desire for triumph over the racism he experienced as a child:

> As far as the racism goes, that was from the very beginning, from kindergarten all the way through high school. We, the Mexican kids, were always, always called dirty names and insulted. I was no exception, especially when I was younger and didn't speak very much English, or none at all. . .
>
> . . . And the reason I did so well in high school and in college was because I was determined to be better than the Anglos. It was that simple. That was my driving force always to be better than the Anglo.

Other typical stories describe name-calling for physical features and skin color, for Mexican accents or speaking Spanish, or for bringing Mexican foods like tortillas and tacos to school for lunch instead of sandwiches. People told about being called "beaner," "taco bender," "greaser," "spic," and other epithets. Many Chicanos, particularly the immigrants and children of immigrants, told about being punished for speaking Spanish in class. And many told about being excluded from dating Anglos when they were in high school.

One of the most common stories told, even by those who otherwise had not experienced substantial racism, was about discrimination in school, particularly from high school guidance counselors. Men told about being directed to take "shop" classes instead of college prep classes, and women told of being advised to concentrate on "the secretarial." And both were discouraged from applying to major universities and colleges and encouraged to attend junior colleges and vocational schools. This story from a lawyer who received a B.A. from University of California at Berkeley and her law degree from University of California at Los Angeles is typical:

They had honors classes for the college bound kids ... and the teacher wasn't gonna let me into the Honors classes. There was only one Asian in the classes, but otherwise everybody was White in the Honors class. . . . It wasn't until my classmates petitioned on my behalf that the teacher let me into the class. I had the grades, you know, but that wasn't it.

. . . We had only one college counselor at the high school. . . . I didn't even know she existed, but luckily I was in these college bound classes, so I found out from my classmates that she existed, so they told me to go talk to her about going to college because I wanted to go to Berkeley. . . .

Well, my mother had talked me into going to Beauty school [while she was simultaneously in high school]. So the college counselor—I'll never forget this—she got my file and record and of course she noted that I was in Beauty school. I told her that I wanted to go to Berkeley and she said, "Well, honey, maybe you should think about that. Why don't you try going to a junior college, finish beauty school, and then if you still feel like going to college, why don't you try going to a junior college. . . . They have a lot of vocational training there. I really think that's what you should do.

And like the dummy that I was back then, I said, "Okay." I didn't question her. I knew that all my friends were going to colleges they wanted to attend, that they were getting scholarships but I felt. . . . I just felt. . . .Well, okay, that's for them because they're White, but this is for me, because I'm Mexican. This is *my* standard. So that's what I'll do.

And I did. I went to junior college for two years.

Notice how she structures the story to demonstrate that while she was a "dummy" back then, she has since gotten smart. The implied meaning is that she has since become exposed to a way of seeing the world which has changed her perception about what happened to her. The rest of this story revealed how this same Chicana began to recognize this and other blocks to her career pursuit as racist, and at times sexist as well, and demonstrated how she had put that guidance counselor (and all other racist/sexist types) in their places by becoming a successful civil rights lawyer.

In another example of school-experienced racism, a public defender who graduated from Stanford, explained how he used to defy the racist stereotypes teachers had of him:

> It [racism] was there in the schools. The teachers didn't know-how to deal with us. You can tell that they'd just assume that you're a dummy. We'd go in and sit in these trigonometry classes–you'd be sitting in the back–and the teachers, they'd just assume that you were an idiot or something, and then when we would do our homework up on the boards, I'd just go up there and just blow everybody away. I'd do these hard proofs up there on the board. . . sometimes the only one that could solve the problems.

Notice how in both these latter stories, the protagonists show how they proved to the "racists" that they were not the expected "dummies." These exemplify the same kind of "I told you so" educational triumph story which made the movie "Stand and Deliver" so popular with Chicanos. At one level, it appeals to everyone who subscribes to the American success myth and the "Rocky" movie ethic that you shouldn't underestimate the "little guy." Yet it goes one step beyond that, suggesting that Chicanos are up against a "big guy" which is even greater, the big guy of racism.

Another Chicano, who grew up in Texas in the fifties and sixties related how he was beaten up at a bus stop for being Mexican when he was a school kid, and about how he endured being forced to sit at the back of the school bus. His narrative is deeply woven through with a historical sense of family struggle against racism going back fifteen generations when his ancestors first owned land "granted them by the king of Spain" in south Texas.

He [his grandfather] had gone with his father to Monterrey [Mexico] and he had trouble crossing the border [back into the United States]. They didn't believe that he was an American citizen and he was crossing the border at Laredo to get to land that the King of Spain had granted his family. But you know, they didn't believe that he belonged there.

And so, that little incident, every once in awhile he would talk about it, but that little incident must have haunted him because when he went senile he would talk about it all the time. He would say, "*¡No me quieren dejar pasar!. ¡No me quieren dejar pasar! ¡Pero soy Americano! ¡Soy Americano!*"[2]

And it was kind of incredible to me that of all the things that had gone on in his youth, that was the thing he remembered most.

Of course, not all the life narratives told by Chicano professionals exhibit such a sense of dramatic struggle, nor do they all acknowledge racism as a strong element in their early years. The second kind of story tends to show how their narrators came to terms with racism usually from observing the experiences of other Chicanos, sometimes their own brothers and sisters, or fellow class mates. Usually this awareness became crystallized into a clearer understanding of racism within an encounter with the Chicano Movement discourse. Miranda Hinojosa is a fairly typical example of a Chicana physician in the Chicano Movement cohort who was not aware of racism until she encountered the movement discourse about racism in her undergraduate years of college:

Growing up, because I was light-complexioned, and when I was younger I had blonde hair that would get blonder in the sun, and I have hazel eyes, I was always. . . . I didn't try to separate myself; I didn't try to pretend I was not Mexican. But because of the way I looked, ever since I remember, from day one in kindergarten, somehow I was encouraged in a special way that my fellow classmates were not [in a predominantly Chicano attended school]. And because of that encouragement and expectation—like we talked about before—when you're expected to perform, you will perform! That's what makes me so angry about the poor expectations of the Chicano community. If we are expected to stay in the jails and the gardens, we will stay there. But if the expectations are given us, we'll do better.

I was always given the golden star. It was straight A's all the way. Whereas my sister Renata, who is shorter than I am, who is stockier than I am, who is darker than I am although she has green eyes, (she was dark and had the dark hair) she was always not expected to do as well as myself and in high school was counseled to go into the army. [This sister ended up getting a B.A. from a university and going on to graduate school].

... But anyway, I wasn't aware of it, but looking back [in college] I became very aware of it. . . . .because then issues like this were talked about. I had never heard anybody talking about it. It had never been presented to me that way. And it was now being presented, the whole thing of racism, and how some, the lighter skin Latinos if you look around the college class, Latinos for the most part are gonna be the lighter-skinned ones. I think a lot of that is true. And I didn't know that.

.... And then recognizing, "Well, wait a minute! The only reason I'm here is that all along I was the "good Chicana" and got passed along because by all rights I should have been back working at Alpha Beta, or working behind a desk somewhere."

Through her intense involvement with the Chicano Movement in college as an undergraduate, this physician learned to think that her success in pre-college schooling was largely due to her light skin, blonde hair, and green eyes. Like this physician, many Chicanos who had not earlier in their lives identified racism as an issue, began in college to see themselves as part of a group which had been discriminated against. Their stories reveal a burgeoning awareness of racism perpetrated against them personally, as well as against their fellow students, patients and clients, and the broader Chicano/Latino community. Exposure to the discourse of racism within the Movement made them see the behavior of individuals and institutions in a new light.

Even the pre-Movement cohort of those over fifty who climbed to professional status without the benefits of affirmative action may tell stories of how they first became aware of racism through the Movement. An elderly surgeon who had given up his practice to work for a Chicano community clinic in a Los Angeles barrio explained that he had never thought about the discrimination he had experienced during his lifetime in terms of racism until he became involved, late in life, in community affairs and began to see racism as an institutionally perpetuated phenomenon. This man was deeply involved in the Chicano Movement culture through his work, although he felt more personally comfortable identifying as a Mexican rather than a Chicano.

In these examples of Movement type story, the teller acknowledges racism either initially or belatedly as part of his or her life experience. By contrast, the stories of those who do not identify strongly with the Movement either make a half hearted acknowledgement of the existence of "discrimination" or deny that such exists at all.

As an example of someone who made a gesture in the direction of being aware of "affirmative action" and discrimination issues, I talked to a judge in his mid-fifties to whom I had gained access through a daughter who was roughly my own age. He told me frankly that he had never participated in any organized Hispanic or Chicano groups and did not see any benefit in that for him personally. Yet he was quick to point out that his own daughter had benefited greatly from all her Hispanic networks and that he was glad that she had been able to benefit from the post-affirmative action years. Furthermore, when I asked him about whether he had ever experienced racism or discrimination he told me how he was locked out of jobs when he first graduated as a Certified Public Accountant in the 1950's because "They didn't take Jews, Mexicans, Orientals or Blacks." And before the interview was over, he insisted that I meet a young Chicano law clerk that he had been instrumental in hiring. He wanted me to know that he looked out for outstanding Hispanic candidates, but that he made sure that they were fully qualified.

While the judge acknowledged having been locked out of certain opportunities in the certified public accountancy field because he was Mexican, he did not put this story in the form of a classic Movement "experienced racism" story and he did not indicate that this kind of discrimination had compelled him to bond with other Mexicans or other minority peoples in any significant way. He was not denying the fact of discrimination, and was in fact eager to let me know that he "helped" his fellow (deserving) Mexicans, but he was not deeply compelled personally by the discourse of race and racism.

Similarly, I interviewed a young Chicano physician in his early thirties, and therefore within the age group of the Chicano Movement generation, who although he acknowledged the fact of discrimination and felt some obligation to counter it in his professional life, yet did not share the race and racism discourse of the Movement. This was a Chicano who had never been deeply immersed in Chicano activism, although not completely alienated from the college Movement culture, and had not networked extensively with other Chicanos during his schooling. He in fact felt that he had lost touch "with all that stuff."

The story he told me about his own journey to "success" did not acknowledge racism or discrimination at all. It was simply a story of working hard and "getting the grades," and "doing the best at what I do." When he did mention a concern for discrimination he said that he felt an obligation to be a good role model as a physician so that "next time when they consider a Hispanic in this [residency] program, they'll remember me as someone who could do the job, and let them in." He was not interested in politics, and was not particularly involved in the any of the Chicano professional physician (or pre-professional) organizations or networks. Yet like the aforementioned judge, he did want to acknowledge a certain sense of responsibility.

> I can understand that being in the position that I am that I have more say and more power than someone who's still in college, but I don't use that power. I'm kind of more of a quiet person who just keeps to themselves and just takes care of their business. You know, like I say, I do my bit for the Hispanics in different ways. I do it by doing my good job so that they can get the opportunities that I had too, in that way. And eventually I'll go back into the community and help people directly.

When I asked this physician toward the end of the interview if he felt bonded to other Chicanos through culture, class, or the experience of racism, he responded to the first two, but ignored the latter, despite my persistence. It was clear that this was not an important part of his sense of ethnic identity.

In the last type of story, unlike these two previous examples, the teller not only does not acknowledge the experience of racism for himself or other Chicanos, but in the process of explaining his own experiences with being dark-complected, constructs an explanation which stands in opposition to the "Experienced Racism" story. This is perhaps not a coincidence, because this professional not only acknowledged openly that he did not feel comfortable with what he termed "activist" Chicano politics or ideology, but described to me in detail his participation in wealthy, conservative L.A. circles.

What unfolded in our interview, which was interrupted repeatedly by telephone calls and knocks on the door, was an interesting story with a glaring internal contradiction which despite my probes, the interviewee was unwilling to address.

First, as he was telling me about his early experiences in school, in which he did quite well, he started to say something about having experienced "prejudice" and then quickly retracted the statement by saying, "I don't know if you can call it prejudice. I think the prejudice may have been my own feeling not as good as anyone else."

Then, later in the interview, when he was speaking about what he called a "natural assimilation process," partly in regard to his children who were half Anglo, he said:

> When I go any place they obviously see me as being Hispanic or something. The difference is that my children don't look like me. They're much more assimilated genetically, much like you would be if you were to go someplace. No one would say, "Ah, you're obviously Hispanic." Whereas if I went any place—there's no question that I'm different, that I'm darker or whatever. So that is maybe an important issue that I had to deal with as a young person and still deal with to a certain degree is how you see someone is what you think of them. And this is something that is my thing that goes back for many years."

It was instantly obvious to me, as I sat squirming in my chair, that what he was saying here contradicted what he had said earlier. In his first statement, he had said he had not really experienced "prejudice" but had rather felt inferior because of his skin color. However, he was pleased that his children, who were lighter than he, (like "me") did not encounter this problem of having to deal with the issue of "how you see someone is what you think of them." I tried gently to push the issue, but he resisted. He was a polished professional, accustomed to interviews. I was a fledgling, female anthropologist.

But as I reviewed the tapes later, I recognized how clearly the contradiction stuck out. He had worried all his life about being treated differently because of his skin color, and was pleased that his children did not have to deal with this issue, but he attributed the problem to his own individual sense of inferiority, and not to the society which judged him differently. This was dramatically different from the position that Movement Chicanos had cultivated. Instead of attributing his feelings of "inferiority" to the racism of the dominant society, and then positively embracing his "racial" identity as a person of color discriminated against racially, he chooses to live with the contradiction by individualizing the problem, claiming that "this is something that is my thing that goes back many years," and hoping that his children will escape the same problem since they are light skinned and "genetically assimilated."

Chicanos of the Movement generation often identify this as what they call the "Richard Rodriguez"[3] syndrome, where someone obviously Mexican looking, even "Indian" in their darkness, refuses to accept the collective Chicano Movement interpretation of the *collective* experience of racism, and ascribes it to their own individual struggle.

EVERYDAY STORIES OF RACISM

During their Movement youth, Chicanos developed an intimate, nuanced "underground" discourse about racism which included banter, jokes, intimate asides, and subtle comments with underlying messages. Now as professionals, Chicanos rely on this subtle understanding to share many stories of their experiences with the dominant society which reflect racism. One example of this occurred at a Stanford Chicano/Latino Alumni Club Meeting. A small group of us were talking informally, when a couple told about going to a Palos Verdes Stanford Alumni Club meeting in someone's home. They were completely ignored, they said, the entire time they were there, even by the hostess. This was a well-heeled, firmly established and successful physician couple who lived in one of the nicer neighborhoods in the L.A. area, and owned their own clinic. When they related their story, everyone nodded in understanding. The assumption between this couple and the small group of people to whom they were speaking, including me, was that this was a racist snub based on their physical (racial) appearance, since no one had bothered to talk to them to determine who they were in any other way. As I discussed in chapter 4, the language of bodies is prevalent in many of these stories.

Chicanos also tell stories about their experiences with racism which include members of other minority groups. For example, at another Southern California Stanford Chicano Alumni meeting one day, the President explained that she and the President of the Northern California Chicano Alumni club had just attended the President's

Council meeting of Stanford Alumni Clubs. She then added, with a large smile, "Noel and I were there, and one Black fellow from some club, and they were sure surprised to see us." The subtext of this comment, which everyone in the room understood without making it explicit, was: "Those racist white people were surprised to see us brown and black people. We're now a force to be reckoned with." The club president was conjuring up an image of distinct-racially defined bodies confronting each other, a majority group of obviously "white"-looking alumni suddenly coming face to face with obviously "brown" and "black" alumni and being forced to recognize the changing ethnic face of Stanford alumni politics.

Another story my husband told illustrates how the bond of experienced racism may work across racial lines with other minorities. He was working in a team as a resident in the hospital with an African-American intern with whom he got along very well. One day, a 73-year-old Anglo woman came into the hospital and was put in their care. She had fallen and bumped her head and remained semi-comatose. When her son came in later in the evening to see her ("liberal looking, laid back" described my husband) the son said to him and his intern: "It serves her right. All her life, all she ever did was bitch about niggers and Mexicans, niggers and Mexicans. And here she ends up with you two guys trying to save her life!" After that incident, said Beto, every time he and his intern needed a laugh, they would say to each other, "niggers and Mexicans, niggers and Mexicans," and "crack up."

Again, this is a story about bodies, since the prejudice that the son ascribed to his mother was a racial one, and their obvious physical appearance as members of "racial" minorities was the only way that the son could identify them as different from other doctors in the same setting. Furthermore, what made the incident so funny to both the residents was their shared perspective about having had racism directed at them all their lives and now being in the position of having to help someone who was so obviously racist.

Stories like this about racist incidents are told and retold in various settings and thoroughly enjoyed by other Chicanos. Another story my husband told about his internship never failed to get a laugh, and illustrated again how people share a sense of experienced racism. In order to get the full benefit of the story, it is necessary to understand that the story works its way up the hospital protocol hierarchy, from emergency room doctor, to intern, to resident.

A White guy gets admitted to the emergency room. He gets worked up by a Black and he said, "I want another doctor, a real doctor." So I come walking in the next morning and he goes, "No, I wanna real doctor!" And so I said, "Okay, let me call my resident [i.e. immediate superior] And so then Tui [the Vietnamese resident physician] walks in, and he says, "Jesus Christ! Don't you guys have any White doctors around here?! " And Tui says to him, "This is it, guy. You don't get any special treatment." Tui and I got a lot of laughs about that.

Again, this is a story about differences between people perceived through bodies and racial metaphors, extended here to include African-Americans, Mexicans, as well as Vietnamese. The humor depends first on the shared recognition that the picture of a racist white male in a vulnerable position and requiring emergency treatment in a hospital is funny because it is a reversal of the normal dominant position of white males. Second, the humor depends on a recognition of the fact that popular culture portrays doctors predominantly as white males. So, the sequential parade of minority and even female doctors in hierarchical order offering their services to this white male patient is funny because it challenges the popular norm and demonstrates a new ethnic and gender reality in medicine, as in the rest of Los Angeles culture. Finally, the humor depends on a recognition that Blacks, Chicanos, and Vietnamese people, in this case, doctors, are mutual victims of racism in their daily lives and, therefore, those incidents where they can use their newly acquired power to put some Anglo male in his place are inherently and triumphantly humorous.

THE POWER OF THE EXPERIENCED RACISM STORY

While I obviously subscribe to the Chicano Movement interpretation of racism, I recognize that it is a cultural force generated by the experiences and energies of a particular cohort, which some Chicanos may choose to resist. It was rooted in barrio experience, shaped in the University sixties environment of rebellion and ethnic assertion, and continues to shape power relationships within the Chicano professional community. The following anecdote is an illustration of how powerfully the Experienced Racism story and the concept of "racism" itself shapes Chicano professional lives, and reaches out to shape the lives of a new generation of Chicano students.

In Spring of 1989 the Stanford Chicano/Latino Alumni Club held its annual reception for Chicanos who had been accepted as undergraduates to Stanford. The meeting's purpose was to encourage students to accept the invitation to Stanford instead of going to a less expensive state school, or another prestigious private school like Harvard or Yale. The meeting was held in the gracious Spanish-style home of two Stanford alumni lawyers in a prestigious part of Pasadena.

During the formal part of the event, parents and their high school senior children were seated in the living room with the twenty or so Stanford alumni attending the event. The president directed the group to go around the room and introduce themselves, which they started to do. Everything was going along smoothly in the expected manner when one mother introduced herself and then haltingly stated that she felt compelled to say something that had been on her mind.

She explained that her daughter was attending a private women's Catholic school and it turned out that she was the only student from the school who had been accepted that year to Stanford. Her daughter was at the top of her class, and the other students who had applied to Stanford, and were rejected, were all Anglas.

She then related how her daughter had returned home from school, the day after she received her acceptance letter, feeling extremely upset because several of her fellow students had told her that the only reason she had been accepted was because she was Mexican.

The woman said that she felt deeply troubled by this incident because she knew that all these other girls were "really smart too," and she had begun to wonder if the fact that her daughter was Mexican was indeed the only reason that she had been accepted. But, she said, this made her angry, because it wasn't fair that these people had made her start to feel so badly about something that was actually so wonderful! She started to feel like it was somehow her fault that she was Mexican and couldn't protect her daughter from this. The acceptance had been tainted for her, so that she didn't feel like sharing it with anyone for fear they would be thinking the same thing.

People were at first stunned into silence with this outpouring of unexpected feeling. It had disrupted the careful politeness between strangers, and jolted them off the track of warm but superficial introductions and pre-arranged speeches about why people should come to Stanford. The group stirred uneasily.

Then suddenly the guest speaker, a prominent Stanford alumni, said in Spanish, "*El racismo siempre está con nosotros.*"[4] The use of the word "racism," coupled with the sudden switch to Spanish when they had all been speaking English, shifted the event swiftly into a different space. Alumni and parents burst out with stories and comments in support of the woman. One middle-aged father with dark, weathered skin and gray hair began to speak: "My English is not so good, so I have to tell you my story in Spanish."

> *Señora, no ponga atención a estas cosas. Yo me crié en Tucson, Arizona durante un tiempo cuando el racismo contra la gente Mexicana era muy fuerte. Yo he mandado tres hijos a Estanford. El primero fue número uno en su clase. El segundo número trés. Y el tercero, el que va a ir este año, es el Valedictorian. Ellos han trabajado mucho para esto, y nadie les pueden decir que no lo merecen. Y yo les digo que no pongan atención a estas cosas.*[5]

The President of the Club took control of the pause which ensued, asking the alumni members if perhaps they wanted to introduce themselves. It was as though she were trying to smooth over the disruption and move back into the expected ritual events. However, all of the next few people who introduced themselves made the subject of racism the focal point for telling his or her story. The first one to speak was my husband, Beto, who told me later that by this time he had a lump in his throat, "cause it made me mad, hearing all this again:"

> My name is Beto Rentería. I'm a physician here at Kaiser here in Los Angeles. I come from a family who grew up picking grapes. I grew up in the Napa Valley. Some of you may have heard about it, you know, because of the wine industry, or since it's gone Hollywood because of Falcon Crest. I grew up in a very small school with a lot of affluent kids, but I was the only one in my class that got into Stanford. And even though I was at the top of my class, all I heard from everybody was that the only reason I got in was because I was Mexican. Well, it hurt, but I didn't let it get to me because these people didn't think I was going anywhere anyway because I was Mexican. So why should I listen to them?

> What you have to understand is that these people are ignorant. They really don't know what they're talking about. You've worked just as hard as anybody else. The stereotype is that you have lower grades than other people, and it's not true. You've got just as good a grades as anybody, and you can't let that stuff stop you from following your dreams.

After him a few other alumni introduced themselves using only their names and job titles, and then another alumni got up and told his story:

> My name is Benjamín Cristobal. This is my home. I have my own law practice six blocks down the road which is very successful. My story is very similar to Beto Rentería's. If it hadn't been for some personal decisions I made a long time ago and not listening to certain people, I would probably still be picking cantaloupes back in Calexico.
> . . . You deserve everything you've worked for and don't let anybody take it away from you.

After everyone had introduced themselves, the President took the matter in hand again and summed up what people had been saying in their testimonies. Sometimes, she said, when parents are told so often that Mexican people are "stupid" they start believing the stereotype, and they question whether or not their kids really deserve getting into such a good school as Stanford. But, she assured them, "You need to understand that your kids are in the top 1% in the nation. They are the best!"

To round out the ritual with an official word of encouragement, the Stanford Admissions officer who was present, also a Chicana, said:

> I want you to know that I have personally read every one of your files at least four times, and every one of you that has been accepted was without any reservations whatsoever. I've worked at Harvard, Yale, and Stanford in admissions and I've also attended all those schools, and I can tell you that Stanford's admissions requirements are the toughest of any of them. Every one of you here deserves their acceptance. I just hope that you decide to come to our school because I think that's the best for you.

When I talked to my husband about this event later, I asked him just what he felt was happening during all this, and he said:

> Well, you know, when that first lady stopped talking, you could feel almost a sense of anger, like, "Goddamit, this is happening again!" but then everybody started raising their hands, and it was almost like comic relief. But then everybody wanted to get serious, because of the nature of the issue. They wanted to make personal contact with her and her daughter to say, "Don't listen to this. Hang onto your dream."

I asked him, "Would you say that people felt closer to each other because of this interaction?"

> Oh yeah. There was an immediate feeling of intimacy because of all the very personal experiences people had shared. I mean, one minute people had come into this very fancy home in a nice part of Pasadena and their only knowledge of the host is that he's a very successful attorney, obviously making a lot of money, and then within half an hour they know the guy was picking cantaloupes not too long ago. I mean, you know, that changes things. It brought everybody closer. It broke down barriers. It emphasized the point we were all making, that even though we alumni were now successful in our careers, and they were just starting, we're all still part of the same family basically.

This "family" is the "*familia*" of Chicano Movement discourse, the family connected by blood "race" ties and the mutual experience of racism. This biological metaphor encompasses all the traits, biological and cultural, for which Mexican Americans are discriminated against: brown skin color and Indian features, Spanish accents or bilingualism, having the last names of "Garcia", "Rodriguez," or preferring *tortillas* over bread and *posole* over chicken soup. The "family" is also one that crosses class boundaries, embracing all Mexican Americans in the mutual experience of racism, as Beto demonstrates by explaining how "barriers" put up by the appearance of the "fancy home" were broken when it was revealed that its owner once *worked in the fields*, the quintessential blue-collar Mexican job.

Beto is speaking the language of the Movement. So was the event's main speaker who broke into Spanish during the awkward silence following the woman's speech about her daughter, swiftly and simply identifying this incident as "racism". This was no idle gesture on his part. He made an instinctive politically-strategic move to counter the question which the woman's story had raised.

The question was a particularly sensitive subject for all the people in that room. It is the question of "how did I get here; to what do I owe my success?" The woman and her daughter, neither of whom, presumably, had been baptized into Movement culture, asked this question in the context of the Anglo backlash against affirmative action. It was clear that the mother had no defense against this backlash, and felt compelled to entertain that point of view. She felt forced to wonder if perhaps her daughter was *not* fully qualified and had been accepted to Stanford only because she was Mexican American. However, the fact that she brought up the question with these Chicano professionals, who were clearly, visibly successful (it was a big, showy, Pasadena house), indicates that she was searching for another way to view her daughter's acceptance and the reaction it had engendered from the White community around her.

By responding to her in Spanish and by immediately identifying the experience as racist, the speaker drew everyone together into a shared sense of both *cultural* solidarity through the use of Spanish, and of *racial* solidarity as a group of people who had all experienced racism. He was also addressing the problem of affirmative action anxiety and the "myth of inferiority" with which everyone in that room had struggled in some way.[6] He was answering with the voice of the Chicano Movement which continued to identify the dominant Anglo position as racist, whether it concerned pre-Civil Rights exclusionary racism, or the latest racism of "reverse discrimination" claims. By continuing to insist on the language of racism, he was making a claim about the continuance of racism in the society, and of the need to collectively combat it through the claims of "racial" solidarity.

The testimonies of the parents and Chicano Alumni which followed all corroborated this Movement perspective. First, as if stepping out of the deepest icons of Chicano culture, spoke a working-class, Spanish-speaking father about his three children who had struggled to get into Stanford and deserved the education they had received. Then came the alumni's stories, those who embodied the Chicano perspective most archetypically, the ex-farm workers, telling their stories in most depth. There was Beto who had grown up picking grapes and was now a doctor, and Benjamín who had grown up picking cantaloupes and now owned his own law firm. These were American success stories with the classic *Chicanismo* twist, the struggle against those people who, as Beto put it, "didn't think I was going anywhere anyway because I was Mexican."

CONFLICT AND CONFESSION: WHY WE NEED THE EXPERIENCED RACISM STORY

The story telling session at this Stanford alumni gathering demonstrates how the "Experienced Racism" genre continues to play out its influence in Chicano professional circles among Movement members, and is being passed down to the next generation in interactions like these.

On one level, the social scientist in me is primarily interested in observing the power dynamics being played out as the Movement generation continues to generate its influence over other generations and Chicanos continue to construct their sense of ethnic differentness through such discourses about experienced racism. However, the Movement part of me, which cannot separate analysis from ethical conviction, is convinced that such stories and the ideology which informs them are the only effective way to combat political complacency and ignorance in the face of the ravaging realities of racism in contemporary United States society.

Here is the problem. It is not only "Anglos" who have difficulties believing that racism continues to limit the opportunities of those who are labeled as "racially" different. Even Chicanos who succeed in American society, like those who populate the emerging Chicano professional class in Los Angeles, are subjected to a tremendous amount of tension in the way that they interpret that success, particularly in light of the question of racism. One of the ways that this manifests is in how people appear to be haunted by the question of why they "made it" when so many others, because of racism, have not. What was it about *them* that was different?

I noticed this concern in people's life stories. They attributed dozens of factors as contributing to their own personal success: light coloring, Protestant background, families who encouraged education, defiance against families who discriminated against them because they were dark, Catholic schooling, older siblings who helped them, middle-class backgrounds, unusually helpful teachers at crucial points in their education and so on.[7]

Another way that such uneasiness shows itself is in how talk about racism is deeply circumscribed by taboo. Sharing deeply personal feelings over former or even present experiences of racism, under most circumstances, is somewhat socially unacceptable, even among one's friends. Everyone acknowledges that racism exists, but it is almost as though it has been relegated to a category of an experience that happens to "other Chicanos," that is, 1) the Chicanos that they might have been before they became professionals, or 2) the "Other" Chicanos who had a harder time than others because of language problems, or darkness, or whatever, but who now don't need to be worried about because they've "made it," or 3) those Chicanos "out in the community" who are still struggling to "make it."

It is as though the culture of Chicano professionalism is somewhat embarrassed by the contradictions in its collective story. On the one hand, all its members are living proof of the American myth of success through hard work. The temptation once one has become successful is to simply accept this version of the story, shed Movement culture, and enjoy the fruits of professional life, feeling that somehow, "you deserve it." For most Chicano professionals, once they have moved into powerful positions in their fields, the question of overt racism seldom comes up, so it is relatively easy to forget the problem on a personal level.

The problem is further compounded by popular literature on the subject of racism and racial/ethnic politics. This includes writings like those of Richard Rodriguez who continues to be the *bete noir* of Chicano Movement culture, with his views that racism is an exaggerated problem[8] and that affirmative action is a mistake [1983: 166]. Adding to this critique is the recent upsurge of popular books by minority members of the affirmative action generation on the subject of race and ethnic minority "racial" politics. These include Linda Chavez's [1991] attack on the Chicano elite, where she claims that they are inventing the problems of the Mexican American underclass in order to make power claims, and of Shelby Steele [1991] with his claim that racism is no longer a powerful force and that the "politics of racism" is creating a class of blacks with victim mentality.

While Chavez simply denies the existence of racism by ignoring the subject, Steele acknowledges racism but claims that it is lessening its hold in this country and is therefore no longer a valid basis for political organizing. What the Chicano Movement view argues is precisely the opposite, that racism and the language of race continues to be a potent tool of the dominant culture and that therefore, the most powerful way to resist this hegemony is with the language of race and racism.

Rodriguez and Chavez do not subscribe to the Experienced Racism story nor the discourse which is generated from its telling. However, they (and African-Americans like Steele) are tapping into the fears and anxieties of many successful Chicanos and other minorities because of the power of the American success story, a story which compels a belief that racism only exists for the "other guy" and that any one who works hard is capable of achieving in our society.

I was jolted into thinking more clearly on this subject one night soon after the Rodney King riots in Los Angeles. I awakened bolt upright from a deep sleep with my mind churning. I remembered a story that one of our friends had told us, one of the most powerful stories I heard from any Chicano professional about experienced racism.

This physician friend told Beto and me that several years ago, when he was driving home one day from the clinic where he worked in a heavily Chicano barrio neighborhood, he noticed that a police car was pulled up behind him with its lights flashing. Our friend was driving a nice sports car and was wearing the tie and dress slacks of the professional work uniform.

Wondering what kind of inadvertent traffic violation he had made, he pulled over to the nearest safe place, which happened to be an alley, and stopped the car. He started to get out, but before he could open the door, the policeman was at the car window pointing his pistol at our friend's face.

While eventually the incident was straightened out, and the policeman let him go, for those moments while he sat there waiting, our friend felt terrified. He realized that by pulling into this alley, he had made it virtually impossible for there to be witnesses to what might unfold. As he put it, this cop could shoot him and no one would ever know what had happened. He was, in that moment, just another "Mexican," and his nice car, extensive education, and professional job made no difference.

Although this kind of incident does not happen that often to professional Chicanos in Los Angeles,[9] the fact that it *could* underlies the consciousness of every Movement Chicano. And the fact that this doctor realized that he could easily be a victim of a racist policeman during this encounter was largely due to the fact that he subscribed to a Movement awareness of racism.[10] He knew, because of the shared discourse of racism, that racism still pervades the workings of the power structure, be it in the police force or the local law firm that is reluctant to hire Mexicans and African-Americans.

What does all this have to do with the Rodney King verdict and the riots? In my household during those days, as we watched and heard the drama unfold on television and over the radio, Beto and I couldn't stop talking about the issues. We came to an agreement late one night in the heat of our discussion, as probably many people with similar feelings about racism were doing, that the problem with that Simi Valley jury was that they didn't believe in racism. Furthermore, no one on that jury (or in the lives of the jurors heretofore) could or would tell the story of Experienced Racism in a way that might have given these jurors some insight into the everyday experiences of black and brown people, particularly men, with the structures of power. There were even two members of "racial" minority groups on the jury, an Asian and a Hispanic woman, but they obviously were not able to tell this side of the story.

What was lacking was someone with a perspective rooted in Civil Rights consciousness, whether Chicano or Black or White or Asian or whatever. This is precisely why I feel that the Chicano Movement with its analysis of racism and its allegiance to "racial" politics, rooted in Civil Rights and affirmative action history, is an important cultural force of resistance to the dominant culture. Those Chicanos who are steeped in this Movement culture have a way to explain and to counter the discrimination they encounter in their lives, and which other members of their families and communities encounter. Those who are not part of this culture, like the woman and her college-bound daughter in the earlier story, who began to think that perhaps she didn't deserve to get into Stanford, are vulnerable to the forces of racism without any recourse or way to resist. The Movement culture offers an alternative, a shared story about the experience of racism which challenges the comfortable stories that most Americans tell themselves everyday, that everyone in our society is given equal opportunity, that only people who are lazy or criminal don't do well in our society, and that racism is something that happened in South Africa, but not here.

Just as importantly, Movement culture, carried in the minds and memories of these professionals, and cultivated by Chicano organizations, offers a different success story which challenges the idea that people who work hard and behave themselves are successful and never experience what some may call "racism." It is a story that won't let them rest easily in their success, that stirs them to remember their own experiences with racism, or their close friends' experiences with racism, or the experiences of students like the girl who was accepted to Stanford and whose friends belittled her achievements and attributed her acceptance to "reverse racism." The culture of *Chicanismo,* like Zarco's mural and the Latinos Anonymous play, nags at these professionals, inspires them, haunts them, and pushes them to remember and to stay *uncomfortable* enough in their success so that they always question the alliances they have made with the American success story. The Movement culture continues to generate concern for the powerless "Other Mexicans" so that it is impossible for Chicano professionals in tune with its imperatives to stake their claims on society without feeling compelled, at some level, to take responsibility for those for whom success has not come, and for whom the terrible power of racism is still a daily, pervasive reality.

NOTES

1. This is not to say that the Chicano student movements of various regions were in every sense identical. For example, Muñoz [1989] suggests that the California movement was more focused on issues of identity than that of Texas, because Californians were culturally more "assimilated" and distant from Mexico than Texans[p.10].

2. "They don't want to let me pass! They don't want to let me pass! But I'm American! But I'm American! "

3. See Chapter 2, footnote #10.

4. "Racism is always with us."

5. "Ma'm, I was raised in Tucson Arizona during a time when racism against Mexican people was very strong. I have sent three children to Stanford. The first was number one in his class. The second was number three. The third—the one that's going this year—is Valedictorian. They have worked very hard for this, and no one can tell them that they don't deserve it. And I tell them not to pay attention to these things."

6. This is Shelby Steele's term from his book *The Content of Our Character: A New Vision of Race in America,* New York: HarperCollins Publishers, 1990. While I do like the term, I don't like his conclusions about what he calls the "politics of race" and the failure of affirmative action.

7. I noticed this same concern about how some Chicanos "make it" and some don't in the comments that many people made and the questions they asked about my research. People often assumed that my research was designed to identify the factors which contribute to Chicano "success." I was usually unsuccessful in explaining that I was doing somewhat open-ended fieldwork in the pursuit of an interpretive, cultural analysis of Chicano professional culture. People wanted me to be writing a statistical, survey-type analysis of why certain Chicanos had made it into the professions. This desire makes sense for practical, problem-solving oriented professionals like the doctors and lawyers I was involved with. Many of them are concerned with obtaining data they can use politically.

8. Rodriguez never quite says this, but I interpret him to mean this when he insists that class is a more important issue than race, and appears to imply that middle-class, dark-skinned Mexicans, or middle-class Mexicans who identify as "different" from the WASP standard in any obvious way are not subject to racism. No one in Movement culture would deny that class is a crucial issue.

9. It may happen more often to African-American males. On one of the television shows reviewing the aftermath of the Rodney King verdict, a black journalist said that over the course of his professional life he had been stopped often by police in various cities across the United States simply by being a Black man in the wrong place at the wrong time.

10. I am not suggesting that only university-educated Movement Chicanos are capable of recognizing racism. Of course many blue-collar Mexicans recognize and identify racism.

CHAPTER 6

Status and the Trappings of Class

One afternoon at a reception for new physicians, I was conversing with one of the hosts when I learned something about her that intrigued me. I knew that this always beautifully-dressed, classy physician came from a migrant farm worker family and was now co-owner with her Chicano husband of two health clinics in the Los Angeles area. They had recently remodeled their house by her design, and I was complimenting her on her architectural success. Her response startled me, accustomed as I was to her usual polished air of self confidence. "Sometimes I feel a bit embarrassed about all this," she confided. She waved her hand weakly around the elegant room with its stunning Pacific Ocean view. I sighed, admittedly a bit envious of such a dwelling, and yet eager to give her the confirmation I felt she was seeking. "But you've worked so hard to get here! You deserve it, Dolores!" I assured her. She nodded half-heartedly with a wry grin, clearly not completely at home in these upper-class surroundings of her own making.

Dolores wasn't completely at home in her own home because the Movement ethic she had carried with her from her student days wouldn't let her be. Movement culture generated a dichotomized picture of class and status: On the one hand, *Anglos*, not Mexicans, were professionals, members of the middle-class, and had white-collar jobs with authority over people. They wore ties, suits, white coats. They were doctors, lawyers, engineers, and business executives. They lived in big houses with fancy furniture. They drove expensive cars and used multiple spoons and forks. Chicanos, on the other hand, were blue-collar, working-class people who took orders from those in authority wearing the business suits. They wore work shirts, khakis or jeans, and uniforms. They were the janitors, the kitchen staff, the mechanics, the farmworkers. They lived in barrios and small houses or apartments. They had used furniture and cars, and often ate their meals with tortillas rather than utensils.

Of course, this dichotomization was rooted in the life experiences of most Movement Chicanos, since the majority of them came from blue-collar backgrounds. As one Chicano from a northern California agricultural town said matter-of-factly about his birthplace: "The Anglos own everything and the Mexicans do all the work." The fact that these same Chicanos now find themselves as members of the professional-class, wearing imported suits and ties, driving BMW's and Mercedes Benz's, and wielding authority with ease, results in a definite contradictory tension within the cultural categories inherited from the Movement.

STATUS AND CLASS AWARENESS

Part of the dominant American mythology is that there are no real social/economic classes in the United States. The Chicanos of the sixties and seventies who, through affirmative action, were boosted from blue-collar backgrounds into elite universities and middle to upper-class futures, were keenly aware of class differences and did not buy into this classic American story. They felt the differences between themselves and other (Anglo) students with painful acuity.

Movement-generated classes and rap sessions helped students to sort out these feelings and identify them as problems not just of cultural difference but of class difference. What this awareness did, however, was to generate tremendous ambivalence and contradiction in student's lives. On the one hand, they were presumably in these elite universities in order to become successful professionals. On the other hand, Movement ideology encouraged them to stay true to their blue-collar barrio roots. It was a difficult contradiction to live. Chicanos monitored themselves and their friends for signs of bourgeois leanings. In the Stanford Chicano Theme House, one of the worst things that could be said about someone was that they were aspiring to "live on a hill in a big white house," in other words, make it financially and separate themselves from the rest of the barrio.[1]

Such class awareness, and the tension it generated, lives on in current Chicano professional culture, as one can see with the migrant worker-become-doctor who felt uneasy with her affluence. Perhaps one of the most poignant and ironic examples that I collected of how this legacy continues to influence Chicano professionals was that of a physician director of a community clinic in East L.A. This doctor felt extremely bitter about what had happened to him as an undergraduate in Chicano pre-professional (university) health circles. He felt that as a student from a middle-class background, he had been discriminated against by the blue-collar Chicanos who felt he did not fit the "Chicano image." His entire motivation, he told me, for becoming successful in "the community health game" was to prove to those Movement Chicanos who had ostracized him that he, from his middle-class background, could be just as loyal and effective in helping the barrio poor as any blue-collar radical.

The irony was that the name he kept citing as one of the most prejudiced of the Chicanos who had allegedly harassed him was that of a Chicano who I personally knew had been raised in the upper middle-class. I couldn't help but tell him what I knew. He was flabbergasted. The Movement blue-collar ideology was so strong that it had blinded him to the realities of the actual students he was dealing with.[2] A Chicano lawyer with more awareness about the politics of university Chicanismo explained its dynamics to me in a way that makes the doctor's misconception more understandable. Many of the "quasi-radicals," he said, the most vocal students in his college, were actually middle-class students who adopted the culture of the real barrio "homeboys," like himself. Their extreme defense of Chicano blue-collar values, he offered, had much to do with defensiveness about what he called their actual "lack of any culture," i.e. true barrio, Mexican background.

A less intense, but no less telling example of how strongly some Chicanos associate Anglos with wealth and Chicanos with poverty, occurred in a conversation my husband and I had with some friends one evening about places to go to celebrate New Year's Eve. One couple said they were going to the "Stock Exchange", a popular downtown Los Angeles club. Later, our friend Luis, who was still in training as a resident physician, said to me, "Gee, The Stock Exchange! That's where all the celebrities hang out and they've got a $100.00 cover charge! I knew Anglos went to places like that, but not *us!*" The most ironic thing about this exchange was that within a year this Chicano physician himself would be making at least $70,000 a year and fully capable of affording a $100.00 cover charge anywhere he wanted to go.

Humor is one of the best examples of the way that Chicano professionals experience and express this status awareness. For example, one night at a planning session for the Latino Lawyers Association's summer reception, the group of five or six corporate lawyers, the majority of them graduated from Ivy League law schools, were discussing where to hold the event. One of them mentioned that the Sheraton might be a good place to hold it, since the hotel had a well-organized staff, good food, and, as one of them volunteered, "I've got connections there."

Someone then piped up in a strong, mimicked Mexican accent: "The *Cheratón?*"

And another chimed in quickly, "What, you've got connections with the waiters?"

Everyone laughed delightedly at this repartee because its humor highlighted the fact that, although they had all come from non-professional families, they were now lawyers for major corporations, people who might have "connections" with someone in the hotel management rather than with the kitchen staff.

The dichotomization of Anglos and Chicanos, rich and poor, finds expression geographically as well. Many Chicanos told stories about growing up on the "wrong" side of the tracks with the Mexicans, and their occasional encounters with the "Other" side. Those Chicanos who have grown up in Los Angeles, or lived there a long time, make frequent references to The East Side vs. the West Side. The East Side is associated, both positively and negatively, with where they came from, *familia,* poverty, barrios, chevies, *vatos* and *cholos,* "real" culture, low-riders, and crime. The West Side is associated with wealth, professionalism, White People, fancy houses, phony commercialism, country clubs, BMW's, movie stars.

Chicano professionals often made judgements about each other by where they lived or worked. If on the East Side, they were still loyal to their people. West Side Chicanos were suspect in their loyalties. When discussing their work and home places with me, many people were either defensive or elaborate in their explanations. "I live on the West Side, but I work in a clinic in East L.A." or, with an obstetrician who worked on the West Side, "I know that people say there aren't any Chicanos on the West Side, but you'd be amazed at how many people there are over here who want to see a Chicano O.B."

These geographical distinctions are not merely symbolic. They are rooted in the concrete realities of people's daily experiences of living and working. I became acutely aware of the tremendous differences in the geographic locations and work settings of where Chicano professionals worked, in particular, as I trekked across the city doing fieldwork; there was such a contrast between the environments of those who worked in the blue-collar community and those who did not. When I visited community health clinics, barrio doctors, public defenders and community lawyers, I drove into areas that sometimes felt alien and even a bit frightening to me. True daughter of the protected Anglo suburbs, I couldn't get the idea of gangs and criminals out of my mind. A community health clinic in East L.A. was nestled into a neighborhood of small shops with hand-painted signs and iron bars across doors and windows. Across the street was "El 7 Mares Restaurant" with paint peeling off the walls, and "Madre Rebecca Espirituista-Curandera" with a blinking neon light in the window, Freddy's Radio T.V. Service, A&F. Auto Parts, and the corner Mexican market with the signs all in hand-written Spanish. The surrounding residential neighborhoods off the main boulevard were blue-collar, small houses with sporadically kept yards, many pickups and older model, large American sedans parked in driveways and on the streets. The clinic itself was neat and functional looking, but completely devoid of the aesthetic graces I was accustomed to in the suburban clinics I had grown up with.

In stark contrast, the upscale downtown neighborhood where I went to interview several corporate lawyers was a highly polished island carved out of some of the ugliest streets in the city. Gleaming skyscrapers thick against the smoggy sky. A slick YMCA with floor to ceiling windows through which I could see yuppies in spandex pumping away at exercise bicycles overlooking the nearby indoor mall. (Several of the lawyers I interviewed worked out here). This beautiful complex, with its restaurants, book shops, bakeries, flower shops, bars and even a vamped-up MacDonalds, was protected and graced by two uniformed attendants at the door to assist people with directions. I was as nervous here as I was in the barrio neighborhoods. It was terribly sleek and upscale. I wasn't sure I was dressed appropriately much of the time and navigating the area geographically was complicated, trying to sort out the dense one-way traffic, the subterranean bowels of huge, hidden parking garages, and the intricate protocols for getting past the downstairs attendant to the elevators. The offices where I was whisked up to the 28th/14th/30th floors in slick, shiny and silent elevators were elegant with wide-carpeted halls, gracious wooden spiral staircases, large upholstered chairs and huge picture windows looking out over the teeming city below. Needless to say, most of the Chicanos who worked in these offices were extremely self-conscious— if not deeply pleased—about their fabulous working environments.

AMBIVALENCE

While only a few Chicano professionals work or live in such obvious splendor, all of them wrestle with the contrasts between their former working-class lives and their present professional lives. One of the most interesting responses to my interview questions about the tensions between class identities was that of a successful Chicano corporate attorney in his mid-thirties. This attorney, leaning over his large wooden desk in his window-lined office overlooking West L.A, wearing a designer suit and silk tie, patiently explained to me that he had no problems living between the two worlds of his blue-collar childhood and wealthy, professional-class adulthood. He lived in an affluent West Los Angeles neighborhood, he drove a Mercedes Benz, and he mixed socially with many of his celebrity and financially powerful clients. However, he also frequently visited his mother, extended family, and numerous childhood friends who still lived in a southern California barrio and remained blue-collar. And, he insisted, he felt no contradictions or uncomfortableness with his new affluence and position vis à vis his barrio family and friends.

> [T]he only three factors that would cause any kind of tension would be my clients, my car, or my clothes. . . .
>
> When I go home, the garage gets closed, the radio gets flipped, and we drink beer and talk and just basically hang out, and in that environment, there's no car, there's no clothes, and there's no celebrity clients unless they bring it up, so I'm right back to where I was. I pick up right where I left off. I speak English, Spanish, jive, and barrio if you will. . . .There isn't any young kid in the neighborhood who can come up to me and think he's gonna get away talking some line of rap to me and think that because I've got a coat and tie on I'm not gonna give it to him right back.
>
> Anybody who is from the neighborhood who happens to be brought into that environment won't know that I'm not just another guy from the neighborhood, unless somebody points me out and

says, "That guy's a lawyer," or unless they say, "Why is that guy wearing a coat and tie?"

Notice how he evokes the classic stereotype of the blue-collar, beer drinking male, joining his friends and escaping the women in the garage where they will talk "jive" to the neighborhood kids and otherwise relive their adolescent triumphs. Even wearing his coat and tie, he asserts, he feels no class tension between the worlds of home/childhood/barrio and career/adulthood/affluence. He goes on to describe the bicultural, bi-class life his children lead as well:

"Well, what I do want for them is to have a very positive but very accurate self image. They have to know who they are based on their parents, their ancestry, their nationality, the culture that they come from, and the environment that they live in today. My kids are growing up today in West L.A in a classic "Leave it to Beaver" neighborhood . . . and they have everything that they need in terms of the basics, and they have the things that they don't really need but which I want them to have. . .

And they go home and they get good solid exposure to the lifestyle that I grew up in 'cause my mother still lives in the same house she lived in when I grew up, and we still have chickens running around in the yard, and we've still got three or four yard dogs chained up, you know, pit bulls, German shepherds and dobermans, and we still have a big dirt lot behind the house, and my cousin lives behind the house that my mom lives in, and we still have a cow and a bull back there, and the neighbors still yell across the fence. . . and there are still gang shootings, and there are still helicopters and big lights in the middle of the night, and I'm not saying that that's wonderful for them in terms of exposure, but when we go to my hometown they get a good solid dose of reality, and it's not sugar-coated.

And sometimes it just means getting dirty and dusty and grungy running around in the yard and the mud with all the kids and getting tossed around, and getting a bump and a bruise here. And speaking Spanish the whole time with my mother, and with my aunt Maria, and with my Aunt Delia, and my Aunt Silvia, and my Uncle and on and on and on.

And so after two days of that, they come back to the comfort of the West Side but with an understanding that the world isn't all

"Leave it to Beaver." I mean, in my hometown, life's a little bit tougher, and it's a lot more fun in some respects because my kids wouldn't trade a weekend there running around with their cousins for almost anything. They think running around the yard and chasing the dogs and chasing the chickens, they think that's just a gas.

And in the process they get a dose of everything that they would be getting if they were there all the time, in terms of the positive things in the environment, the love, the closeness, the camaraderie, the family ties, the cultural awareness, the exposure of who they are, the languages they get to speak, and then they get to come back and enjoy the other part of their life, which is having a nice home, and having a nice yard, and having toys and going out and seeing movies and going to lunch at the swim club with their mother and all the rest that goes with it.

Now I think the mix, for my kids is so far turning out to be a real solid, healthy combination of the best of both worlds. My four-year-old daughter is fully bilingual!

This wealthy lawyer describes here his children's relationship between the barrio home environment he grew up in, and in which most of his family still lives, and their present life in a wealthy Westside suburb. This contrast is a perfect example of the classic dichotomized Movement idea about the difference between "Chicano" and "Anglo" lifestyles. This lawyer's barrio home depiction epitomizes the blue-collar background idealized by the Movement culture. And his description of his children's current life in the suburbs is typical of the upper-class lifestyle idealized and somewhat demonized by Movement culture as students anticipated their future lives in comfortable upper middle-class environments as professionals.

Images that the lawyer conjures up about the barrio experience of his children (a replication of his own experience as a child) include farm animals, tough dogs, dirt, rough-housing children, yelling neighbors, extended family, gang shootings, and cops, all part of a nostalgic picture of the stereotypically more natural, earthy, chaotic and dangerous ("dose of reality") life of the blue-collar Mexican American. In contrast, his description of his children's life back home is devoid of any substantial elaboration. He instead employs terse code words and phrases like "the Westside" and "Leave-it-to-Beaver" to encapsulate the cliché upper middle-class, all American [Anglo] life of fifties prime time television, complete with manicured lawns, big trees, and two story houses with wide staircases, formal dining rooms, and big kitchens.

Up to this point in his monologue, this lawyer projected confidently that he did not feel any of the tension between these two worlds, either for himself or his children. However, as he continued talking, he began to subtly indicate a certain uneasiness with his children's upbringing in affluence. This included his admission that at times he is amazed at how his four-year-old daughter is such a little "MAP," [Mexican American Princess], fully comfortable with her "Leave it to Beaver" life.

> I'm not sure I'm comfortable with it yet, but it's an accurate self image. The same little girl who loves running around the back yard with the chickens and the dogs in my hometown is the same little girl who loves swimming at the Club and who is very comfortable with the notion that her dad wears a tie and drives a Mercedes and goes to the office so that he can have money so that she can go to the Club.

Here he elaborates on the accoutrements of the professional "good life," i.e. belonging to private recreation clubs, wearing ties, driving a Mercedes, working in an office. These images contrast sharply with those of hanging out in the garage with his blue-collar cousin sipping beer. Yet while he claims no disjuncture between these worlds for himself, he is clearly coming to terms with the idea that his daughter is becoming as comfortable swimming at the local prestigious club as she is running around in the backyard of a barrio neighborhood chasing chickens.

This lawyer's statement is an example of a fairly well-crafted response to my question about comfort between two worlds and the problem of assimilation. Whether or not he was totally comfortable with his new class position, he was enough a part of the Chicano Movement cohort to understand the necessity for a well-shaped defense of the fact that he found himself on the West Side living an affluent lifestyle and moving in powerful Los Angeles circles. Furthermore, when he relaxed enough to admit some of the contradictions in his position, he revealed that he was still not totally at home with the idea that his daughter was growing up in such a different way from the way he had grown up.

Unlike this attorney, most Chicanos I talked with were somewhat more candid about feeling a certain disjunction between their former and present class identities. For example, in an interview with one Chicana physician who had once been an active participant in the Movement, we discussed this issue:

Miranda: I think that when I was going through college I equated any kind of financial security or financial affluence as being the same as being a traitor to our culture.

Anthropologist: Being a *"vendida."*[3]

Miranda: Absolutely. Very much. People would go around saying, "We're going to go back to the communities. We're all gonna eat rice and beans." A lot of that stuff. . . .

When I got to medical school and there were months when it was difficult to pay the rent, it was hard, it was real hard. That's when I started thinking and appreciating what it feels like to have money to be able to pay the bills. That was my feeling, like, "I cannot wait until I can go out and buy something that I see that I like, and not have to plan for it a month ahead of time, or when I know I'm going to have money for groceries, or when I can go buy frozen yogurt and not worry about it! Although I'll still worry about bills and stuff. That's something I'll always have.

So, my view has changed, has shifted, and I don't know if it's because of this global thing that's happening to our community. . .

Anthropologist: You mean in the sense that now there's a Chicano middle-class and upper middle-class?

Miranda: Yes, yes. That has become more accepted. Or it might be because I myself am changing.

Anthropologist: Do you ever feel guilty or uneasy about that? Being one of the Chicano elite?

Miranda: No, I feel like I still have very definite limits. There are still some things that I cannot see myself doing.

Anthropologist: Like what?

Miranda: Well, like going out and spending lots and lots of money on a car, you know, buying a car in the sixty or eighty thousand range. To me that's unthinkable. I just can't see myself doing it. And I think that's just because of the background that I'm from. People that I know don't spend money like that.

Anthropologist: What about a house? Could you have a nicer house than your parents live in?

Miranda: Oh, absolutely. In fact, that's one of my goals now. That's part of my. . . not reward, if you will, but something I'm going to do for me. . . .

But I can't say I feel guilty about that. Because I think it's something that, at one time I might have felt guilty, but now, I don't. And I guess if that's assimilation, then that's what it is. Or maybe anybody who feels like they've put their life on hold for so long feels that it might be time for some kind of reward for what you've done.

. . . . I'm saying that it's not so unacceptable any more to be able to say, "Hey, I make a decent living and I can support my wife and kids, or I can support my family, or whatever, and I live in a nice house. That's not something to be ashamed of. It doesn't mean we're *"vendidos."* It doesn't mean we're taking advantage of anybody. It doesn't mean that we're out to stab our people in the back so that we can eat good, or live good. I don't think it means that anymore.

Miranda, like many Chicano professionals first beginning to make a pay check after long years of training, was wrestling with the Movement view she had learned as an undergraduate, that wealth was evil. However, after suffering through difficult financial problems through four years of medical school, she was beginning to question her earlier judgement and look forward to being able to buy a house and live comfortably. However, she did have limits, she felt, to how she could see herself living, like spending sixty or eighty-thousand dollars on a car.

Clearly, she was concerned about abandoning her earlier Movement judgements, since she spends so much energy talking about her changed belief that people who make a "decent living" and have a "nice house" are not necessarily *"vendidos,"* or "sell outs," eager to exploit the Chicano working-class for their own benefit. In that same vein, one of the reasons she felt she needed to work in a public health clinic which catered to under-served Chicanos was in some ways to ameliorate some of her guilt feelings. She was going to "put back into the community" some of the things she had received from it in terms of support. This was a commonly expressed sentiment among Chicanos.

Other evidence of the uneasiness about class status was evident in the stories that people told me about their lives. Time and again, people eagerly told me accounts of their initial "culture shock," the first time they experienced the different world of "White people," or upper middle-class Anglos. For example, I had this conversation with a Chicano physician in his early thirties who grew up in North Hollywood where many of his schoolmates were middle-class and his own extended family was blue-collar:

> *Doctor:* I became friends with a couple of guys [Anglos] and going to their homes, it was like going to a museum or something. When I grew up, we never had a T.V. T.V. was fancy stuff. God, I must have been eight or nine years old when we had our first T.V. and then it was an old black and white one that could hardly work.
>
> These were really affluent people. Since I didn't interact very much with them socially, most of what impressed me was socioeconomic, what they had versus what I had.
>
> *Anthropologist:* Like concrete things, like they had a big T.V. and you didn't?
>
> *Doctor:* Yeah, and so much of what they talked about was different. Like, going out and playing tennis and doing all these kinds of activities that were totally another planet for me.

A Chicano lawyer told me a similar story about a college experience:

> *Lawyer:* I had a girlfriend who was from San Diego and I went to visit her at her home. And what I didn't realize at the time was that she was from a wealthy family
>
> *Anthropologist:* Was this an Angla woman?

Lawyer: M hmm. She was Irish. . . . And so I went down to meet her family one time and she gave me the directions, and as I was getting closer and closer the houses were getting really nice, and I was going, "Gosh, this is something else! This is a nice drive having to go through here."

She told me that I should look out for double glass doors which I thought was interesting because nobody had double glass doors! And so I couldn't conceptualize it. . . .

Anthropologist: These were the front doors?

Lawyer: These were the front doors. And then I see this house that to me looked like a mansion, kind of a half moon driveway, and these double glass doors and it was huge! And I thought . . . you know, they had a formal living room, a formal dining room. The thing that impressed me was the master bedroom. Her parents' bedroom was as large as my mother's living room and dining room put together. And their master bathroom was as big as my mom's kitchen, you know.

And it's the only time I remember lying down in bed at the end of the day and goin', "What the hell am I doing here?" And that's the only time that I've really ever felt what you might call out of place.

This attorney has since become accustomed to black-tie receptions on the White House Lawn, and mixing with the wealthy and powerful in various Los Angeles settings through his work with a public interest law organization. But he, like many Chicanos of his generation, vividly remembers this first experience with the "Other" world of the "Anglo."

Of course, not all professional Chicanos express such ambivalence about their professional status, and many do not apparently feel either apologetic or defensive about class issues. For the most part, these are Chicanos who for one reason or another—generation, personal choice, going to school where there was little Chicano activism—were not deeply touched by the Chicano Movement culture. For example, one wealthy Chicano surgeon in his mid-fifties, who had recently been elected to the Boards of several major corporations, expressed only enthusiasm and self-congratulation about his rising status and financial situation, despite my probing questions.[4] This same man has been known to arrive at a Chicano function in a limousine, a bit of gossip which causes numerous Movement twitters of incredulity. Another Chicano, a young lawyer who had attended undergraduate and graduate schools outside the Southwest and indicated he had had no real involvement with Movement culture as a student, had this conversation with me:

> *Anthropologist*: Do you feel that upward mobility is what is most threatening to a loss of cultural values?

> *Lawyer*: No. Because I definitely make the counter argument. . . . First of all, I feel that I'm Mexican. There's Mexican blood in my veins. I'm not barrioish, or whatever, so you don't have to live in the barrio, you don't have to be poor, you don't have to speak bad English and bad Spanish, you don't have to write on walls, you don't have to wear your hair straight back . . . to be Mexican. And maybe that's because my Mexican background is . . . somewhat middle-class in orientation, if not in means.

This lawyer indicates that he believes his reason for not feeling any cultural tension about his professional status and his Mexican identity has to do with the fact that his parents both came from fairly middle-class Mexican backgrounds, although they raised him as blue-collar immigrants in the United States. However, I have noticed that many individual Chicanos from relatively middle-class backgrounds nevertheless identify with Chicano Movement values and express their feelings of tension concerning class identity. The difference appears to be, as I have suggested, in whether or not the individual has ever identified with the Chicano Movement culture. This attorney had attended East Coast schools for college and graduate schools, and had never been immersed in Movement attitudes and values. I was actually a bit shocked at his blatant and somewhat arrogant bias against blue-collar Chicanos, speaking about what he called "barrioish" traits like slicked-back hair, writing on walls, and bad Spanish and English. Unlike most Chicanos, even of his own post-Movement generation, he showed no real ambivalence about his new class status as a professional.

CHOICES AND STRATEGIES

In working out their ambivalence about class allegiance and the trappings of status, Chicano professionals often structure their lives with conscientious creativity. Many choose to live on the West Side and work on the East Side, feeling they can have safety, status, and good schools for their children while at the same time working in barrio areas with and for people who have not had the same advantages. Others choose nice neighborhoods in the heart of the East Side, like Monterey Park, which may not be as safe or prestigious, but make them feel they are still among friendly, familiar faces. One wealthy, elderly surgeon who had grown up in L.A. described to me proudly how he had always lived in the same neighborhood in East L.A. and been involved in community work with the working people from whom he had earned his excellent living.

I was amazed at the ingenuity of an aspiring young Chicano lawyer/ politician in his choice of living place when I drove to his apartment in Highland Park to observe a meeting. When I got off the freeway at the designated place I was baffled, even appalled, at what confronted me. The area was seedy-looking, with ramshackle houses and apartments in bad disrepair, and scraggly, down-and-out characters wandering uprootedly around the neighborhood. It was one of the most depressed looking areas I had seen in L.A. I couldn't imagine an upwardly-mobile Chicano making at least $50,000.00 a year living in such an area. I drove around and felt lost. Finally, I noticed a driveway going up a hill alongside the freeway in exactly the place where the address I was looking for should have been. I drove up and was confronted by a huge cement wall and a seriously threatening iron gate. I spotted an intercom and negotiated my way inside with the help of a few more instructions.

The apartment complex was a handsome, gated enclave on a hill with a 360 degree view of the surrounding wretched neighborhood and the teeming freeway below. This enterprising lawyer had managed to find a safe, attractive haven with a barrio location. This undoubtedly eased his Movement conscience and gave him political credibility with an address on the "right" side—the Chicano side—of town.

Sometimes such a living strategy may back fire. One doctor friend of ours bought a house in an East Side neighborhood, because it was both affordable and he and his wife liked the idea of living in a neighborhood with other Chicanos. I must admit that when Beto and I went to visit him one afternoon, we were skeptical about the location. The neighborhood was definitely poor and blue-collar, surrounded by litter, small stores fitted with window grills, and tiny, ramshackle houses clinging like barnacles to a barren hillside.

His house was nice, much nicer than our student apartment on the West side. But six months later our friend had been robbed twice and was vowing never to live in a Chicano neighborhood again. "Forget this Chicano neighborhood shit!" he growled to me over the phone. "We live in their neighborhood and look what they do to us. Forget everything I told you about the *gente* and community!" We were both laughing at that point. How quickly the "Us" of belonging to the barrio could become the "They" of class distinction and indignation.

While I relish this last story, my favorite in the battle of strategies for dealing with class change is one devised by a doctor living in a posh, upper-class home and neighborhood. This doctor was an old time radical of the Movement, with a legacy of hot Chicano rhetoric. However, his fancy house and lifestyle did not fit the image. I had been told by chuckling friends, and then corroborated it for myself, that while he and his wife owned two nice foreign cars suitable to their yuppie status, the doctor actually drove a third car to his work at an East Los Angeles clinic in the heart of the barrio. The car was a classic fifties chevy in mint condition, one that would have been the pride of any barrio homeboy. I was told about this by some Chicanos who were critical about what they called their colleague's hypocrisy, but I, as anthropologist, was delighted with his creative solution to some of the tensions between his dual and dueling class identities.

Whether or not a Chicano wrestles consciously with these dilemmas of the Movement culture's legacy, if he or she is involved with Chicano professional networks to any extent, he/she must be conversant with the discourse of class awareness. Actions and conversation must be shaped in relationship to the subtle uneasiness which pervades attitudes about upward mobility and financial success of those Chicanos who have been affected most by the Chicano Movement culture. This is because the Chicano Movement defined being "Chicano" as being blue-collar and poor, thus leaving those touched by its values with a sense of ambivalence and contradiction about their own social mobility. This uneasiness, in turn, however, continues to fuel Chicano professionals' concern with their less fortunate blue-collar compatriots.

NOTES

1. I must admit that as a freshman student and Angla from a sheltered middle-class background, I did not understand what all the commotion about class at Casa Zapata was about until I was invited to visit the family of a dorm mate one spring break. My friend was an intelligent, articulate, well-dressed Chicana who wanted to teach me a lesson. When we arrived at her house I was shocked to see the run-down neighborhood, the cinder block ugliness of the house, the weeds and the washing machines and car parts in her front and back yard. She told me proudly that her father had built the house himself. Innumerable other small indications of poverty that I had never encountered before assaulted my middle-class assumptions for the rest of the week. Her father was a disabled warehouse worker; her mother a school aid. They were both intelligent people without formal education. Until that week I had, in my typical upper middle-class ignorance, associated tidy yards and full refrigerators with intelligence and goodness.

2. These two Chicano physicians ended up becoming allies on several health projects, interestingly enough.

3. *"Vendida"* is the feminine singular form meaning "sell out."

4. I am not implying that age necessarily indicates a lack of identification with the Chicano movement. For example, in contrast to this man, another wealthy Chicano surgeon in his sixties had a much more developed sense of class issues, although he did not identify with all aspects of Chicano Movement culture.

CHAPTER 7

Serving the *Gente*:
An Alternative Professionalism

One of the more profound ironies that pervaded the Chicano Movement and which now haunts Chicano professionals, is the fact that, while they were going to college precisely for the purpose of becoming professionals of one type or another, they were deeply suspicious of professionalism. Some of this was inherited from their blue-collar backgrounds, but much of it was cultivated in the Movement itself. There were numerous ways that the culture played out this tension. One was to consciously promote values that were perceived as more blue-collar, or that critiqued the "Anglo/professional" way of doing things. This included everything from celebrating "Chicano time," which meant arriving at, or starting events later than scheduled, to cultivating a deliberately more egalitarian, anti-elitist way of organizing clubs and political projects.

Another way was to advocate only certain kinds of professional careers, those that most clearly served the interests of blue-collar Mexican Americans. If you were going to be a lawyer, then you should go into civil rights law, or public interest law, or public defense, areas of law that were believed to benefit blue-collar and disenfranchised people. You should not go into private practice law for the money, or public prosecution and argue for the government, or above all, corporate law, because that would demonstrate an allegiance to the wealthy and powerful. If you were going to be a doctor, then you preferably should be a family practice doctor and work in a community low-income clinic, or serve as an obstetrician or pediatrician in a county clinic where you could help under-served Mexican American women and children. And, above all, whether a doctor or a lawyer, or

143

whatever profession, you should work in a Chicano barrio in order to "help your people," or "serve the *gente*."

These judgements about what kind of professional one should be are still part of Chicano professional culture; however, they have undergone considerable changes since the Movement generation's members were undergraduates. Most of these changes have been shaped between two poles of influence. On one side are the Chicano Movement's values of allegiance to the working-class Mexican and a student Movement culture which both explicitly and implicitly critiqued professionalism. On the other side are the expectations and influences of professional life. These expectations and influences, what I call "pressures," can be divided into four different areas.

First is the particular job a Chicano chooses. If she chooses to work as a Civil rights lawyer, the conflict with Chicano Movement values is minimal. However, if she chooses to work in a major corporate law firm doing mergers and take-overs, it is much harder to reconcile the way she makes her living with the values of the Movement. Chicanos who participate in Movement culture talk about their choice of work in terms of a tension between choosing a career out of personal interests vs. out of a sense of obligation to help "the community" (i.e. working-class Mexicans) in some way.

Second, there is the pressure of professional training, the rigorous, specialized education which shapes the skills and values of its trainees to conform to the requirements of each profession. This training involves shaping general "professional" values, as well as the more specific values of a particular profession and/or specialty. This "professionalism" comes into conflict with "Chicano" values in interesting ways, and in some cases, Chicanos have turned it on its head to serve their own sense of professional commitment.

Third, there is the pressure to do something for the community using volunteer time. Those Movement-oriented Chicanos who work in jobs that can in no way be construed as helpful to blue-collar Mexican Americans—such as corporate lawyers—often feel a weighty obligation to participate in and organize activities outside of their work schedules. Other Chicanos whose jobs are obviously involved in helping the community, may still feel the need to do more in their private time.

Fourth, there is the pressure of time. This was a constant lament that I heard from Chicano professionals, that their lives were so consumed by work that there was little time for family and personal recreation, much less for doing the things "for the community" that they wanted to do.

THE CAREER TRACK

Before discussing these four arenas of conflict for the Chicano professional, it may be helpful to briefly describe just what the usual training and career track of attorneys and physicians involves in order to give an idea about the institutions which so strongly influence Chicano professionals' values and choices. The first hurdle is gaining admission to a law school or medical school, which involves, at a minimum, achieving competitive grades as an undergraduate and receiving an adequate score on either the M.C.A.T. (Medical College Admissions Test) or L.S.A.T. (Law School Admissions Test). Medical School admission is perhaps more competitive than law school, simply because there are only eight medical schools in California. For attorneys, education usually involves three years of law school, and in some cases, several years of business school as part of preparation. For physicians, education includes four years of medical school, and then a minimum of one year internship and two years residency training in a hospital and clinic setting in order to qualify for most jobs. The minimum of three years is for family practice doctors; the maximum of ten or more years is usually for surgeons in some specialty area. All other specialties require something between three and ten years.

After training, the lawyer has multiple options. Many Chicanos choose the government track, where they may work as public prosecutors, public defenders, in the attorney general's office etc. Others choose public interest law like those who work for the Mexican American Legal Defense and Education Fund (M.A.L.D.E.F.) or The California Rural Legal Assistance (C.R.L.A.). Still others may choose to work for small or large private firms doing various kinds of litigation and family law like divorces, wills, estate planning. And still others may choose to go into corporate law for major law firms.

Attorneys progress in their careers in different ways according to the specific field and their particular career goals. Many from various law backgrounds aspire to be appointed or elected as judges or as politicians. Others work to become partners and then senior partners in their law firms, whether small or large. Still others may labor to own their own law practices. Others who work in bureaucracies, whether public interest organization or government agency, may aspire to management or supervisory positions.

Physicians have a similarly wide range of options, depending on their specialties. Some may opt to work for a health maintenance organization (H.M.O.) like Kaiser Permanente. Others may work for private clinics, small or large. Others may choose to work for community clinics. Some choose academic medicine. A few even start out on their own, opening their own private practices.

In terms of career advancement, physicians who work as employees for private groups aspire to partnership in the practice, and possibly, in the larger HMOs, some kind of supervisory bureaucratic position. Some may work for others until they can get the resources together to strike out on their own and begin a private practice. Those in academic medicine work for research success and tenure, like any academic. Those in private practice struggle to maintain a patient base and economic stability, and in some cases, to attain the possibility of hiring other physicians to work for them.[1]

From the time Chicanos are undergraduates, if not sooner, their career choices influence their values and behavior. At the college level, it is primarily in terms of making good grades, joining appropriate organizations or doing some kind of work in the field, as well as learning the ropes of how to apply, how to interview, and what schools have what reputations.

In order to help educate and support each other through this entire process—which Movement Chicanos, in particular, perceive as something to which most Anglos have an inside track, in contrast to themselves—Chicano pre-medical and pre-law students form organizations, study groups, and networks. Individuals lobby for leadership positions in these groups, carefully cultivating their credentials for medical school and law school applications.

Besides such obvious self interest, part of the glue which binds these organizations is the Movement culture, which includes a discourse of concern for those who are coming behind them on the career track, and a conviction that they will "help their people" and "go back to the community" when they "get out," that is, become professionals. But this commitment is not usually left at the level of discourse. Often these associations organize community projects, or send students into the communities to work in health and legal clinics for the under-served, or to tutor barrio children. This too, it is recognized, may bolster professional school applications by showing community service. In these ways, these pre-professional organizations serve to combine an ethic of concern for the larger Chicano blue-collar community with the career ambitions of young people.

Similarly, in law and medical schools, Chicanos continue to organize to help each other get through school and find good residency programs (in the case of doctors) and future jobs (in the case of lawyers). These organizations, like their undergraduate equivalents, manage to combine self interest with the Movement ethic, and are thus highly successful in terms of involvement and influence.

However, at the professional level, physician and attorney organizations begin to differ. I once asked a physician who was trying to revive a California Chicano physician's organization, why he thought the lawyers had been so successful in organizing themselves; the lawyers' organization, M.A.B.A., was almost thirty years old but the physicians' attempts to organize over the past ten years had continuously floundered. He pointed out to me some significant differences between law and medicine: law organizations at the professional level can continue to serve dual purposes, since in order to advance in their careers lawyers usually need wider political connections, whether they are working for partnership in a major law firm that is seeking clients and political allies, building their reputations as litigators in the court system, or networking for a judicial appointment. Doctors, on the other hand, he suggested, don't need to network as much in order to be successful and advance in their careers. Thus he felt that it was easier to get Chicano lawyers to organize and rally around the cause of helping their people, since they would simultaneously be boosting their careers, whereas with doctors, most of the appeal for organizing had to resort primarily to their Movement values, rather than self interest in the form of prestige, a new challenge, or an increase in salary. His point was that physicians were hard to organize, but it is also interesting in terms of showing how various points on the career tracks of both professions are stages for different contests between the values of the Movement and the values of professional advancement.

CHOOSING A CAREER

The shift from youth to age, and Movement to professional attitudes about career choice, is captured beautifully by this quote from a public defender of the Movement generation as he contrasts how he and other

Chicano students felt about the subject back in college, and how he feels now:

> We felt that people who wanted to go into the mainstream were kind of just ripping us off. We had a certain number of slots available, and there were certain numbers of us who got into school, and if someone were to go out and work with a corporation, it was like, "Well, that guy is just stealing a spot from somebody that might go work in the community."
>
> But that just simply isn't reality. When everyone graduated, everyone went and did what they wanted to do anyway. And so many of the people who were the hard-core radicals ended up working for some big corporation. And so many of the people who were just dismissed as being just corporate, you know, 'sell outs,' are really good people and are in their own way contributing a lot to society, and the Raza community. They're out there doing good things, and so you can't make those kinds of judgements about other people. That's ridiculous.

This same sentiment was expressed by numerous other former "radical" Movement Chicanos who had come to realize, by their own observations, that those who had participated the most vociferously in Chicano nationalist organizations were not necessarily the ones that went on in their professional lives to adhere to the values of the Movement in their lifestyles or career choices. It was clear that even those who chose "non-Movement careers," such as surgery or corporate law, might be those who ended up doing the most good for the Chicano community. Furthermore, some of the people that student Movement Chicanos had ostracized or judged as "sell outs," (*vendidos*) were now deeply committed to careers which were perfectly aligned with Movement values.

One of these was a friend of mine from the Chicano Theme House at Stanford who had experienced much criticism by Movement Chicanos when he was there because he was from a professional, middle-class family and was able to mix comfortably with both Anglos and Chicanos. He and I reminisced about the way he had been judged as an undergraduate and chuckled deliciously over the irony that he was now a lawyer for the Mexican American Legal Defense and Education fund (M.A.L.D.E.F.), a classic Movement job. In fact, he told me a story about going to a Casa Zapata reunion at Stanford and meeting up with one of the "heavies" of our Movement days, who was now a lawyer for California Rural Legal Assistance. He said he found it "hilarious" that they would find themselves "talking together as fellow attorneys" doing the same kind of Civil rights work for Mexican Americans, when the other lawyer had been one of those upperclassmen during the early seventies who had "come down" and "intimidated" fellow Chicanos like himself to conform to the Movement norm: "This is what a Chicano is and if you do not do these things then you're not Chicano."

However, despite the fact that most Chicanos as professionals had learned to nuance and temper their judgements about the "commitment" of other Chicanos, there was still a clear hierarchy of values concerning career choice expressed by Chicanos both in public and in private. Movement careers were still valued the most highly. This meant that at public functions and meetings those that were praised and lauded most were the M.A.L.D.E.F. lawyers and the family practitioners working in the barrio. It was clear that a Chicano could not be successful politically with his own peers unless he was visibly involved in activities which complied with Movement values. So the corporate lawyer who did pro bono work, or who worked in city politics for Chicanos could be honored in Chicano circles, and a surgeon who left his lucrative career to run a community health foundation could likewise be praised by his peers.

Gossip between Chicanos about each other's "commitment" similarly invokes Movement values. For example, some friends of mine who worked in Civil rights law warned me about some lawyers who ran a firm who had "made their living off the backs of poor immigrants. They'll deny it, but that's the truth. They made money off of immigration." Some family practice doctors who worked on the "East side" where most of the poorer Mexicans and Latino immigrants lived, loved to criticize Chicano doctors who worked on the "West side" and tried to "pretend" they were helping Chicanos.

Within the interview situation, Chicanos also expressed these Movement values in terms of career choices, their own as well as other Chicanos' choices. Chicanos with "Movement careers" were the least likely to express any ambivalence about their work. At one extreme were the Civil rights lawyers and the barrio family practitioners who felt no conflicts about their work and their "commitment" to the community, because they knew that their daily living involved helping other Mexican Americans in a way with which no Movement Chicano could quarrel. As a Civil rights lawyer put it:

> "I like being a Civil rights lawyer because you have the luxury of being pure. . . . You can tell everyone in the world, 'This stinks; this legislation's bad.' Or you know, 'Goddang it, clean up your act,' and you have the luxury and you don't have to worry about whether or not you're going to be elected," [or lose your job)]. [my addition in parentheses].

Family practice doctors who work with working-class Mexicans feel particularly "clean" in terms of compatibility between their work and their Movement values. My husband and his friends love to tell each other stories about the little old ladies "just like my grandma" who come into their clinics daily and blessed them with gratitude for being able to speak Spanish and understand their complaints.

However, not everyone with a "Movement career" feels complete compatibility between their work and their Movement values. I had a frustrating (but ultimately fascinating) interview with a Chicano public defender who I knew had been involved in the Movement as an undergraduate. Throughout our interaction I kept pressuring him to tell me that he felt he was "helping the people" by being a public defender. He eluded my pushes in that direction until he was apparently fed up, and said:

> I don't have any misconceptions about what I do. I mean,. . . who is the criminal gonna rip off? He's not gonna take a bus and go over to the West side. He's gonna rip off people close to his neighborhood. I've also dealt with that, being both victim and defendant. That's been my background. That's the way I grew up. I can kind of understand both sides, but I don't have any illusions about this kind of romanticized defendant that kind of goes out and rips off because he's hungry, or that kind of thing. On a case by case basis, sometimes that's the case. But you can't romanticize the criminal. Is there a crime or is there not? It's a very technical area. And you deal with it like that. I don't romanticize it.
> . . . I've had my car ripped off, and I don't romanticize the guy who did that. I want to get him and beat his ass, but on the other hand, I can kind of step back and say, "Well, these people haven't had as

many opportunities or whatever and I don't help 'em by putting him
out on the street, but I don't see how jail is gonna help him either."

This public defender knew my background in relationship to the
Chicano Movement, and was clearly trying to set me straight about
any "romanticized" notions I or any Movement Chicano might still
have about the nature of his work, which, he insisted, was not about
helping the underdog, "hungry" defendant, but rather a "very
technical" job in which guilt was determined through the intricacies of
the law. Whether or not he himself had ever romanticized criminals
when he was a student in the Movement or benefited from others
romanticizing his own background growing up "on the streets," he
was now strictly a professional doing a job, not a Movement Chicano
helping the *gente*.

What this public defender was more concerned about was the fact
that his job was so time-consuming and exhausting that he didn't have
time or energy to get involved in community activities that *really*
"helped the community," like voter registration and political
leadership.

This kind of concern about helping the community outside of
one's work setting was more prevalent in Movement Chicanos who
worked in clearly non-Movement careers, like public prosecutors or
lawyers who worked for large private law firms. For example, I had
another interesting interview with a lawyer who worked with wealthy
entertainment clients. First, he went into great detail to me about why
he had chosen to work for a large firm instead of doing what he had
intended in law school to do, which was work as a public defender or
in a small firm in his barrio community with Mexican people. To
make a long story short, he discovered, on the advice of some friends,
that many progressive law firms would allow and even encourage their
associates and partners to be active politically in community affairs. So
he decided that perhaps through working in such a firm he could
"work in a sphere of influence that has political and economic contacts
at high levels" and in this way he could do the "social engineering" he
had always aspired to do on a large rather than small scale, because at
this level, "sometimes a decision that you make will impact a hundred
thousand people in one fell swoop." He joined a large firm, became a
partner by age 35, was making a generous living, and was active in
City politics and L.A. Mexican American affairs. His walls, floor, and
desk were covered with plaques and awards for community service.

However, when I asked him what feeling motivated all this activity, this is how the interview proceeded:

> *Attorney:* Oh, I think it [the feeling] can be anything from a facetious comment like "guilt" all the way through sincere commitment and everything that falls in between. Certainly not being a legal aid lawyer and not being a public defender, and making more than a reasonable yearly income, I feel an even greater obligation than before to not lose sight of my commitment. That could be easily interpreted by some people as guilt. You know, "you've got yours. What are you gonna do about the rest of us?" A.k.a [also known as] 'guilt.'
>
> Or simply, that I found a better way to do what I had always intended to do, which is to have as positive an impact on the quality of people's lives with the same energies that it would take to help one family at a time.
>
> *Anthropologist:* But you say *some people* might interpret it as guilt . . .
>
> *Attorney:* Well, *I* might even interpret it as guilt, 'cause I'm sitting here in a ten-story office with a panoramic view of the Pacific Ocean on the west side of L.A., wearing a nice suit with a very nice office with celebrity clients and a nice car and a nice home on the West side, and it would be very easy to get lost in the shuffle of the ivory tower never to be heard from again . . . ah . . . but I feel like hell about it, so I make sure that I get out there doing that which I committed to do when I first got to law school.

Most of what this attorney said in this section of interview was glibly spoken in controlled lawyer fashion, expressing feelings only indirectly. However, when I gently led him on, he admitted (however obliquely) to feeling some guilt. A few words later he concedes a bit more guilt feeling when he says, "but I feel like hell about it. " His tone here had no facetiousness and seemed to be one of the few sincere and straight things he said to me throughout the interview.

Career choice for Movement Chicanos is clearly a decision which is complicated by Movement values. For those who are fortunate enough to be able to combine their personal interests and circumstances to work in careers which are compatible with these values, the need to justify or work out guilt is much less (or non-existent) than for those who feel compelled for various reasons to work in areas which are less clearly Movement approved.

What makes "pure Movement" choices so difficult are a competing set of values which, although not as openly acknowledged—or at least not openly praised among Chicanos—are nonetheless compelling enough to provide intense competition with Movement values. These include the values of personal fulfillment, which may guide someone into a non-Movement career because they are "interested in," or challenged by a certain area. A Chicana public prosecutor explained to me how she painfully came to the decision to shift her goals from public defense to prosecution, in spite of the fact that she had always felt "defense-oriented" and knew that she would suffer criticism in the Chicano professional community, particularly in M.A.B.A. As she explained it, a job had come up, and it sounded challenging, so she took it, and now enjoyed her work thoroughly.

Other competing values were the desire for financial stability and success, which includes in many cases the need to pay off high student loans and/or support parents and siblings financially, but also has to do with the all-American urge to have a "nice car," a "nice house" and to wear "nice suits." Another strong value is that of professional prestige. Although legal-aid lawyers are admired by Movement standards, successful corporate lawyers who move in high political and financial circles are also admired. Similarly, while family practice doctors are lauded for their choice to do culturally sensitive "family," and "preventive" medicine in the Chicano community, the few Chicanos who go into surgery or some esoteric branch of internal medicine (both areas which are thought of as more prestigious than lowly family practice in medicine) and make a name for themselves, are also admired for their ability to "make it" in such difficult fields.

However, while some Chicanos struggle with professional values which compete with their Chicano values, some non-Movement oriented Chicanos find themselves struggling *against* Chicano values in order to maintain their professionalism. This is due to an ironic influence of the Movement on some prospective employers, who may expect Chicanos to be Movement oriented whether or not they give any indication of such an orientation, and thus scrutinize them more closely as potentially unfit for a particular job. For example, one Chicana who had avoided "political" Chicano activism in law school said that she resented that in her interviews with corporate law firms they kept asking her if perhaps she really wanted to do Civil rights law or legal aid work. Her resume, she said indignantly, was clear that she had a long-term, single-minded interest in business. Another Chicano working as a new associate for a large law firm, who was deeply immersed in Movement values, said that he kept all his Chicano activities very "low profile" because he did not want to be stereotyped by the partners in his firm.

PROFESSIONAL TRAINING

As Chicanos become more deeply involved in their respective professional training and practices, they wrestle out the meaning of that involvement in their own minds as well as in conversation with other Chicanos. Much of this discourse, for those who identify with the Movement, has to do with conflicts between the Movement's anti-professional, or counter-professional values and the intense assault those values encounter in the process of professional training. These pressures are particularly intense during the years of graduate school and the first years of law practice or medical residency, when the values first begin to clash.

The values at the extreme of the Movement, when it was in its youth in the sixties and seventies, were anti-establishment, anti-rules, anti-anything "Anglo." Movement heroes were the *cholos* who smoked *"mota"* (marijuana), survived street fights, and might steal a few things now and then from the undeserving rich. Or they were revolutionaries like Emiliano Zapata, Pancho Villa, and Che Guevara fighting oppressive oligarchies. Or they were American "social bandits" like Joaquin Murieta or Gregorio Cortéz who turned to crime because of being unjustly treated by the law. Or more tamely, but no less radical, they were union men like Cesar Chavez fighting for farm worker rights against greedy capitalist growers, or inspirational leaders like Reies Lopez Tijerina fighting to restore land to the northern New Mexican Hispanics whose land rights had been violated by unscrupulous Anglo Americans.

Chicanos in the Movement felt antagonistic toward "the System" and justified in feeling no special allegiance to the rules and regulations of the educational, governmental, and private institutions from which they aspired to wrest what they felt was their just due. Ultimately, the Movement inculcated deep suspicion of those in power and thus posed a paradoxical challenge to those Chicanos who aspired to have power, i.e. become successful professionals, or, as one lawyer put it, "enter the belly of the beast," and yet wield that power for justice rather than self-aggrandizement.

By the time most movement Chicanos got out of law school or medical school, much of the fire and fervor of their anti-establishment feelings had been muted by the requirements for conformity which are an integral part of professional training. However, the tensions between professional and Movement values remain for most of them, bolstered by the force of Movement culture, and manifesting themselves in different ways.

For many, "the job" and its intricate requirements virtually swallow up any latent Movement critique of "the System" or any sense of an alternative professionalism, although they may participate actively in Chicano organizations and at one time may have identified with the Movement. For others, the clashes between values emerge in particular situations or settings. A small incident at the C.M.A.C. conference in 1989 is a simple example of how values may change, and how Chicanos feel about those changes. I was wandering between rooms on the first morning of the conference, taking note of the proceedings and not too subtly eavesdropping. The first session was already about twenty minutes late, and I heard two Chicanos complaining about this, joking about "Chicano time." "Chicano time," as I mentioned earlier, was what Movement Chicanos jokingly termed the casual attitude of their student days toward beginning and arriving at parties, classes, and get-togethers well past their official starting time. It was a more subtle aspect of the critique of "White" people's perceived obsession with punctuality, particularly professionally oriented Anglos.

However, now that they were professionals themselves, accustomed to being ruled by the clock, these Chicanos were displeased that the conference was getting off to a bad start, by professional standards, in being so late. By joking the pronouncement "Chicano time" they were expressing both judgement as professionals and a sense of irony as former Movement students who had once prided themselves on observing "Chicano time."

Another example of conflict between Movement values and professional ones is a story told to me by a young attorney in a large firm. He explained that when he had first started the job, he learned that the other Chicano in the firm was being criticized by other members for dressing and acting "too barrio." This included, he said, a heavy accent, slicked-back cholo-style hair, and suits that were not conservative enough. Instead of allying himself with his fellow Chicano, the neophyte lawyer felt that expressing solidarity with someone who was clearly untutored in, or insensitive to, the cultural requirements of corporate law practice, might jeopardize his own credibility and opportunities for advancement.

A more pervasive example of such value conflicts is in how many doctors and lawyers in various work settings express some sense of conflict about whether or not—or to what extent—to socialize with the Mexican janitors, nurses, cooks, and secretaries at their places of work in the name of identification with the blue-collar or wider Chicano community. While some congratulate themselves on their easy camaraderie with "the help," others feel that such "fraternization" with underlings might undermine professional authority, or jeopardize professional seriousness in the eyes of colleagues. I watched my husband Beto shift his attitudes somewhat toward mixing with nurses, orderlies, and the kitchen staff at his training hospital when he was an intern and resident. When he started out as a lowly intern, he felt little distance from them, and identified with their status at the bottom of the hospital hierarchy. Then he would come home with stories about joking around in Spanish with the guys in the back of the kitchen, and talking the Chicana scheduling nurse into giving him a light load of patients at the clinic.

However, as he progressed in authority, and became more deeply immersed into the professional structure, he came home with other kinds of stories. He started to worry that one of the Chicanos who served him breakfast in the cafeteria everyday was asking for drugs, and that he couldn't let that kind of pattern get started because he was afraid he would be inundated by behind-the-scenes requests. One day we were in an elevator at the hospital when a friendly Chicana nurse introduced herself to me, striking up a pleasant conversation. I asked Beto later why he had barely spoken to the woman, since she obviously worked with him, and he said that she was the kind that liked to get "too close" to physicians and ask them favors.

Many neophyte doctors and lawyers describe an initial difficulty, at the start of their careers, in establishing their "authority," or the proper professional relationship, to staff in the work place who are lower in status. One corporate lawyer with strong Movement values expressed his discomfort with talking to Mexican custodial staff, for fear that they might be judging him as a presumptuous elite. Another felt awkward with them because he did not speak adequate Spanish, and was afraid he would "let them down" when he spoke in his broken dialect. Chicana (female) physicians often described their difficulties in gaining respect from nurses, particularly fellow Latinas. One of my friends in particular struggled for several years with her role with the Latina nurses at her hospital while she was in training. Eventually, she learned to balance her roles, "exerting her authority" where it was necessary, particularly under emergency conditions where it was her responsibility as a physician to take charge, and then letting loose with giggles and gossip behind the scenes with those Chicana nurses she had learned to trust.

However, out of the tensions, compromises, and strategies which Chicano doctors and lawyers employ to make peace between their warring loyalties and values, a few exceptional Chicanos forge a clear path for the combination of their Movement and professional values. Some do it by working within existing institutions and resisting the pressures of professionalism wherever they violate these values. Such is the case of Noelia Suarez, an obstetrician who first trained as a nurse at a major Los Angeles county hospital and then returned to that hospital when she became an intern and resident in order to help "right the wrongs" she had experienced and observed there:

> When I was working at the County I developed a very, very strong sense of justice, patient care, and care for third-world women in the medical system. Defending what we called patient advocacy at the County was a big, big responsibility because you're not just a nurse,[2] you have to defend patients in the system. You know, I've witnessed people being assaulted, being slapped, being told to shut up by staff [by "staff", she means physicians].
>
> . . . This was a very bad group of physicians, just always going around slapping women. This was the same hospital that ten years prior had a class action suit for mass sterilization of Mexican women. . . . I was in the brunt of a bad group that was disrespectful, hated patients. [There were] no minority physicians when I was there. . . . Always very racist remarks, open hostility toward the patients. And for me, I internalized the experience and it made me very aggressive, assertive, and again, a clean cut image about what's right, what's good, what makes a good physician and how I could make a difference.

At the county hospital, this doctor not only advocates for patient's rights, but also teaches undocumented people "survival tactics," like "where to get food, where to get free clothes; how to get their ability-to pay-program and not have to go through a welfare system and sacrifice their documentation process." She involves nurses in patient care in a clear violation of the usual rigid doctor/nurse hierarchy, asking their opinions and "giving credit where credit is due." The price she pays professionally for her loyalty to patients and staff members below her in the professional hierarchy is a reputation as a "trouble maker," a sobriquet with which she has gracefully learned to live.

Because of her demonstrated commitment to Movement values, this woman has a reputation in the Chicano medical community for integrity and is also known widely as an impassioned speaker for Chicano causes. She is one of the few people in that community who can still bring sober Chicano physicians to their feet in a standing ovation with her invocations of protest against particular injustices against the Mexican American community.

Besides this "thorn-in-the-side-of-the-system" way of retaining loyalty to Movement values within professional practice, other Chicanos are creating alternative professional institutions and ideologies. Such is the case with the White Memorial Residency Training Program and the formation of the Family Care Specialists group in East Los Angeles.

The story begins in Spring 1988 when a group of seven Latino family practice physicians, most of them Chicanos, organized themselves as a private medical group and contracted with White Memorial Hospital in East Los Angeles for hospital privileges and the management of an inner-city residency training program. While I did not closely observe either the program or the new medical group, I was acquainted with some of its issues and struggles through one of its residents, Luis Duran. Luis and my husband were long-time friends, and over the years of their medical schooling and internship/residency training I witnessed, and in some cases participated in, countless conversations between them about the process of balancing Chicano values with the rigors and responsibilities of professionalism. In addition, Luis and I spent hours on the phone several times a month discussing various problems and happenings of his life as a doctor in training.

One evening that spring Luis was at our apartment for dinner, relating some of the details of the plans for the residency and medical group. Luis and Beto were excited about the program because it would be the first residency training program with a predominantly Chicano staff and Chicano residents, and it involved several of their acquaintances and close friends from various school and organization networks.

Luis began by explaining to me that White Memorial Hospital had been known as "The Chicano clinic" for years, and had been put down by other [Anglo] doctors for its alleged mediocrity, but the tables were being turned now that this group of Chicanos had enlisted the help of a Los Angeles family practice academic [Anglo] who was widely known for creating one of the best residency training programs in California.

I asked if this kind of program was more feasible here in Los Angeles than in northern California, and Beto and Luis responded affirmatively, saying that it was primarily due to the fact that Los Angeles has a large population-base of Mexicans who can pay for Spanish-speaking, culturally-sensitive services, and who are eager to find doctors who offer such services.

So I asked Beto how he felt about the program, and he said,

> It's exciting because it's something that I've always wanted to do, or would do if I could. Just to know it's going to happen is great. It's accredited by the Board of Family Practice! This is as significant as when Martin Luther King demonstrated and got rid of segregated bathrooms! It's as close to a minority hospital as you're gonna get!
>
> They really are gonna make one helluva difference to that community. They'll get the best care at a decent price, with doctors who speak their language and understand their culture.

He launched into a story to illustrate how important that cultural sensitivity was. He explained how one evening when he volunteered at the Venice Free Clinic he saw only Spanish-speaking patients, and they kept asking him if he would be back so that they could see him again. "They want somebody like me because I can understand them." He told how a woman came in complaining of abdominal pain and headaches. After examining her, he talked to her and asked her gently about how things were going and she said that her husband wasn't in the house, but that he was "trying to come back." From that little bit he understood that she meant that her husband had been picked up by Immigration ("the *migra*").

"No wonder she was depressed!" he said. "She's asking for help." He explained that he had had to "read between the lines" in order to understand what her real problem was, and he felt that an Anglo would never have caught the nuances, or if they had, would not have handled it correctly with understanding. "At least I'm able to understand her situation and offer sympathy, even if I can't really help her. " He said to the woman, " *Ud. tiene mucha razón por tener dolor de cabeza porque su esposo no está en casa.*" [3]

Then Beto went on to explain how great it would be to work with Chicano faculty, and how much one of the Latino faculty people at his own program at Kaiser Sunset understood him and was helpful: "He won't criticize the way a white guy might, 'Oh, he has a language problem,' or being critical of the way you don't 'assert' yourself."

Then I turned to Luis and asked him how he felt about the new program, and he said:

> First, it's important because they are bringing together a faculty that never existed before, an all minority, exclusively minority faculty (although there are some black medical schools that might have done it before) but never any exclusive Chicano faculty and second, the purpose is to train Chicano residents.

Furthermore, he went on to explain, residency programs like the one in which he was *currently* training as an intern, although they had a large Chicano population, did not address Chicano issues "as a whole". In fact, he, an intern, was always having to teach the White residents [who were superior to him in rank] about Mexican American issue. For example, he explained, they thought that all Chicanos used *curanderos*, generalizing falsely from what they had read in medical journals. Although these Anglos were sympathetic, said Luis,

> What they don't realize is that socioeconomic factors play a role in the use of *curanderismo* as much if not more than cultural factors; the average Mexican only uses *curanderismo* when they can't afford western medicine.

Luis went on to complain about other problems with his current program, and expressed optimism that this Chicano group of faculty would have more concern for him not just personally, but as a Chicano.

Then Beto jumped in and said that the program would offer role models for people like himself, someone to look to from your own background. Again he brought up his own Latino resident and described how he gave Beto hints about presenting patients to faculty with the right style, "Because when you deal with Anglo staff, you have to present it right, so that people will not think you don't know when you do know."

Luis concurred: "If you stammer, or hesitate, they'll cut you off, and say something like "lack of fund of knowledge," or they'll question your "data base." Both Luis and Beto started laughing at this. "The greatest compliment they can give you is that you have an "adequate fund of knowledge," Luis explained. There was an implicit judgement here about "Anglo" professional emphasis on memorized medical knowledge in contrast to their Chicano values of empathy and concern for cultural understanding. Then Beto said:

> This program crystallizes all the goals that people who interview for medical school, like himself, said they wanted to achieve, going back to the community (in this case East L.A.) and . . .

> Luis jumped in: . . . commitment, and how it's done: sensitive, bilingual and putting the patient at ease.

> Beto: . . . wanting to be a role model, making a difference in people's lives. And also, everyone says "I want to build my own clinic." Well, these guys are doing it!

> Luis: There are two different exciting things about it. Number one, the formation of an H.M.O. and number two, the formation of the residency program.

He went on to describe how they are setting up the private practice group as a Health Maintenance Organization when I asked him about it:

> They are contracting with little medium sized "Mom and Pop" businesses, like *tortillerias*, bakeries, restaurants. They already have "King Taco" and are getting other groups, local businesses around White Memorial which is the only private hospital in East L.A.

Evidently they have already brought a practice and are planning soon to lease a building.

. . . And for my own ego, I'm the first resident they ever hired. For me, that's really important. It's like a sacrifice, 'cause I'm not getting a lot of pay, but the compensation is to be part of something that's never been done before, like being the first man to walk on the moon. No other Chicanos have ever done this!

Beto: The ultimate ramifications are that if it takes off, it will question the way that Anglos train residents. And it will also justify all the affirmative action activism of the sixties. . . . If it succeeds, physicians who see it as competition will be scared, because of the competition. They [the Chicanos] will be taking away their minority patients!

As they talked, they were both getting increasingly animated and enthusiastic. At one point Luis exclaimed: "This is getting me even more excited than I was!"

Then they went on to talk about how three of the physicians in the group were leaving Kaiser Permanente in order to form this practice. One of the leaving doctors was actually going to inform the Chief of the Family Practice program at Kaiser that one of the reasons they were all leaving was that Chicanos had not been promoted to faculty positions, and that qualified Chicanos had been overlooked repeatedly for Anglos.

Beto: So, we're saying, 'Well, screw you! We'll create our own!

So then I asked Beto and Luis to tell me what was the real difference between a bunch of White guys getting together to start a clinic and a bunch of Chicanos:

Luis: Whites go to school 'cause they look forward to mixing with doctors. Chicanos go because they want to relate to a certain patient population.

Beto: Chicanos believe in the motivations they have always felt, when they were kids and went to the doctor, and he or she didn't speak Spanish.

Luis: You're working with people more like your family.

Beto: That sense of shared values and goals are what kept these people going through all they had to go through.

Luis: For example, what will keep you going when you don't do as well in school, or have to retake exams. I'm here for a reason other than satisfying my ego, not just money. I am needed by people like my family. For example, my grandmother goes to a clinic where an old friend is her doctor. We have a big sense of loyalty, family, working hard, not for money but because it's good to work hard. [Luis's expression was heightened and animated]

Beto: There's no doubt that there's a group who are screwed by the medical system that exists. People are literally dying. [At this point he is excited and passionate in tone]. It's things like that that keep you going when you have a hard time in school or whatever. For example, you hear White guys talking about wanting to go to a particular county hospital so they can "experiment" over high volume. They wouldn't think the same way about a hospital that served rich people, upper middle-class people. The poor have no choice, and don't necessarily know better.

I have rendered this dialogue in depth because it is saturated with the richness of the Movement Chicano doctor's experiences and values, particularly in the training stages when first being confronted with the realities of the professional world. I have also rendered it in order to contrast it with later dialogues which Luis and Beto had about the same residency program, after Luis had been working there for several months. In comparing these two dialogues, I will illustrate how Movement values are shaped in relationship to particular professional pressures.

In this first dialogue, Luis and Beto have only a few things to say which uphold traditional ("Anglo") professional values. The main area where they seem to uphold them is where Beto gleefully asserts that the White Memorial Program has enlisted the expertise of a leading Anglo family practice residency specialist who will be able to give the Chicano faculty a hand in creating a residency program which is *respectable to the wider community*. He is likewise pleased that the program is *certified* by the Board of Family Practice.

Also, Luis and Beto admire the fact that these Chicano doctors are financially savvy enough to be starting their own practice just like any other up-to-date professional doctors, on the model of the Health Maintenance Organization, contracting with businesses and obtaining privileges with a large hospital.

Except for these areas, however, the rest of the discussion about the potential virtues of the new program centers around Movement values, particularly in contrast to "Anglo" professional ones. For example, both Luis and Beto express the hope that these "Chicano" doctors will train residents without all the professional harumphing about "fund of knowledge" and the proper kind of "presentation."[4] I heard this criticism of professional training time and again by various Chicano doctors. "Anglo" doctors (read "the professional standard") admired book knowledge, how many articles a person could cite, how up on the literature they were, and how smoothly and authoritatively they could present their cases. Chicanos, by contrast, were more sensitive to the interface of psychological and cultural issues with health, and recognized that one's ability to cure and help people was more important than the way in which one cited the literature and bluffed through a patient presentation to a superior. Beto sums this attitude up when he says, "The ultimate ramifications are that if it [the residency training program] takes off, it will question the way that Anglos train residents."

Even more specifically, the residency program and the all-Chicano family practice group would provide models and a pathway for training Chicanos to work in their own communities to provide health care in a way that Anglos had never been able to do. Luis and Beto clearly felt that Chicanos, trained in their own programs and working in their own clinics, would be free to develop a different way of practicing medicine with Chicanos and other Spanish-speaking, blue-collar and poor people. Not only would they provide care where often no care was available, but the medicine they practiced would be culturally sensitive and non-exploitative. They would be *Movement* physicians, different from the Anglo book-oriented, money-making technicians who went into medicine "to relate to other doctors," (i.e. for status) and who see the poor as "populations" on which they can experiment rather than family and friends who deserve healing.

The Chicano physicians that I knew personally, and those whom I interviewed in depth, always shaped their sense of professional identity in relationship to this issue of being a "different" kind of physician to the Chicano community. This was true whether they were steeped in Movement culture or somewhat peripheral to the culture but simply recognized the benefit of identifying as a bilingual/bicultural specialist in a California population that was increasingly Latino and poor. In the cases of both Luis and Beto, who identified strongly with Movement culture, their respective struggles to successfully get through medical school ("what will keep you going when you don't do as well in school, or have to retake exams") were motivated by a sense that they were in medicine "for a reason other than satisfying my ego, not just money," (quotes from Luis) and that their standards for being doctors were very different from those which had been imposed on them throughout medical school.

However, as a conversation at my house three months later between Luis, Beto, and another Chicana family practice doctor, Miranda Hinojosa, demonstrates, once they are making judgements about a "Chicano" training program, or are judging the behavior of a fellow Chicano whose behavior may be perceived as "too Chicano" and not professional enough, the issue of what is "Anglo professional" and what is "Chicano professional" may become more complicated.

In late summer that same year, when Luis had just started working as the Chief Resident at the new White Memorial program, he called Beto and told him he was having a hard time with one of his interns. Beto related some of the problem to me. A month later, I came home one afternoon to find Luis, Beto, and another friend, Miranda in deep conversation about Luis's problems with the interns in his program. As the conversation evolved, Luis described how this one intern in particular was always late for rounds[5] in the morning at the hospital, didn't do her "pre-rounds", complained about working in the clinic after she had been "on call"[6] the night before, and "presented her patients" in a sloppy, informal way. Furthermore, she was a "know it-all" that refused to ask questions.

After Luis's description of her, Miranda and Beto jumped all over the intern in question. Beto was furious because he thought the woman was trying to get away with something simply because she was working with someone of her own "race," that she thought that Chicanos would be more lenient on her and let her "off the hook" because they would understand the pressures she was under as a minority.

Regardless of race, this is totally unacceptable behavior for a physician because she is directly responsible for making decisions that affect people's life and death and you can't take those lightly. You've gotta be serious. There is no doubt in my mind that if this person were surrounded by and working with all Anglo people they would be working harder, because they would know that they were being judged as inferior from the start.

It's a reverse kind of racism. Their attitude is that we're inferior because they apply a different set of standards to what they think is expected of them by people of their own race than what they think is expected of them by people of another race, and they value the opinion more of White people. And I won't put up with that shit. As a Chicano physician going through my second year I'm seeing how much responsibility there is in my program, and I see how important it is to really stay on top of what is going on and not take short cuts, because if you don't try to do your best, you're just reinforcing the stereotype that people have of you anyway.

Miranda concurred and lamented that with the kind of behavior that this girl was presenting, and the way she was making trouble, she could give the whole program a bad reputation. "That's exactly what people on the outside are gonna be looking for—a bunch of Chicanos doing a lousy, sloppy job. We always have to do it better because we're being watched."

Luis said that one of the things that was hardest for him was that she was assuming that, because it was a Chicano program, that they would be doing things the "Chicano way." It turned out that she had participated in a Chicano free clinic which Luis had also once been a part of, and he felt that she was trying to appeal to the egalitarian, informal atmosphere of that Chicano student run clinic. This is what had caused some conflict in him, he explained, about establishing his own authority and a strict protocol for intern and resident behavior. To add to the problem, said Luis, the attending physicians [the senior staff who had started the program in the first place] had told the interns at the beginning that this would be a collegial atmosphere, and so now, complained Luis, the interns think " we're freed from the White medical system. We can do it the Chicano way."

The "Chicano way" meant the "alternative way" which had been practiced by undergraduate, and sometimes graduate Chicanos in their student organizations where hierarchies were eased, where people could arrive on "Chicano time," (late), and where criticism of the status quo was expected and cultivated. Beto and Miranda were unequivocal in their judgment of this intern's inability to realize that the stakes were different at the professional level. Said Miranda:

> If one of those guys fucks something up like that, it just takes one lawsuit and the program is gone. She could sabotage the program. And you know, she's the kind of person that if she gets kicked out or disciplined, will pull out the Chicano brotherhood rhetoric.

What Luis was looking for from his two fellow Chicano physicians, and obviously received, was confirmation that this woman was going too far with her appeal to "the Chicano way." They supported his judgement and went on to articulate what they felt were the appropriate standards for a Chicano residency program. First and foremost, the professional standards of conduct shared by Anglos had to be cultivated. Seniority and authority needed to be respected because just one year of experience could make a tremendous amount of difference in terms of "knowledge" and "ability to anticipate problems."

"It's like the military; you have to respect discipline and rank," said Luis.

It has to be, because "lives are at stake," concurred Miranda.

In this conversation, three Movement-grounded Chicanos come to terms with the realities of professional standards and the conflicts that Chicano Movement values and practices can cause when brought into the professional arena. One of their concerns is that Chicano projects not be discredited in the professional world by Chicanos who do not understand or appreciate the delicate balance necessary between "Chicano" values and behavior, and the "professional" standards necessary to be accepted by the wider society.

Furthermore, they reveal a process of professional evolution in this conversation. All of them had worked in free clinics and been enmeshed in undergraduate and graduate Chicano organizations. All of them had been bitterly critical of their medical schooling for its "Anglo" standards and insensitivities. However, in this threshold between student life and full professional life while they are residents in training, they have come to some of their own conclusions from experience about why professional training is disciplined the way it is, and why certain aspects of that are necessary. So while Luis and his compatriots were open to the idea of a more collegial residency program where Chicanos would be more sensitive to the trials of their fellow physicians and to the problems of their Latino patients, he was not willing to sacrifice certain professional standards and thus jeopardize, not only the credibility of the program, but also the lives of patients.

In this way, while these Chicano physicians were beginning to accept some of the standard values of their profession—promptness, willingness to work long hours, acceptance of authority and hierarchy—they were doing so selectively, with a fine-tuned sense of discrimination between what professional values were necessary due to the nature of the profession, and what were dispensable as accoutrements of power. In this way they were not submitting to professional education without questioning its premises and challenging its traditions.

This conversation was only one of thousands of conversations being carried on all over Los Angeles by other Chicano physicians and lawyers trying to balance their values and find a different way to be professionals. The White Memorial Residency, as an "all Chicano" program was the perfect experimental ground to wrestle out some of these ideas and to come up with new solutions to the problem of being a professional and continuing to serve the *gente* in a new way.

VOLUNTEERING OUTSIDE OF WORK

The Chicano ethic of working in the community to the limit of one's capacity influences the everyday life choices made by most professionals. Even those whose daily bread is earned serving their blue-collar compatriots feel compelled to spend much of their free time volunteering in other capacities. People spend evenings, weekends, lunch hours and snagged minutes on the job to do volunteer work.

This work falls into several different areas. The first and most obvious includes donating money and/or participating in multiple Latino functions in the city. Chicanos pride themselves on attending as many fundraisers, community festivities, and professional events as they can cram into their busy schedules. People often express guilt about missing a particular event. Donating money is usually a more private affair, so it is difficult to know-how many people actually give money to Chicano organizations, but wealthy doctors and lawyers are often acknowledged publicly for donating to help host conferences, parties, alumni organizations, and political campaigns.

Probably the most popular area of volunteer participation is in professional organizations. It is widely believed and reiterated that people are "showing their commitment" by attending monthly meetings of these groups. Of course here one's self-interest and community interest may coincide, since career networking and politics are part of the function of such organizations. However, these associations also spend a tremendous amount of time and effort educating people on political happenings, and organizing political campaigns and events which benefit the wider Chicano community. For example, at one MABA meeting two of the evening's speakers were present to recruit people to work on voter registration and a parole sponsorship program. I met lawyers who volunteered for both. MABA itself takes stands on state and city legislation effecting Latinos, and endorses particular political candidates. Similarly, CMAC in its fledgling state, was organizing to help influence state lawmakers on issues like scholarship programs for students from blue-collar Mexican American areas, with the idea (backed up by research conducted by Chicano doctors and scholars) that Chicano doctors often returned to work in minority areas with doctor shortages. CMAC also sponsored leadership training for medical students to teach them to think and act critically about how medical school policy affects them and subsequent applicants.

Chicanos feel passionately about this professional organization work to benefit the community. At the first CMAC meeting, held at Tamayo's restaurant, the invited speaker, a public health professor from UCLA, gave a stirring speech about working to make public health policy in a unique Latino/Chicano way. Health care, he emphasized, was a cultural issue, and Latinos had their own history and discourse about health going back to the first medical school in the New World, founded in Mexico City in the 16th century. Latinos, he said, looked at sexual identity, diet, gender roles, sexual behavior, and raising children, in different ways from Anglos. Chicano doctors needed to press the wider community and its public health policies to reflect this different cultural perspective. It was a stirring speech that left the audience pumped up and enthusiastic.

Another volunteer area could be called role modeling. Role modeling is something that Chicano professionals are intensely aware of, and in some sense, many see their entire lives as role models. As my husband often tells me, he feels it is important just "being there" meaning in the hospital and in the clinics in his doctor's coat, to show in a blatantly visual way, to both Anglos and Chicanos, that brown skin is compatible with being a professional. The more formal way of being a role model primarily encompasses speaking and mentoring at high schools, colleges, and for other organizations. Chicano professionals are diligent about participating in such activities. Chicano doctors I knew could be seen at college and medical school graduations either as speakers or (paying) banquet participants, at undergraduate premedical conferences, and at local and hometown high school career days and graduations.

While giving time to these volunteer activities is time consuming and demanding, most people seem to enjoy it, not just because they feel they are participating in the important job of helping those behind them, but also because the socializing, mentoring, and networking is fun in itself. I remember one undergraduate premedical conference put on by the Chicano premed societies of five different L.A. area colleges where I had a great time running into at least five or six doctor friends who were speakers that day.

"Role Modeling" has come under some scrutiny and critique recently. Law professor Richard Delgado, in a 1991 essay in the Michigan Law Review,[7] suggests that Chicano professionals who participate in classic role modeling serve the dominant society's desire to keep minorities complacent about the status quo. Role modeling, he argues, is part of affirmative action, and affirmative action is a tool of the majority "White" society to let only a controlled and conforming few minority members into the professional class. I agree with Delgado that affirmative action is in some sense a tool to control the discontent of minorities by offering the carrot stick of possible success and role models who are complacently successful. However, his argument is too functionalist and ignores the complexities of human culture and history. Chicanos who participated in the Movement culture have never passively accepted the hand-out of affirmative action. Chicanos undergraduates, graduates and professionals in both law and medicine have actively participated in campus protests and the more subtle internal political struggles of admissions committees etc. to control affirmative action as much as possible to serve their own Movement ends. The Chicano professionals I observed who were immersed in the legacy of Movement culture were seldom role models in any passive, compliant sense, but rather constantly struggled to be professionals and mentors of a unique kind, consistent with the value of loyalty to the blue-collar Mexican American community. Certainly some of them reveled in the classic role model's role, but most of the Chicanos I observed, at least in the Chicano Movement generation, saw their role as getting more Chicanos into the professions, and helping them survive professional education without losing the critical awareness of the disenfranchised communities (and class) from which they came.

Beyond role modeling, or mentoring, Chicano professionals spent much time actually out in the community doing volunteer work of various kinds. The politicians I met—two City Commissioners—considered their political work a means to benefit the Latino community in large, structural and policy areas. Many lawyers in particular participated in the more nitty-gritty political work of voter registration in barrio areas on their weekends. Many doctors worked in their off hours at community clinics which primarily served Latinos. Almost every Chicano professional I knew had at one time or another participated as an honoree or speaker at a community Cinco de Mayo festival, a role which after the first flattering time often became more of an obligation than a privilege. Most Chicanos considered it important to support by their money and their presence local Chicano art, theater, authors and much of their social time doubled as community service in this sense.

TIME

While many of the pressures of professionalism which shape the lives of Chicano doctors and lawyers have to do with a shifting set of values from their Movement days, one of the strongest inhibitors of their activism is an element which in some ways seems obvious and cliché, but which deserves some careful attention.[8] As I discussed earlier, during the student Movement years, one of the ways in which Chicanos celebrated their anti-Anglo, anti-professional status was by observing "Chicano time." This term was used to describe a leisurely attitude toward punctuality, but there was another kind of "Chicano time" which was enjoyed by Movement students and which is now lost to them as professionals.

A former Movement Chicano lawyer who once lived in Casa Zapata expressed it well when I asked him about his sense of community, and he contrasted his life in the Stanford Chicano community in the mid-seventies and his life now as a professional:

> The problem with defining community is that . . . you go to work, you do your job for however many hours a day, you go home and you're burnt out. You don't have a lot of time to hang around, shoot the bull, and have that sense of community. Like we used to hang around the stairwells and stuff at Stanford.
>
> . . . Everybody kind of gets into their own little spots and warehouses themselves after you get home from work, and you still have that community, but it's not very active right now, unless you really make that a part of your life.
>
> . . . You get more into the mainstream, and I don't know if that's good or bad, but that's just what happens.

This lawyer expressed regret about the shift from student days when he had the time to sit around with his friends and "create community," and as he told me earlier in the interview, work actively in MEChA. He also told me later that he looked forward to a time when he didn't feel so tired and he could put some serious time into voter registration or other M.A.B.A. activities.

Faustino's lament about the lack of time to not only create community with his peers, but to work in the "outside" community, is shared by many Chicanos, including those that are far more active than he in Movement-oriented activities. A young Chicano attorney deeply immersed in Movement values and politically ambitious, told me one day on the phone that he had resigned from his political appointment in Los Angeles government, and was cutting back on many of his activities because he found that it was conflicting not only with his personal life, but also with his job performance. "I found out the hard way that I'm not God's gift to the Chicano community," he said introspectively.[9]

However cliché this problem of time constraints for the busy professional may seem, the fact that professional jobs require substantial amounts of energy and time beyond the "9:00 to 5:00" commitment popularized in songs and movies has a serious impact on the ability of professional Chicanos to practice their Movement values off the job. As Faustino Negrete put it:

Certainly I'd like to accomplish a lot more, and I'm working toward
that hopefully, but for the time being I'm tired, I'm gonna go home,
and I'm gonna rest. And it's hard to think about going over and
doing this for M.A.B.A. or . . . it's just not the same.
  . . . It's not just Chicanos. It's everybody in our society. We're
so alienated. Everybody's working more.

My Chicano physician friend, Luis Durán, as a student used to
recurrently express a similar sentiment about feeling tired, alienated,
and working too hard, wondering out loud to me whether or not he
might be better off just working as a blue-collar plumber like other
members of his family. Then he would have plenty of time to do the
things he wanted to do, including family and Chicano activities. We
agreed that the trade-off for professional pay and prestige is a work
week which often exceeds forty hours, and obligations which often get
taken home after hours, and both wondered if at some level we were
"being sold a bill of goods" by the System in taking paths toward
professional careers.

The fact that we could talk like this reflected our dual perspectives
on class identity and the pursuit of professionalism, attitudes which
had been cultivated in both of us through our immersion in Movement
values which questioned professionalism.

However, like many Movement Chicanos, the way that Luis
"resolved" his ambivalence toward professional status and the
constraints of time was to plunge more deeply into Movement
activities and submerge his conflicted feelings about time constraints.
This is a typical solution which is publicly encouraged by many
Movement professionals. A telling example of this attitude is this open
letter written by a Chicano physician encouraging his fellow Chicano
physicians to make an extra effort to support the newly forming
C.M.A.C. organization. In these two paragraphs, this Movement
Chicano sums up the feelings of many of his fellow professionals about
the constraints of time and the shared desire to find time to sustain an
organization with the goals of helping the community.

As a practicing physician, I am very much aware of the time
constraints as a result of busy office schedules compounded with the
obligations of family life. Let's be frank, as professionals we have
arrived into the real world of meeting financial and professional

deadlines which impinge on our ability to devote time to desired
social issues which we all hold dear to our hearts.
The survival of C.M.A.C. is critical. As individual health
professionals we have respect and varying degrees of influence in
the community. Imagine the political impact we could have
collectively! However, it must be sustained and goal specific. To
succeed, we must have input from all members to develop extensive
strategies to attack our goals in an organized fashion. The
organization cannot depend on the energy of a few active members,
but if we all contribute a little, the outcome will be dramatic. We
must sustain each other and continue to push forward. We must
never give up!

"We must never give up!" This is the rallying cry of the Movement
which spurs Chicanos to greater efforts to juggle their time
commitments as professionals just a little more, in order to "sustain
each other and continue to push forward" in the struggle toward a
different kind of professionalism.

NOTES

1. Recently, the pressures of professional choice for doctors have been
changing. Fewer will be going into private practice, and more will work for
HMO's because of the increased complexities involved in managed care.
2. This physician was a nurse before she went to medical school. She
returned as a doctor to the hospital where she, as a nurse, had seen such
terrible abuses of patients.
3. You have a lot of reason to have a headache, because your husband is
not at home.
4. "Presenting a patient" is the formal way that physicians discuss cases
with each other. Students in internship and residency training programs are
taught how to "take a history", "write up" a patient, and then "present the
patient."
Taking a history: find out what is bothering the patient (the "complaint"), and
ferret from them key elements of their medical history
Writing up a patient: Write what the patient's "complaint" is, what you
determined from taking their "history," what you note from their previous
medical record, what your diagnosis is and what treatment you prescribe in
the appropriate way on a "chart" which becomes part of their legal medical
record.

Presenting the patient: Describe the history (symptoms and medical history) of the patient, your analysis and diagnoses, and your proposed treatment orally to a group of your peers and/or superiors. In teaching hospitals this procedure is highly ritualized and there is tremendous pressure to present with both the appropriate style (in a direct, authoritative way) and substance (citing numerous recent studies, and being able to refute any questions or arguments based on your superior "fund of knowledge.")

5. "Rounds" refers to the practice at training hospitals where interns, residents, supervising doctors, and specialists walk around the hospital together from patient to patient to discuss the cases. Interns and residents are expected to do "pre-rounds" before "rounds" in order to be able to learn the latest developments in the patient's progress and to thus be able to adequately "present" their patients to the rounding group of doctors.

6. "On call" for residency training programs means that the intern or resident is on hospital premises taking care of patients on various wards during off hours like weekends or all night. It usually means that the resident or intern gets little or no sleep, although they are usually allotted a bed and room in the hospital from which they may be reached by phone. ("On call" in other situations, like private practice, may involve working at the hospital during off hours, or simply being available by telephone or beeper to take calls from patients asking advice, or being available to come to the hospital on an "on call" basis.)

7. "Affirmative Action as a Majoritarian Device: Or, Do You Really want to Be a Role Model?" [89 Mich. Law Review 1222 (1991)] Delgado challenges the classic affirmative action role model which advocates that professionals inculcate their protege's with the dominant society's values. I would argue that the more immersed in Chicano Movement professional culture that a Chicano professional is, the less likely he or she will be to serve as a classic puppet role model. Chicano professional culture, as I have argued throughout the book, serves as an alternative and critical point from which to shape one's role as a professional and as a "role model."

8. A friend, after reading this section, commented that the time issue was not really unique to Chicanos and this section seemed unnecessary to her. I argue that while all professionals struggle with time in terms of family, job, and community obligations, minority professionals have stronger pressures on their time than most professionals because of their small numbers and the demands placed on them, as well as their Movement-cultivated sense of obligation to serve the community.

9. Yes, this is the same Chicano from the LLA that in Chapter 1 was appointed to a city commission

CHAPTER 8
Tortillas, Beans, and Bilingualism: Transformed Meanings

One afternoon at a H.I.S.M.E.T.[1] barbecue hosted in a beautiful Pasadena home, I was perusing the buffet table, laid out amply with fruit, breads, cheeses, and barbecue chicken, when suddenly the hostess burst out of the kitchen with a distracted look on her face, carrying a large bowl and a covered basket. "I forgot the beans and tortillas!" she said ruefully, looking around for sympathetic faces, and then deftly nestling the steaming dish of refried beans and basket of hot tortillas in with the rest of the food on the table.

It was a simple incident, but it stood out as a singularly symbolic moment to me. On the one hand, she was lamenting her forgetting the beans and tortillas as the essential side dishes to any Mexican meal just like my Alabama mother might chastise herself for forgetting the biscuits and gravy, the required accompaniment of all Southern cooking. Yet, on the other hand, tortillas and beans carried much more cultural weight then the average ethnic or regional food, particularly when they were being served by an obstetrician who had cut her college teeth on the Chicano Movement and was hosting a party with clear Movement orientation. Forgetting the beans and tortillas at a Chicano event was like forgetting why you were there in the first place. Tortillas and beans were the food of poverty, of Mexicanness, of the barrio and of the Movement. They were the foods that Anglo kids made fun of when you brought them in your lunch to school. They were the foods you fought to get included on the menu at your college dorm. They were not simply a remnant of the culture you left back home; they were a steaming, gustatory link to "the struggle," the struggle of Mexican farm workers and urbanites to rise above poverty,

177

your own struggle to get out of the barrio and into a profession, and the collective Movement struggle to help your fellow Chicanos "make it."

In this discussion of beans and tortillas, I suggest that while some cultural practices in Chicano professional life are nostalgic bits and pieces left over from blue-collar ethnic life, others have become transformed in their meanings through their use within the Chicano Movement, and their subsequent adoption in the lives of Movement doctors and lawyers. So there is a subtle but qualitative difference between a sixty-year-old Mexican American physician who listens to Linda Ronstadt in Spanish because she sings songs that remind him of his childhood, and those Chicano yuppies in their late thirties who flock to her concerts and play her at every barbecue. The difference between their respective enjoyments of this music is that Movement Chicanos love it not only because it reminds them of their childhood, but because Ronstadt is a Chicana who barely speaks Spanish but sings these songs with such relish and authenticity that her singing is a symbol of their own cultural pride. This is a pride which is rooted not only in the ethnic practices of blue-collar Chicano and immigrant Mexican families, but in the transformed cultural practices of Chicano student life within the Movement, practices which revolutionized and politicized the meaning of enjoying what is Mexican.

The Chicano Movement made a point of glorifying Mexican culture in conscious, cultivated contrast to Anglo American culture. A whole set of practices was established by Movement culture as "Chicano" in direct opposition to "Anglo." These practices included things like speaking and/or valuing the Spanish language, learning about and cultivating the Chicano/Mexican arts, and enjoying Mexican food together. Of course, it also included things about which Chicanos were less conscious, attitudes, feelings, and practices which were elements of culture in a more subtle sense. This included values like those I have discussed in previous chapters, like those of *"familia,"* [family] and *"corazón,"* [heart] through which Chicanos attributed to their culture a unique concern with family and community, and a feeling of responsibility and warmth for that collectivity, in contrast to what they perceived as the apparent family and community anomie and emotional coldness of "Anglos." It also includes the value of solidarity with the wider community based on an awareness that Mexican Americans as a group experience racism, and that this experience may not be understood or may be denied by the larger American society.

Chicanos consciously cultivated these kinds of collective practices and ideas of Mexican and Chicano culture during the student movement years in redress of the fact that their education had been dominated by the English language and "Anglo Saxon" culture. As adult professionals, most Chicanos now seem to take this cultivation of their ethnic uniqueness more for granted; it has become a daily, comfortable way of life, reinforced by the presence of substantial numbers of Chicanos from similar backgrounds who share similar practices and values.[2]

SPEAKING SPANISH

One of the strongest values cultivated by the Movement culture was that of speaking Spanish. Many college Chicanos who did not feel fluent in the language took Spanish classes, and even those who were fluent often took Spanish, Latin American, and Chicano literature classes to enhance their familiarity with the language. Similarly, Chicano students made trips or arranged studies in Spain and Mexico in order to enhance their language skills in Spanish.

The ability to speak Spanish was also cultivated as a deliberate challenge to the dominant monolingual culture and in redress of specific childhood experiences with English-speaking Anglos. Many Chicanos tell stories of how they were punished in elementary school for speaking Spanish. This was what a lawyer in his late twenties told me:

> I remember going through kindergarten, first and second grade, being terrified, because I didn't understand what was being said around me. And those were the good old days when teachers still punished Mexican kids for speaking Spanish. They used to make us sit in the corners, or stand in the corners—that type of stuff— anything they could do to humiliate us.

The ability to speak Spanish continues to be highly valued by Chicano professionals. I found that in my interviews the cultural attribute most valued by everyone with whom I spoke was speaking Spanish, whether or not the person was bilingual him/herself. Several Chicanos talked about studying in Spain and Mexico when they were students, and being proud of their subsequent fluency in Spanish. Others talked wistfully about their dreams of taking six months off from work and living in Mexico to polish up their Spanish, or more practically about sending their children to spend time with relatives in Mexico and take Spanish classes in school to ensure that at least they spoke the language.

Many times Chicanos whose Spanish is rusty end up having to polish it up for job situations which require its use. For example, many Chicano physicians I knew were delighted at how quickly their Spanish "came back to them" when they began working in barrio clinics with primarily Spanish-speaking patients. Several corporate lawyers saw it as an asset in their work with wealthy Mexican clients. In fact, many Chicanos take great pleasure and pride in being able to use Spanish in their work situations either formally with clients and patients, or informally catching up on the gossip with each other or greeting the kitchen staff and custodial help.

However, despite the high value placed on Spanish, the language is used in public situations primarily only in symbolic ways. This is apparently because many California Chicanos are not proficient in Spanish.[3] For example, speeches are often opened or closed with a bilingual greeting or leave taking like *"Buenas noches. Good evening,"* or *"Gracias. Fue un placer estar con Uds. esta noche."*

Those Chicanos who are fluent in Spanish may play a central role in the cultural texture and rhythm of public social interaction. In one small group of lawyers I observed, a Chicano who was fluent and literate in Spanish often used his comfortable facility with the language to interject comments or to break up a serious moment with humor. Spanish is often used in jokes, or in asides, both in public situations or in private. In small groups, a joke told in Spanish, or a few words quickly passed between people, indicates intimacy and ethnic belonging. People switch to Spanish in crowded elevators, or whisper gossip or comments to each other in Spanish when they assume they are among non-Spanish-speaking people. In large groups, Spanish can be used to make a strong statement, or to emphasize a particular point. In all these interactions, Spanish works as a signal which sets ethnic boundaries; those who understand, belong, and those who don't, do not.

One night at the 1989 M.A.B.A. installation banquet, a comedian named George Lopez kept the entire crowd of 500 people (a majority of them Chicanos and lawyers) laughing until many of them were close to tears. Most of his jokes required either a knowledge of Spanish and/or an intimate acquaintance with the local Chicano culture. For example, one of his longer jokes hinged on the word "*huevos*," slang for a man's testicles. Once the point of the joke had been made—obviously only understandable by those who were bilingual—he gestured out to the crowd, which was already roaring with laughter, and said condescendingly, "For those of you who don't understand Spanish, it's like a *fajita*." He said the word "*fajita*" in a flat Anglo American accent which sent the crowd into new gales of laughter.

The juxtaposition of the word "*fajita*" against a joke hinging on the word "*huevos*" incited laughter for several reasons. As with all his jokes, Lopez was setting up an insider/outsider tension. Those who were savvy enough to understand the joke, i.e. understand street Spanish, were the "insiders." Those who couldn't understand the joke because they didn't know Spanish were the "outsiders." Furthermore, the word "*fajitas* " was a code word for things that were artificially and commercially Mexican, just the kind of word to which the partial understanding of "outsiders" would be limited, since "*fajitas*" had recently become trendy on the menus of southwest nouveau cuisine restaurants and fast food places like Jack-in-the-Box. The message was one of exclusion/inclusion, that "we"—i.e. those that understand this joke because we know street Spanish—know about the "real" Mexican culture, unlike those "Anglos" or anglicized Chicanos, whose only knowledge of the culture is a popularized, trendy, commercial one.

This "insider/outsider" tension on which the humor of George Lopez hinged, reflects a tension in the Chicano professional community concerning the Spanish language. The fact that so many Chicanos do not speak fluent Spanish, although they value the skill highly and want their children to be bilingual, causes a certain amount of guilt or mild stress in people's lives. Often at work they may be expected to speak Spanish simply because they have a Hispanic last name. Or other Chicanos may subtly indicate judgement of another's inability to speak or understand the language. At a C.M.A.C. conference in 1989, an elderly Chicano physician named Samuel Galindo started his lecture with a story about a fellow Hispanic physician. As he related, once he and this colleague had been participants together on a medical panel at a conference. At some point people in the audience began denouncing the government and insulting the speakers in Spanish. Galindo described how his colleague calmly endured the ordeal, so much so that afterward Galindo asked him how he had handled himself so coolly. The man answered, "Well, you know, Sam. I don't understand Spanish very well."

Upon hearing this story, the C.M.A.C. audience burst into laughter. A Chicano who didn't understand enough Spanish to know when he was being insulted was an object of hilarity, if not of pity.

However, many Chicanos without fluent skills in Spanish respond to the problem in various ingenious ways, trying to improve their Spanish, some by reading novels and newspapers in the language, others by vacationing often in Mexico, others by speaking Spanish openly whenever they are with another Chicano who speaks it also. Still others find their Spanish improving when they work increasingly with Spanish-speaking clientele or patients.

In terms of their children, most Chicano professionals make a point to try to raise their children bilingually, even those who are not fully bilingual themselves. This is facilitated by the fact that Los Angeles is plentifully supplied with Spanish-speaking female immigrants who can be hired at minimum expense for both housework and childcare. Additionally, many parents take advantage of Spanish-speaking relatives and grandparents to tend their children. I recall the satisfied, almost smug expression of one Chicana lawyer's face when she explained her child care arrangements to me:

> Their grandmother takes care of them during the day. She speaks only Spanish to them. We've got only bilingual kids in this family, *¿verdad, mi'ja?*

She said the latter line in Spanish (right, my daughter?) as she swung the baby up in her arms and nuzzled her neck, confident that her child was well on the way to a satisfactory ethnic future.

"CULTURE," ARTS AND HISTORY

Along with valuing Spanish, the Chicano Movement emphasized an awareness and knowledge of Mexican and Chicano history and culture [Reich 89-93]. Chicanos organized their own classes on Chicano literature, art, and history and lobbied university campuses for Chicano Studies programs and/or departments. Drawing on the art forms they encountered in their studies of Mexican and Mexican American culture—Aztec and Mayan sculpture and architecture, Latin American, Spanish, and Chicano novels, Mexican murals and barrio street painting, Mariachi music and salsa—they experimented with their own art forms and relished their unique cultural expressiveness, so different from the forms offered them by a general college or university education.

Of all the cultural attributes valued by the Chicano movement culture, this is the area where Chicanos as professionals continue most strongly (or most consciously) to cultivate their ethnic uniqueness. A general awareness of Mexican and Chicano history and the arts is assumed among professionals, and those who are particularly knowledgeable are admired and sought out for their opinions. Chicanos proudly display Mexican and Chicano artwork and crafts in their homes and offices, meet each other in Mexican restaurants, rave about their Mexican vacations to resorts and pyramids, and share the latest novels of their favorite Chicano authors. Couples go to Linda Ronstadt (in Spanish) and Los Lobos concerts, and dance to salsa and cumbias at nightclubs like "*El Caché* " and "Miami Spice". On weekends they tote their children to Mexican and Chicano art exhibits and cultural events like the Cinco de Mayo celebration on Olvera Street. And of course, almost everyone appears to enjoy Mariachis (and an occasional strolling trio), since this is the preferred music for weddings, graduations, and professional banquets.

A perfect example of this continued love of Mexican culture is how professional-class occasions may be punctuated by earthy, traditional Mexican cultural expressions. At the same M.A.B.A. installation banquet which I mentioned earlier, during the pre-dinner hour, sleekly tuxedoed men and elegant women in fancy dresses (spangles, sparkles, bouffant puffs of shiny and metallic fabric, jewelry, pumps, and elaborate make up) were lingering and mingling decorously around a fountain-decked reception room, sipping dainty little cocktails. Suddenly a mariachi band broke into a rousing chorus of "*Volver.*" Within seconds, the low murmuring decorum of the assembly became focused on the music, and several full-throated, rowdy "*gritos*" (shouts) broke into the air from the sedate crowd. This interaction sent people around me into giggles and frankly pleased smiles. It was as though these successful professionals were delighted at this touch of blue-collar Mexicaness in the midst of their sophisticated celebration of upper-class status. It was a shout that registered a certain sense of humor and ironic perspective about all this professional glitz and glitter. And it was a reminder of what their organization was supposed to represent beyond pats on the collegial back and boosts up the career ladder; that is, providing resources and leadership for the Mexican American underclass who as yet had no such opportunity to strut in sartorial splendor on Saturday night at the downtown Sheraton.

A frank enjoyment of, and pride in, many other elements of Mexican culture is demonstrated by many professionals in their patronization of Mexican restaurants throughout the city. Tamayo's restaurant in downtown East Los Angeles, in particular, has become the preferred meeting place for casual drinks after work, or dinner on the weekend, as well as a popular place to hold professional meetings. I attended many C.M.A.C. and Stanford Chicano Alumni meetings in their back room for weeknight suppers of *"pollo rostizado"* from the huge open fireplace rotisserie, and Sunday morning brunches of *huevos rancheros*, mango juice, and chile salsa. Tamayo's is a large, old Spanish-style mansion, with dark beams and warm pastel walls, and paintings by the Mexican painter Rufino Tamayo hanging throughout. According to the explanation on the back of the menu, the restaurant was started under the sponsorship of a group of East Los Angeles Chicano businessmen who wanted a high class Mexican restaurant for Chicano professionals to patronize within the barrio. Every time I visited Tamayo's, the clientele appeared to be primarily Hispanic, and it is one of the places most frequently mentioned as a meeting spot by Chicano doctors and lawyers.

It is not just eating in Mexican restaurants that binds people in culinary ethnicity, but also talking about and sharing favorite Mexican foods at home with the family and with each other when people entertain. These foods usually include blue-collar Mexican standards like beans, rice, tortillas and *carnitas*, or something a little more special like *posole*, or *mole*, or the favorite for recuperating from a hard night's partying, *menudo*. Some people make a point to experiment with more gourmet Mexican and southwestern cooking, sharing recipes and ideas with their friends.

Patronizing Latino theater and art is widely enjoyed as well. While back in their Movement days, Chicano students learned about the Mexican muralists and painted their own murals in dormitories and on barrio buildings, they now take their children to see community murals and patronize the growing Chicano art scene. Several professional couples I knew followed up-and-coming Chicano artists faithfully as they were being discovered by the wider art community in Los Angeles. I attended numerous art openings with these friends, and it was fun to mingle and meet with other Chicanos interested in their community's art. One professional couple preferred to spend all their discretionary income on Chicano art rather than furniture, seeing it as both a cultural and monetary investment. Their relatively empty apartment had walls covered with exciting Chicano pieces.

Chicano theater was likewise becoming increasingly visible and popular in Los Angeles during this time. Some of it, as I talked about in Chapter 4, was a direct legacy of Chicano Movement street theater and paid homage to it in various ways. A major Los Angeles Latino theater project was in the works, I heard, just before I left Los Angeles in 1990. I learned this from a Chicano lawyer who worked at a major corporate law firm. He had volunteered his services as legal advisor to the group.

Not all involvement in arts and culture is so obviously elitist. Chicano professionals enjoy participating in weddings, parties and music in the blue-collar communities of L.A. People love to go to East L.A. to shop for Mexican cuts of meat, look for a piñata for their kids' birthday, enjoy a meal in a family-style restaurant, and listen to strolling mariachis. At a Los Lobos concert at the Hollywood Bowl, where I went with some physician friends, we were surrounded by screaming, dancing grandmothers, vatos, and babies from all the Los Angeles barrios. We were right in there with them.

However, no matter how often the Chicano professional dips into barrio Mexican life for his cultural pleasures, the fact remains that many of his arts and recreational activities strike an ambivalent elitist note. One of the most pleasant and visually beautiful celebrations of Chicano professional culture that I attended during my fieldwork was a MALDEF fundraising barbecue held in the beautiful backyard of a prominent Latino L.A. physician. This elegant function demonstrated Chicano professional culture at its finest and its most contradictory. It was a fundraiser for an organization that spearheaded civil rights legal battles, particularly for the disenfranchised Chicano masses. And yet, it was also a celebration of, and for, some of the most elite Chicanos in the City of Los Angeles. This was not a homeboy, back-yard, barrio barbecue with *carnitas* and Miller beer.

Everybody who was anybody in Chicano professional circles was present, because 1) MALDEF was widely acknowledged as a "pure" Chicano cause that everyone should support and 2) it was going to be a fabulous affair. The Pasadena house was a somewhat pretentious stone mansion with a long tree-lined driveway, a large swimming pool, gracious flower beds and flowing lawns. It had been featured recently in a local magazine.

Everywhere there were Mexican/Chicano decorative and gustatory touches. The backyard's wide green lawn was spread with tables, each graced with red, green, or white tablecloths and umbrellas, the Mexican national colors. The food was catered by Pollo Loco, a popular fast food Mexican franchise. Seagrams had donated huge icy barrels of their fruity coolers. A strolling *palleta* (popcicle) vendor, the kind ubiquitously seen in every barrio neighborhood, wended his way through the tables. The band was local and Latino, and a dance floor had been laid out on the grass and decked with an arch of brown and white balloons. Several of the women lawyers attending had turned their professional business suits in for beautiful, long embroidered traditional Mexican dresses, and some of the men wore *guayaberas*, the Mexican traditional dressy shirt. A visiting Mexican movie star attended and spoke for a few minutes. (I was never quite certain about the purpose of this particular touch of culture). Even the children were considered. A hired clown, tying balloons under the trees, amused the children with her bilingual antics.

Everything was organized and carried out to perfection. We met many friends there and had a lovely time. However, several incidents lent an ironic twist to the occasion for me. First, it was an expensive affair, requiring a ticket purchase of $50.00 per person, or affiliation with a major corporation that had bought an entire table of seats. Of course it *was* a fundraiser, but it was an exclusive party, nonetheless. I myself could not afford the ticket, and had to wangle my entry with some friends in the organization. Beto and I were allowed entrance if one of us would help park cars for an hour. Beto volunteered, so that I could conduct fieldwork. He later expressed some feelings of status disjunction to me about being both the hired help and a physician guest at the affair, but his dual role allowed me both time to observe, and a glimpse into another bit of telling cultural detail.

While he was parking cars, he overheard two of the hired musicians talking as they headed down the driveway. One of them had been asked to move his car to help ease some parking problem. Beto heard him comment to his friend sarcastically, in Spanish, something about moving his "Mercedes." It was clear, said Beto, that he was commenting from the "other side" (that of the working-class community), on the whole ritzy upper-class affair and the long line of BMW's and Mercedes Benz's parked on the elegant driveway. Beto himself was feeling fairly ambivalent about the whole elitist event, and empathized with the musician, since on his resident's salary, he couldn't afford to attend.

It must be admitted that the celebration of Mexican culture, professional style—whether or not it raises money for the Chicano masses—is not without its class-based ironies.

FAMILY

Chicano professional culture promotes the belief that "family" is a more important value to Chicanos and Mexicans than to Anglos. In Chapter 2, on networks, I talked about how the metaphor of *"familia"* is applied and extended to various levels of Chicano community. *"Familia"* is also used widely as a metaphor of contrast between "Chicano" and "Anglo" categories. This idea relies on a nostalgic sense that professional Chicanos have lost the blue-collar, Mexican childhood of close familial ties, a closeness encouraged by shared poverty and the Mexican value of extended family.

As one Chicana physician put it:

> I've always felt that a strong family value was very Latino, very Mexicano. Just that kind of commitment. Sure there are strong families in this country, but never to the degree that I was raised with, that I see in Mexico.
>
> . . . Every time we go down there [to Mexico], the nostalgia that I feel, the group support . . . Every time that we leave Mexico, it's a hard emotional bond to break. We go there and all the relatives pour out and they come and they receive you and all of a sudden you feel the strength of your family ties, and then when you go back to L.A. it's always a trauma.

In this vein, the *"familia"*—whether Mexican extended family for those from first generation immigrant backgrounds, or the barrio extended family, for those from later immigrant generations—serves as a foil to the enemy "Anglo" culture in the stories professionals tell about their lives. Chicanos tell about how they started out in the bosom of their families, usually extended families, and were gradually compelled, through their drive for educational success, to battle their way against what they perceive as the typical "Anglo" anomie of upward mobility. Sentiments like the following (paraphrased by me) are often expressed:

> Anglo parents kick their children out of the house at eighteen and don't help them, but our families support us through thick and thin.
>
> Anglo children abandon their parental and family obligations as they move up the educational and career ladder, but we send our financial aid checks home to help pay the rent and send our brothers and sisters to school.
>
> Anglos move all over the country and lose touch with their families, not even keeping track of their brothers and sisters, while we maintain close family ties.
>
> Anglos just aren't as warm and caring as Mexicans and Chicanos. They care more about independence and rules and regulations than they do about family and community.

Many Chicanos tell stories which support this strong "Latino" or "Mexican" commitment to family and community, dramatic stories of working late hours to put sisters through Catholic school, or stopping out of medical school to tend a dying grandmother, or buying a house with student loan money for parents living in federal projects. However, other Chicanos relate stories of divorce, child abuse, alienation from family, sibling rivalry and the like. As one Chicano lawyer (deeply immersed in Chicano Movement culture) said to me vehemently: "That "familia" stuff is bunk . . . .I came from a dysfunctional family with mild child abuse, and I hate my parents. And I know a lot of Chicanos who would say the same thing if they were honest about it."

The point, of course, is not whether or not Chicano families are stronger or more closely knit than putative "Anglo" families. I would not presume to judge that. The point is that within Chicano Movement culture, the value of "*familia*" is strongly idealized, and furthermore, that being separated from one's family, or not feeling responsible for family members—often including the extended family—is considered an "Anglo" trait.

What makes this value potentially troublesome for professional Chicanos is the fact that their pre-professional and professional lives often take them out of the neighborhoods and family networks which sustained this sense of family and community togetherness. As professionals in training, they ordinarily left home to attend school, and then as professionals, they usually buy homes outside of the barrios where they grew up. However, many have in a sense "transferred" or extended some of this sense of family obligation, as I suggested in the chapter on Networks, to their Chicano friends, colleagues, clients/patients, and the Mexican/American community at large. This extension has included the notion that somehow they as Chicanos have stronger bonds to their extended "familia" of friends and community than "Anglos" in similar positions, and this sense serves as a powerful sympathetic bond between them.

Again, this is an example of how an ethnic blue-collar value has been transformed through the Movement. The *"familia"* of extended genetically tied family has been transformed to include both the *"familia"* of friends and comrades forged in the struggle to get through school, and the *"familia"* of the wider Chicano community for whom one struggles as a Movement-oriented professional.

LOSING OR CREATING CULTURE?

While I as an anthropologist, as well as a Chicano Movement enthusiast, feel strongly that cultural practices even as simple as serving beans and tortillas are important forms of cultural resistance, not all professional Chicanos feel the same. In one conversation with a Chicana family practice doctor with whom I felt very comfortable, I talked volubly about my ideas of an emerging Chicano professional culture, and was surprised and disappointed that she, as someone who was so active in Chicano professional circles, did not see my point at all. In fact, she lamented that she was "losing" her culture, that she had left it back in her home town with her aunts and her mother making tamales and other "goodies" at Christmas, and that she would have virtually nothing cultural to pass on to her children. In a similar vein, a Chicano judge made a laughing remark when I brought up the subject to him, about "Chicano yuppies," who might send their kids to ballet *folklórico* class, go to Mexico for vacations, and visit the Cinco de Mayo parade, but whom he felt were gradually "assimilating" and "looking like everyone else."

My friend Luis Duran, who is an activist in Chicano medical circles, dedicated to a unique Chicano way of doing medicine, likewise laughed when I asked him if there were other cultural elements which were important to him besides the value of "helping your people." He said, "What, you mean—like rain dances?" For him, Spanish was a tool for helping under-served people, and cultural practices like art and literature were extraneous to what was really important in Chicano life.

I do not think it is a coincidence, however, that those Chicanos who felt that unique cultural practices and traits were not an important part of Chicano professional "resistance" to the dominant culture of professionalism, were Chicanos who had not participated in the undergraduate movement in California during the sixties and early seventies. They had missed the unique Chicano cultural renaissance which occurred on most campuses. This cultural movement was combined integrally with the political movement, so that Chicano art, food, theater, dance, and the subtlest cultural practices were considered important elements of political defiance against the Anglo system, if not the most important vehicles for that defiance.[4]

However, probably the most important reason that so many Chicanos, even those Movement educated individuals who continue to enjoy Mexican and Chicano cultural life as professionals, believe that they are losing at least some of their "culture," is that they have a limited definition of "culture." Chicano professionals often perceive culture as a collection of elements which belonged to them when they lived in the barrio with their blue-collar, usually first or second generation families. "Culture," in this sense, is understood as something they *had* in their childhood, and then often *lost* in the process of becoming educated and changing class position.

This attitude is classically American, rooted in the common experience of most of us as children (or children's children) of immigrants. It assumes that what our ancestors practiced and believed in "the old country" was "culture," and to the extent that we change our beliefs and practices from those of our parents and grandparents, we are "losing" culture. Culture is thus perceived as an heirloom chest of pure traditions that can be carefully handed down from one generation to another, or can be irretrievably lost.

Modern anthropologists see culture as something much more fluid and changing. Individuals inherit certain practices, beliefs, feelings, and attitudes from the generation that raises them. But parents are not handing over an untouched and unaltered treasure to their children. They have adapted, modified, trimmed, selected, and transformed this cultural inheritance in relationship to their own and their generation's experiences. What they pass on is a changed and ever-changing set of ideas and traditions.

One of my favorite incidents involving the way culture change and continuity is experienced and expressed by Chicano professionals occurred one day at a Stanford Chicano Alumni barbecue. It was a mixed group of about fifteen people—lawyers, bilingual translators, doctors, college administrators, and the like—all Chicano except for myself, and all except for two spouses, friends and acquaintances from Casa Zapata, the Stanford Chicano Theme House.

At one point in the afternoon, the males in the group began to gather around the door stoop, draped on stools, chairs, and leaning against the house wall, sipping beers and joking in a soft, slurred staccato of code-switching and throaty laughs. The women remained at the periphery, eating, chatting in pairs, or cleaning up.

Until that moment, the afternoon had passed like any other gathering of college friends, men and women mingling, eating, throwing balls around with their kids. But this closed clustering of males, beers, and joking bilingual repartee was qualitatively different. I immediately felt a stab of recognition, and without thinking, jumped into the middle of the group waving my hands, laughing, and saying, "Hey, wait a minute! This reminds me of something! All these men gathered around with their beers . . . and the women running around cleaning up!"

There was a moment of silence. Then one of the cockier males took my challenge up: "Hey, man, the culture's not dead!" he declared, holding his beer can up. The moment dissolved into laughs, and I left the circle shaking my head and chuckling with the rest of them.

No, the culture wasn't dead, and in spite of the patriarchal, atavistic undertones of that circle of males, I was delighted. The culture wasn't dead because it was alive in the memories and practices of Chicanos like this, and it fueled a sense of solidarity and opposition to the dominant culture even in the ranks of such successful professionals as these.

NOTES

1. The Hispanic Education and Training Program is a California statewide program which trains medical students to practice medicine in shortage areas of California. The program rotates to different shortage areas, and works with local, primarily Chicano doctors, placing students under particular physicians as preceptors, and involving them in seminars and

classes about health care and career choices. It is part of the California Area Health Education Center System (A.H.E.C.).

2. The elements of culture with which this chapter deals are those most commonly understood as "culture", by Chicanos as well as Anglos—language, arts, family values, history. See the next chapter for a discussion of the definition of "culture," and how common misconceptions of what culture is contribute to assumptions about assimilation.

3. One lawyer originally from south Texas contrasted how different the use of Spanish was in California from its use in Texas. In Texas, a majority of Chicanos grow up speaking Spanish, and use it in their daily social intercourse with each other. Here in California, he explained, a lot of Chicanos don't speak the language, so those that do are afraid to use it too much for fear of not being understood.

4. An art show which traveled around California in 1991 called C.A.R.A.: Chicano Art, Resistance and Affirmation documented the depth and creativity of this symbiotic relationship between politics and art. Most of the Movement Chicanos I knew saw the show and it was a popular topic of conversation.

CHAPTER 9

Assimilation Revisited

Like many members of the Movement generation, I am concerned about *assimilation*, about whether or not Chicanos are "selling out," losing contact with their Movement values and practices and becoming like "all the other" professionals. What I discovered in Los Angeles, and record in this work, is that the answer is far more complicated than a simple "Yes or No."

The first problem is the concept of "assimilation" itself. Movement Chicanos in their university years loaded the word "assimilation" with ideas as diverse as exchanging tortillas for white bread, joining a successful corporate law firm, living in a neighborhood outside the barrio, exploiting blue-collar Mexicans for one's own gain, marrying an Anglo, and wearing a suit and tie. "Assimilating," "selling out," or "becoming a *vendido*" were catch all phrases used during Movement years, and then later by Movement Chicanos as professionals, in innumerable different situations to judge and make claims on the activities and ideas of oneself and other Chicanos.

The idea borrows heavily from the classic American myth about assimilation and ethnicity. The myth assumes that being economically and socially successful in American society means losing cultural uniqueness and becoming a generic middle-class American. The idea, at least as Chicanos developed it, also borrows somewhat from classic Marxist analysis which equates belonging to a particular class with being exclusively concerned with that class's interests. Influenced by both the popular tradition and Marxist analysis, Movement Chicanos were saturated with the notion, during their university years, that becoming successful professionals was a serious threat to their unique identity as Chicanos who both practiced an alternative ethnic culture, and cared about the fates of their fellow working-class Mexican Americans.

Most Movement Chicano professionals continue to feel the tension generated by this notion of assimilation and the contradictions such a belief creates in their conceptions of themselves as successful professionals. A perspective widened by an anthropological view of culture may offer a way out of the dilemma.

The first assumption to tackle is the tendency to equate culture with blue-collar Mexican practices. Chicanos often feel that to the extent that they "lose" these practices, they are "losing" their cultural uniqueness. As I explained in the preceding chapter, such an idea betrays a limited notion of culture. Chicanos during their university years shaped their own culture out of the elements of their former blue-collar "Mexican" lives and the new elements they encountered in universities during the turbulent, exciting years of the late sixties and early seventies. The culture they created within their Movement helped shape a unique generation of individuals which would carry that culture into their later lives as professionals, transform it to fit their own new realities, and spread its influence on other generations of Mexican Americans. Chicanos never "lost" their culture; culture is not something you carry around in a backpack and exchange for a briefcase when you become a lawyer or doctor. Culture is a way of looking at the world which both endures and changes as people grow older. People of the Movement generation forged a culture of tremendous power in the days of their youth, which continues to cast its influence on the personal lives and politics of Chicano professionals today.

The most important way that Movement culture endures within the Chicano professional class is through the value of identification with, and sense of responsibility for, the blue-collar Mexican American. Of course this value is not simply about altruism; while some Chicanos quietly sacrifice time and energy to helping their "*gente*," other Chicano professionals carve out reputations, jobs, and political careers from the claim to be serving the interests of the under represented, under-served "Chicano community." Most Chicanos actually live out the value with a mix of self-sacrifice and self promotion.

The point is that Chicanos from the Movement generation, as well as Chicanos who are not from that generation but who have been influenced by the strength of Movement culture, are creating an alternative form of professionalism which challenges old notions about ethnicity and assimilation and which serves as the basis for claims to political power in the Southwest. This alternative *culture* is manifest in various dimensions of Chicano professional life, as I detailed in the chapters of this book, i.e. through shared ritual and mythic forms, through the genre of experienced racism stories, through speaking Spanish and code-switching, through a cultivated set of networks experienced as "family," and so on.

Furthermore, this alternative culture has been, and is being shaped within the boundaries of a unique confluence of historical events. The most seminal historical circumstance was the political and cultural upheaval of the Fifties, Sixties, and early Seventies, particularly the Civil Rights and affirmative action struggles. A new generation of blue-collar Chicanos, the first significant group in terms of numbers, entered universities and created a cohort of educated ethnic professionals with a unique culture and a compelling ideology. This group is currently beginning to make great inroads into politics and culture in the Southwest.

More recent historical factors also contribute to this professional culture. The fact that there is increasing immigration from Latin American countries, particularly Mexico, creates a need for Spanish-speaking, bicultural professionals and the possibility of a political and cultural constituency for an emerging Chicano elite. In the wider, national political arena, ethnic politics in general has been gaining influence steadily, as various groups increasingly make claims on the identity and direction of American politics today; Chicanos are becoming one of the most vocal of these groups. The Free Trade Agreement with Mexico has opened up business and vocational opportunities for Chicano professionals as well, whether they are involved directly in promoting and benefiting directly from its business and legal effects, or are involved in services and political activism seeking to protect and defend the interests of working-class Mexicans and Mexican Americans who are being affected by its implementation.

The latest challenges include an increased public hostility toward immigrants and non-Whites, as reflected in propositions 187 and 209 in California, affecting immigrant status and affirmative action, respectively. What this backlash against non-whites means to the Chicano professional community remains to be studied in detail. Proposition 209 will effect the Chicano professional class most directly, since it will mean a diminishing population of new recruits into the culture, not to mention to the political arena. It will undoubtedly also effect how Chicano professionals feel about their own historical privilege and their obligations to those behind them who have even less chance of "making it" in the current political climate. All of these historical factors create an environment in which Chicano professionals continue to shape a professionalism, a politics, and a culture uniquely their own.

Of course, in this particular study, I make claims only about what is happening with the Chicano professional-class in Los Angeles. This is not a comparative or all-inclusive analysis. I am confident that although Mexican Americans in Texas, New Mexico, Colorado and other states experienced and created a Chicano Movement in the 1960's and 1970's, what has happened to those Chicanos who have since become professionals is undoubtedly different in many, if not all respects.

In summary, I argue that neither laypersons nor scholars should make assumptions about assimilation based on theory. Ethnic life in the United States needs a different kind of analysis and understanding. It is in the intricate warp and woof of historical and particular details, given shape loosely by theoretical and structural models, that we ultimately see most clearly, the rich, diverse cultural patterns that make up our world. Simplistic assimilation models based on American myths about social mobility and culture, or rigid models of class identification, are not adequate to explain what is happening with Chicano professionals today.[1]

The professional Chicanos who now control Mexican American politics in Los Angeles are the products of their own cultural creation in the Chicano Movement. Their consciousness was forged in their youth during a unique period of history, and the cultural practices and beliefs which shape both their personal and their political lives today are still influenced by their experiences as a particular and unique generation. They are "assimilating" in the sense that many are successfully moving into the professional class, putting on ties, living in middle-class and wealthy neighborhoods, driving expensive cars, hiring maids and gardeners, and taking exotic vacations. But they are not "assimilating" in the sense that they are becoming like the average, "Anglo" professional. Chicano professionals, at least in Los Angeles, are creating their own organizations, rituals, and cultural forms which are unique to themselves. The force which binds them in their uniqueness is Chicano Movement culture, a blend of practices bound by an ideology of concern for the Mexican American blue-collar community and generated by a profound sense of history and destiny as a people.

NOTE

1. Micaela di Leonardo has made a similar plea in her book on Italian-American ethnics, "The Varieties of Ethnic Experience: Kinship, Class, and Gender Among California Italian-Americans," 1984.

CHAPTER 10
Postscript: Participant Observation in a Postmodern Chicano Context

As every anthropologist knows, even those who are new at the profession like me, doing ethnography is not like it used to be. "Natives" talk back. Sometimes they don't let you into their countries. Many of them feel hostile at just the mention of the word "anthropologist." And in the case of Chicanos, since 1971 when Octavio Romano-V. [1971a, 1971b] first blasted Anglo anthropologists for their biased analyses of Mexican American culture, Chicanos have done much of their own research on their communities, warily guarding the door to Chicano social discourse from what they perceive as the potentially exploitative and culturally-biased Anglo researcher [Rosaldo 1985].

The legacy of the Romano-V. critique makes it difficult for Anglo anthropologists like myself, who are sensitive to "native" critique, to do ethnographic analysis of Chicanos without at least some explanation, or justification, or positioning of themselves up front as cultural observers within particular historical and political contexts. In this dilemma we are not alone. Largely because the non-Western "natives" who have traditionally been the subjects of ethnographic research are becoming educated and are insisting on defining themselves to the world without the mediation of western intellectuals, recent trends in anthropology encourage "dialogic" ethnography, including a nuanced understanding of the intricate historical dynamics of the colonized/colonizer relationship.

My explanation, or justification for feeling that I can write with integrity, if not knowledge, about Chicano professionals, has a personal history. In 1972 I was placed in the Chicano Theme House at

Stanford University as a freshman. At the time, Anglos had no choice about whether or not they would live in this dormitory, but I was actually pleased at the opportunity because I spoke Spanish, having lived in Mexico City for a summer, and was interested in Mexican culture.

However, I was not prepared for the culture that I encountered at Casa Zapata. It wasn't "Mexican", and it wasn't "American." It was something entirely new, and it challenged the depths of my very Anglo, middle-class, WASP identity. Despite the concern of my parents, I stayed in the dormitory for three years and, strangely enough, came of age within the Chicano Movement culture. I now consider myself a member of that cohort, biological inheritance and pre-college cultural training notwithstanding. I make that claim because I encountered the "World" as an impressionable, sheltered young adult within the discourse of the Movement, among Chicano peers, and my perspective on politics, class and many other things has continued to be more "Chicano" than anything else.

However, good member of the cohort that I am, and yet still very much a self conscious "Gringa," I can't help but remember with a rueful laugh a brief conversation which occurred during fieldwork. It sums up some of the ironies of my situation. I was attending a M.A.B.A. banquet honoring Latino judges. That night, I had not been able to persuade my husband to play (Chicano/male) escort, so I found a place at one of the tables next to a physician friend who was attending with her lawyer husband. Gracious lady that she is, she introduced me around the table as an anthropologist studying Chicano professionals. As I smiled and nodded to each person in turn, a judge sitting across from me, who looked about my own age, muttered under his breath: "Oh, so they're studying *us* now, huhn?"

"*They*." "*Us*." I get tired of explaining myself sometimes. Whereas my long term Chicano friends tell me they don't think of me as "Anglo," in every new situation I am just another "gringa." There will always be tension. It reminded me of the words of the Movement poet José Montoya:

> Rosa, te quiere mi 'ama cause
> The social worker's here!
> Dios mío! A visit from the gava!
> Alsen la mesa, levanten
> Esas garras . . .

Americans were always at my
House. The ones who came to
Strip my Indian flesh from me
And to crucify me with germ-bearing
Labels more infectious than rusty
Nails . . .

AMERICANS AT MY HOUSE!

Cuando no era el probation officer
Era el councilor de la escuel,
La jura or some long haired,
Lostlamb, manic chick offering
Us the world so she could write
Her thesis.

—Its' My Turn to Kick the Can!
Montoya 1972 [1]

I would like to think that I stand in a different category from this
"lostlamb gava" of the poem, but maybe I'm kidding myself.[2] Anyway,
I have felt compelled to write this book, to explore my own thoughts
and observations of the community and culture within which I came of
age, and to share them with a wider audience. This is simply the
intellectual fruit of my own complex and contradictory relationship to
the Movement community.

And yet, I still feel the need for some sort of justification, or
explanation, particularly because of the kind of analysis I engage in
here. This is because I am working on two possibly contradictory
levels of participation/analysis in this work. At one level I reveal my
cultural positioning as a "believing" member of the Chicano
generation, moved to tears at such celebrations of the Movement myth
as the C.M.A.C. reunion, and angered at the usurping claims of the
younger generation of Chicano lawyers in the M.A.B.A./Latino
Lawyers conflict. However, I also may appear to betray my position as
an outsider—as anthropologist more than Angla—to the extent that I
expose the contradictions within the professional Chicano culture,
deconstruct the Movement myths, and practice the kind of observant
anthropology which to Movement Chicanos may appear to be the
essence of disengaged, exploitative ("Anglo") social analysis.

The problem is one with which many anthropologist wrestle today. In his introduction to the collection on politics and postmodernism, *Universal Abandon?*, Andrew Ross [1988: vii-xviii] points out how the politics of color, gender, class, and gender identification remain largely tied to essentialist notions of respective group political identities and he cautions the postmodern analyst, engaged in the process of deconstructing these identities, not to be "blind" to the historical and political efficacy of such claims. Ross is making a carefully-couched point to his fellow leftists turned postmodern deconstructionists, that the claims that such groups as Chicanos, Blacks, gays, women, and workers make on the political scene are valid "subject positions" within the "radical pluralism" of postmodern politics [xi]. It is an important precaution, and one that I take to heart, particularly since I participate directly in the subject position of "woman" and indirectly in that of "Chicano."

But nevertheless, I contend that it is possible to both take a particular subject position, complete with its essentialized and usually biologized claims to identity, in order to make political claims and challenges on the existing system of inequalities and injustices, and at the same time to understand how that subject position relies on culturally-constructed notions of identity which are intellectually untenable according to the paradigms of current academic discourse.

This is crucial in the case of Chicano professionals today, since the Movement myths based on culturally constructed, essentialist notions of Mexican/Mexican American/Chicano/ "racial"/ cultural/national/class identity are being challenged by a new generation within a new post-modern historical context. I have documented how such universalist categories as "race," "class," "family," and "gender" have been employed by the Movement generation to shape ethnic unity, and are now being challenged. "Race" has become a slippery concept, since it is up for debate just who belongs to this "*raza*" now—does it include Puerto Ricans and Nicaraguans? "Class" is problematic since it is apparent that Chicanos who have changed classes are not necessarily behaving in predictable class-determined ways, as it was feared in Movement years. "Family" ideas are questioned as some Chicanos challenge the whole family unity myth at both the biological level and the metaphorical community level. And "gender" questions are cracking wide open the question of nationalist opposition, as women no longer tend the hearth fires of the Movement and insist on their own roles as political actors and not just symbols of a culture which needs "defending" by its "males."

Although my analysis highlights the contradictions in Movement culture, I do not challenge the continued need for a culture of opposition generated by Chicanos, particularly a culture rooted in an awareness of the shared experience of racism. However, the Movement culture is no longer adequate to address current realities. The argument between generations which I describe in this thesis, as revealed in ritual contests, living room conversations, and debates over ethnic labeling, is shaking up the old order of thinking and moving the ethnic debate into new, untried political territory. The question is whether or not the fire of resistance which characterized the culture of the Movement generation and forever changed the face of politics in the Southwest, can be passed in some form to the next generation without quenching its urgent alterity.

I see this analysis as a contribution to the task of passing on what was most important, most radical, most *ethical*, if you will, about the Movement culture. I speak both from within, and from outside, the Movement generation culture, describing what I see, analyzing through what I know from experience, and calling for deeper self examination of our/their cultural assumptions. Perhaps here I cross the border from ethnography to something else—politics, ethics, religion, teleology—but in this sense my work follows the spirit of "Chicano" social science, where it is assumed that no science is value free, and where research for the purpose of bettering the "community" carries the highest value. I can only hope that my analysis contributes to a richer discourse and a greater understanding of the recent cultural history of Chicanos and Chicano professionals in Los Angeles and the greater Southwest.

NOTES

1. Crude translation:

Rosa, my mother wants you 'cause the social worker's here!

My God! A visit from the White girl! Clear the table, pick up those stockings . . .

Americans were always at my House. . . . When it wasn't the probation officer it was the counselor from school, The judge, or some long haired . . .

2. Actually, I like to think of myself in terms of a more "native" category. A hard-core Movement lawyer, who was now a mover and shaker in L.A. politics, introduced me politely one evening to some friends as a "metiche." In English, this means a gossipy, nosey, interfering woman. I can live with that.

Appendix

MEXICAN AMERICAN BAR ASSOCIATION

M.A.B.A. was founded in 1960 and celebrated its 30th annual officer's installation banquet in February 1990. Its members annually elect a President, President-Elect, Vice-President, Secretary, Treasurer and Newsletter Editor as well as a Board of Trustees. This board is structured to represent not only long-time members and law practitioners, but also newcomers to the organization and to law practice . The leadership of M.A.B.A. currently represents a wide variety of people who were educated in various law schools. There does not seem to be a monopoly by any one clique or group on the organization, although this is a matter of controversy, as I note in chapter seven.

Its 1987 membership directory listed 250 attorneys and 32 judges as dues-paying members, and the newsletter goes out to over 700 other people. Membership is confined to California Bar Association certified attorneys and law students.

Monthly attendance at weeknight meetings varies from a minimum of fifty, to over one hundred people. Meetings are often held in conjunction with other ethnic Bar associations. Attendance at the annual officer installation banquet included about five-hundred people.

M.A.B.A. states as its goals the following (from a 1990 brochure):

Improve the professional skills of Latino attorneys
Increase the number of appointed and elected Latino
    judicial officers.
Provide leadership opportunities for the youth of our
    community.

Promote social, economic, and legal equality within the
Latino community.

M.A.B.A. has several active committees: Communications,
Community Relations, Fundraising, Immigration, Judiciary, (makes
recommendations to the Governor's office for judicial appointment)
Latina Lawyers, Law Student Relations/Youth Outreach, MABA-PAC
(raises funds for Latino/a attorneys running for judicial office) and
Membership/Professional Development.

The organization sends out a monthly newsletter, a yearly
membership directory, and invitations to innumerable special events.
It also sponsors continuing legal education seminars, as well as public
service projects like a Domestic Violence Clinic, Law Student Mentor
program for first year law students, and providing public service
announcements addressing immigrant rights, consumer protection and
other concerns of the Chicano/Latino community.

Membership offers benefits to its members of discounts on
disability insurance, Credit Union membership, a consumer protection
plan and a few others.

CHICANO/LATINO MEDICAL ASSOCIATION OF CALIFORNIA

C.M.A.C. was founded in December 1988. It has a President, Vice-
President, Secretary and Treasurer; also a 12-member Board of
Directors, and a set of by-laws. It holds annual statewide conferences,
usually in Los Angeles, although occasionally in northern California
and for a time it was meeting monthly at Tamayo's restaurant.

In 1990 C.M.A.C. had 150 dues-paying members, and it has
southern and northern California divisions, although the Los Angeles
branch is the most organized and active.

The organization's stated goals are the following:

1. To address the health care needs of the Chicano Latino
   community.
2. To promote greater access to quality health care for the Chicano
   Latino populations.
3. To provide continued support and guidance to the Chicano Latino
   residents and medical students.
4. To provide continuing medical education programs for health
   professionals practicing in Chicano Latino communities.

5. To promote Chicano Latino health policy issues at state and local levels.
6. To expand professional and career opportunities for it's members.
7. To support Chicano Latino faculty development and research.

C.M.A.C. has several standing committees: Legislative, Education, Fundraising, Publications, Public Relations, and Membership. It has a northern and southern California division.

LATINO LAWYERS ASSOCIATION

The L.L.A. was started by a small group of first year Latino (primarily Mexican American) corporate lawyers, most of them recent graduates of Stanford, Harvard or other Ivy League law schools, as an organization to support the concerns of Latino lawyers working in corporate law firms. It sponsored its first annual "Latino Summer Associates Reception" in August 1987 to welcome Latino lawyers who would be coming to work in Los Angeles corporate law firms after they graduated from law school. In the Fall of 1988 this association became a committee under the Mexican American Bar Association.

THE STANFORD CHICANO/HISPANIC ALUMNI CLUB OF SOUTHERN CALIFORNIA

This club is an official affiliate of the Stanford Alumni Association. It has a President, Vice President, Secretary and Treasurer, as well as an official Historian and a Board of Directors. It has an occasional newsletter, and hosts several yearly events, such as a reception for prospective Hispanic Stanford students in the spring, and a reception for new Hispanic Stanford students in the late summer. It also hosts more spontaneous events like Christmas parties and summer barbecues.

In June 1989 it had 55 regular, dues-paying members.

Bibliography

Anderson, Benedict
1983   *Imagined Communities: Reflections on the Origin and Spread of Nationalism*. New York: Verso.

Barrera, Mario
1979   *Race and Class in the Southwest: A Theory of Racial Inequality*. Notre Dame: University of Notre Dame Press.

1982   Chicano Class Structure. In *History, Social Structure, and Politics*, pp. 40-55.

Blauner, Robert
1972   *Racial Oppression in America*. New York: Harper & Row, Publishers.

Briones, Angelina
1974   "A Token Education." In Chicanismo, Volume 6, Issue 2, pp. 4-5. Stanford: Chicano Press Stanford.

Chavez, Linda
1991   *Out of the Barrio: Toward a New Politics of Hispanic Assimilation*. New York: Basic Books, HarperCollins Publishers.

Cruz, Patricia
1974   "A Mis Hermanas" in *Imágenes de la Chicana*. Stanford Chicano Press. Menlo Park: Nowels Publications.

Delgado, Richard
1991   "Affirmative Action as a Majoritarian Device: Or: Do You
        Really Want to be a Role Model?" In *89 Michigan Law
        Review 1222.*

Di Leonardo, Micaela
1984   *The Varieties of Ethnic Experience: Kinship, Class and
        Gender Among California Italian-Americans.* Ithaca and
        London: Cornell University Press.

Ehrenreich, Barbara
1989   *Fear of Falling: The Inner Life of the Middle-class.* New
        York: Pantheon Books.

Enloe, Cynthia
1989   *Bananas, Beaches, and Bases: Making Feminist Sense of
        International Politics.* Berkeley and Los Angeles: The
        University of California Press (1990).

Fanon, Franz
1967   *Black Skin, White Masks.* New York: Grove Press, Inc.

Gann, L.H. and Peter J. Duignan
1986   *The Hispanics in the United States: A History.* (Hoover
        Institution on War, Revolution, and Peace, Stanford,
        California). Boulder and London: Westview Press.

Gibson, Charles, ed.
1971   *The Black Legend: Anti-Spanish Attitudes in the Old World
        and the New.* New York: Knopf

Gilman, Sander
1992   *The Jew's Body.* New York & London: Routledge.

Hayes-Bautista, David E.
1992   *No Longer a Minority: Latinos and Social Policy in
        California.* Los Angeles: U.C.L.A. Chicano Studies Research
        Center Publications.

Hietala, Thomas R.
1985   *Manifest Design: Anxious Aggrandizement in Late
        Jacksonian America.* Ithaca and London: Cornell University
        Press.

Hinkson, John
1990   "Postmodernism and Structural Change? "In *Public Culture"*
        Vol. 2 No.2. Spring 1990, p. 82-101.

Horsman, Reginald
1981   *Race and Manifest Destiny: The Origins of American Racial
        Anglo-Saxonism.* Cambridge, Mass. and London: Harvard
        University Press.

Islas, Arturo, ed.
1974   *Miquitzli: A Journal of Arte, Poesia, Cuento, y Canto.*
        Volume 2, Issue 1. Winter Quarter. Stanford: Chicano Press,
        Stanford. p.5.

Limón, José E.
1981   "The Folk Performance of "Chicano" and the Cultural Limits
        of Political Ideology." In . . . *And other Neighborly Names:
        Social Process and Cultural Image in Texas Folklore.* Eds.
        Richard Bauman and Roger D. Abrahams. Austin: University
        of Texas Press. Pp. 197-225. Also appears in *Language and
        Speech in American Society: A Compilation of Research
        Papers in Sociolinguistics.* Eds. Richard Bauman and Joel
        Sherzer. Austin: Southwest Educational Development
        Laboratory, 1980, No.62.

1982a   "History, Chicano Joking, and the Varieties of Higher
        Education: Tradition and Performance as Critical Symbolic
        Action." In *Journal of the Folklore Institute,* 19, pp. 141-166.

1982b   "El Meeting: History, Folk Spanish, and Ethnic Nationalism
        In a Chicano Student Community." In *Spanish in the United
        States: Sociolinguistic Aspects.* Eds. Lucia Elias-Olivares and
        Jon Amastae. Cambridge: Cambridge University Press, pp.
        301-332.

Mannheim, Karl
1952   *Essays on the Sociology of Knowledge.* New York: Oxford
        University Press, pp. 288-318.

Mares, E.A.
1973   "Myth and Reality: Observations on American Myths and the
        Myth of Aztlán," in *El Cuaderno,*(De vez en cuando) Vol. 3,
        No. 1, Winter 1973, Journal from La Academia de La Nueva
        Raza, Dixon, New Mexico, pp.35-50.

Montoya, Jose
1972   *El Sol Y Los De Abajo and other R.C.A.F. Poems.* San
        Francisco: Ediciones Pocho-Che.

Muñoz, Carlos Jr.
1989   *Youth, Identity, Power: The Chicano Movement.* New York:
        Verso.

Paredes, Américo
1978   "On Ethnographic Work Among Minority Groups." In *New
        Directions in Chicano Scholarship*, ed. R. Romo, R. Paredes,
        pp.1-32. La Jolla: University of California San Diego,
        Chicano Studies Monograph Series.

Paz, Octavio
1961   *The Labyrinth of Solitude: Life and Thought in Mexico.*
        Trans. by Lysander Kemp. New York, London: Grove Press,
        Inc., Evergreen Books Limited.

Powell, Philip W.
1971   *Tree of Hate: Propaganda and Prejudices Affecting United
        States Relations With the Hispanic World.* New York: Basic
        Books.

Reich, Alice H.
1989   *The Cultural Construction of Ethnicity: Chicanos in the
        University.* New York: AMS Press Inc.

Rodarte, Irene
1972   "Machismo vs. Revolution." In *Chicanismo*, Volume 3,
        Number 2, April 14, 1972, Stanford: Chicano Press.

Rodriguez, Richard
1982   *Hunger of Memory: The Education of Richard Rodriguez.*
        New York: Bantam Books.

1988   "Success Stories: Voices from an Emerging Elite," in *Los
        Angeles Times Magazine*, November 6,1988, pp. 8-19,55-56.

Romano-V., Octavio Ignacio
1971a   Social Science, Objectivity, and the Chicanos. In *Voices:
        Readings from El Grito: A Journal of Contemporary Mexican
        American Thought, 1967-71.* Octavio I Romano-V. ed.
        Berkeley: Quinto Sol Publications, Inc., pp.30-41.

1971b   The Anthropology and Sociology of the Mexican-Americans: The Distortion of Mexican-American History, in *Voices: Readings from El Grito: A Journal of Contemporary Mexican American Thought, 1967-1971.* Octavio I Romano-V. ed. Berkeley: Quinto Sol Publications, Inc. pp. 43-56.

Rosaldo, Renato
1980   *Ilongot Headhunting 1883-1974: A Study in Society and History.* Stanford, California: Stanford University Press, pp. 110-112.

1985   "Chicano Studies, 1970-1984." In *Annual Review of Anthropology,* 14: 405-27.

1989   Culture and Truth: The Remaking of Social Analysis. Boston: Beacon Press.

Ross, Andrew, ed.
1988   *Universal Abandon? The Politics of Postmodernism.* Minneapolis: University of Minnesota Press.

Ryder, Norman B.
1965   The Cohort as a Concept in the Study of Social Change. *American Sociological Review.* (Dec.) 30(6): 843-861.

Sanchez, Ricardo
1973   *Canto y Grito Mi Liberación: The Liberation of a Chicano Mind.* Garden City, New York: Anchor Press/Doubleday & Company, Inc.

Steele, Shelby
1990   *The Content of Our Character: A New Vision of Race in America,* New York: Harper Perennial, HarperCollins Press, 1990.

Williams, Patricia
1991   *The Alchemy of Race and Rights: Diary of a Law Professor* Cambridge, Mass. and London, England: Harvard University Press.

Yanagisako, Sylvia Junko
1978   Variance in American Kinship: Implications for Cultural Analysis," in *American Ethnologist,* Vol. 5 (1).

1985   *Transforming the Past: Tradition and Kinship Among Japanese Americans.* Stanford, California: Stanford University Press.

Index